Rock Island Public Library
401 - 19th Street
Rock Island, IL 61201-8143

SEP - - 2015

D1258002

50 FAMOUS FIREARMS

YOU'VE GOT TO OWN

RICK HACKER'S
**BUCKET LIST
OF GUNS**

Copyright ©2014 F+W Media, Inc.

All rights reserved. No portion of this publication may be reproduced or transmitted in any
form or by any means, electronic or mechanical, including photocopy, recording, or any
information storage and retrieval system, without permission in writing from the publisher,
except by a reviewer who may quote brief passages in a critical article or review to be printed
in a magazine or newspaper, or electronically transmitted on radio, television, or the Internet.

Published by

Gun Digest® Books, an imprint of F+W, A Content + eCommerce Company
Krause Publications • 700 East State Street • Iola, WI 54990-0001
715-445-2214 • 888-457-2873
www.krausebooks.com

To order books or other products call toll-free 1-800-258-0929
or visit us online at www.gundigeststore.com

ISBN-13: 978-1-4402-3990-8
ISBN-10: 1-4402-3990-8

Cover Design by Dane Royer
Designed by Sandi Carpenter and Sharon Bartsch
Edited by Jennifer L.S. Pearsall

Printed in China

Other Books by Rick Hacker

The Muzzleloading Hunter

The Ultimate Pipe Book

The Christmas Pipe

The Ultimate Cigar Book

Rare Smoke-The Ultimate Guide to Pipe Collecting

Pipesmoking-A 21st Century Guide

Dedication

*Dedicated to my loving, patient, and always beautiful wife, Joan
(better known among our friends as St. Joan),
who has put up with me and my multiple interests
for lo, these many, many years.*

ABOUT THE AUTHOR

Although Rick Hacker was born in Chicago, Illinois, he grew up in Phoenix, Arizona, and, thus, became a son of the Southwest. For it was there that he developed his lifelong interest in the shooting sports and an appreciation of its importance to our American way of life. As a teenager, he wrote a column for his high school newspaper, but really began his writing career when he won grand prize for the Boy's Life writing contest with a short story, "The Cowboy And The Steer." He went on to organize the Boy Scouts of America's equestrian Mounted Explorer Post 44, as well as a trick shooting and fast draw club, The Arizona Young Guns.

While attending Arizona State University, among his many jobs, Rick wrote science fiction and western stories to help pay expenses. Later, while working as an advertising executive in Los Angeles, he met the late Robert E. "Pete" Petersen, whose Petersen Publishing enterprises included *Guns & Ammo* magazine. When Pete learned of Rick's practical shooting experiences with muzzleloaders, sixguns, and lever-action rifles, he commented, "I've got a lot of gun writers doing articles on these things, but few of them know anything about it. How'd you like to start writing for me?" As a result, Rick began writing for *Guns & Ammo* in 1976. Today, after years of writing for that publication, he is Field Editor for both *Handguns* and *Rifle-Shooter* magazines, which were originally part of Petersen Publishing and are now owned by InterMedia Outdoors.

In 1979, he also began writing for The National Rifle Association's flagship publication, *American Rifleman* and, eventually, became Black Powder Editor for its sister magazine, *American Hunter.* Today he is Field Editor of both *American Rifleman* and the NRA's newsstand publication, *Shooting Illustrated*. In addition, he is the author of the best-selling book *The Muzzleloading Hunter*, and he's been a longtime contributor to other national firearms publications, including *Gun Digest* and Safari Club International's *Safari* magazine. He also writes extensively on whiskies, wines, pipes, and cigars for numerous consumer lifestyle magazines.

The author is a Benefactor Member of the National Rifle Association, a Life Member of the Single Action Shooting Society, has been inducted into The National Muzzleloading Rifle Association Hall of Fame, and, among his many other accolades, was knighted in Germany. He collects 19th and early 20th century firearms and has hunted with both originals and replicas of these historic arms on the North American and African continents. Needless to say, Rick Hacker is a firm believer in and a staunch supporter of the United States of America and its Constitution, without which, the freedom to write a book such as this could not exist.

Table of Contents

PREFACE

WHY I WROTE THIS BOOK

The author has been shooting, collecting and writing about firearms all his life.

There are few absolutes in this world, but one of them is that whenever you get two or more people in the same room and let them talk long enough, there will eventually be a difference of opinions. I have seen this phenomenon manifest itself whenever a lengthy discussion drifts onto the rocky shoals of a topic of extreme personal importance, such as what is the best single malt Scotch, the best cigar and, perhaps most opinionated of all, the best gun.

Indeed, few things are as individualistic as a firearm. Shape, design, purpose, function, and feel all come into play. And yet, there is no common denominator. A shotgun, for example, that may be great for trap shooting may not fair as well when it comes to upland game, just as a handgun purchased for plinking might not be the best choice for self-defense. Even if they all shared a common purpose, there are enough variables to fill a gun rack so that it would stretch around the world—which, in itself, is not a bad thing to visualize.

Even though we all have our viewpoints, the reality is, there isn't really a "best" gun. It all comes down to an unscientific determining factor known as "What I like." There are lots of those—great guns that excite or inspire or tantalize us, guns that we might want to have, if for no other reason than we want to have them. Which, when you think about it, is reason enough.

For me, the situation is compounded by the fact that I write about guns I admire, whether it's the western nostalgia of a Colt Single Action Army, the James Bond intrigue of a Walther PPK, or the undercover allure of a Smith & Wesson Model 36 snubbie. I get totally immersed in the gun, its history, its shootability. The end result is that immediately after finishing an article about a particular firearm, I become overwhelmed with an uncontrollable urge to go out and buy it—not an easy task, given mandated waiting periods, proximities to gun stores, availability of the guns themselves and, well, there is also the matter of finances. Thus, my fantasies usually go unfulfilled. As a result, I often lie awake at night, eyes closed but with a faint smile playing across my lips, as I visualize the many guns I wish I could have—but have yet to possess. I am sure some psychologists would have a field day with this scenario; even they would agree, one must have goals in life.

Then, not very long ago, I started to think that I can't be alone in this ongoing yearning. There must be others like me, who have coveted certain firearms after seeing them on the shooting range, in the movies, or pictured in a gun magazine. And then there are those friends who, when not asking me what cigar they should smoke or what whiskey they should drink, want to know what gun they should buy. After going through the prerequisite qualifying discussion—what's it for, how much do you want to spend, and so on—I start to list my many, many favorites, which either elicits enthusiastic agreement or glassy-eyed indifference. In every case, though, they want to know what these guns are.

Of course, my choices rarely have anything to do with my actual need, but, rather, are given merely because I like them and therefore, must have them. Notice I'm dealing in plurals here, because just as one can never have too much money, there is no such thing as too many guns. That's why I always admonish fellow firearms enthusiasts to buy the biggest gun safe they can afford, because they're going to eventually fill it up.

So, given my almost four decades of experience writing about, collecting, and shooting what I think are some of the greatest guns in the world, I thought, what about putting together a list of my personal "Fabulous Fifty Firearms," a hand's-on book that doesn't focus on out-of-reach museum pieces, but on popular guns that can be obtained, new or used, by any qualifying law-abiding reader with a valid credit card.

And that's what I've done, drawing in large part from my many "The Classics" columns that have appeared over the years in the NRA's *Shooting Illustrated* magazine, although I used my own photography for this book and rewrote and updated much of the copy since it was first published. Nonetheless, I would wholeheartedly like to thank the Publications Division of The National Rifle Association for their kind permission to reprint these articles.

By that same token, I would urge every freedom-loving American, whether or not they own a firearm, to join the NRA as a gesture of support for an organization that has fought so hard and so long (since 1871) to protect our nation's Second Amendment. I find it difficult to believe that anyone who enjoys firearms is not a member. But, if you're not, that's easy to rectify. Simply go to www.membership.nrahq.org and sign on. It's that simple, to help keep our freedoms intact.

All that said, now, please join with me as I tell you about fifty firearms I feel you absolutely, positively, unequivocally have *got* to have. You may not agree with all of them (if

In this photo from the 1950s, the author proudly poses with his first Colt Single Action and Winchester 94.

not, please let me know via the publisher and give your alternate choices—we may have enough for another edition), but think of this as a basic wish book for every gun guy and gal in America to use as a guide in buying another gun. Or, better yet, a couple or more. And, if you happen to own one or more of the rifles, pistols, and shotguns included in my "Fabulous Fifty" list, well, there's nothing like seeing your favorite firearm in print, then showing that page to family and friends and saying, "I've got one like that." Thus, you'll be on the way to completing your own bucket list to hand on down through the generations, thereby keeping our American tradition of private firearms ownership alive.

—*Rick Hacker*

SMITH & WESSON
MODEL 36
CHIEF'S SPECIAL

The Model 60 is the stainless steel version of the Model 36 and makes a perfect personal-defense or backup revolver.

Aside from Nancy Reagan's memorable description of the "cute little gun" President Reagan had given her for protection, few people refer to handguns as "cute." Yet "cute" is exactly the descriptive adjective that comes to mind, when viewing the Smith & Wesson Model 36 (although this was probably not the specific handgun to which the former First Lady was referring).

With its stubby 1⅞-inch barrel, compact five-shot cylinder, and rounded butt, this little pocket pistol tips the scales right around 20 ounces. Even so, I doubt the tens of thousands of law enforcement officers and civilians who have packed this diminutive but rugged revolver would call it "cute." Certainly not Jack Webb, who, as Sergeant Joe Friday, flashed his Chief's Special with authority on the old Dragnet television series. Or Gene Hackman, as Detective

Jimmy "Popeye" Doyle, who swapped his Col[t] Detective Special in the French Connection fo[r] an S&W Model 36 in the French Connection I[I] sequel. In real life, this little Smith & Wesson is [a] lawman's handgun, and rightfully so, for it wa[s] named by a room full of police chiefs.

In 1948, Smith & Wesson president C.R[.] Hellstrom realized there was a need for a snub[-] nosed revolver, similar in size to S&W's Terrier[,] but revamped to handle the more powerful .38 Special. The Terrier was built on a .32-calibe[r] frame, but was chambered for the .38 S&W car[-] tridge, a short-range, relatively anemic roun[d] that originated with S&W's top-breaks, in 1877[.] The new revolver Hellstrom envisioned woul[d] have to retain the Terrier's compactness, but b[e] able to handle the more popular .38 Special, [a] favorite with lawmen of that era. In fact, it wa[s] the rival Colt Detective Special, specifically i[n] its .38 Special chambering, that was the impe[-] tus for Hellstrom's new revolver.

Smith & Wesson's engineers went to work[,] using the Terrier as a jumping-off poin[t] but beefing up the gun by lengthening an[d] strengthening the cylinder and frame (thu[s] making it a true .38 in size), while still retainin[g] the smaller cylinder's five-shot capacity. In addi[-] tion, the Terrier's flat mainspring was replace[d] with a sturdier coil spring. As the Terrier wa[s] built on the slightly smaller "I" frame, this newe[r] revolver became the first of the "J" frame serie[s] and carried its own set of serial numbers. But[,] as part of a very clever marketing plan, the gu[n] was not given a name designation.

Having created the new .38 Special to ap[-] peal to off-duty policemen and plainclothe[s] detectives, it was decided to let the decision[-] makers among these potential purchasers se[-] lect a name. The first gun, completed on Octo[-] ber 24, 1950, was unveiled that same mont[h] at the International Association of Chiefs o[f] Police conference in Colorado Springs, Colo[.]

rado. There, Smith & Wesson invited the assembled chiefs of police to suggest a name for the new revolver. Perhaps inspired by the already well-established Colt Detective Special, the overriding choice from the attendees was to call it the Chief's Special.

The guns were blued with case hardened hammer and trigger, or nickeled, and came with rounded, two-piece checkered walnut grips. The front sight was a fixed, no-snag serrated ramp that extended the length of the barrel, while the rear sight was simply a groove milled into the topstrap. After all, this was a close-range weapon meant for fast offensive or defensive shooting. Nonetheless, due to numerous requests, by the end of the first year, the factory was also producing a version with a three-inch barrel.

There were enough complaints from those with beefier hands, as a slightly less concealable square-butt version was introduced in 1952, starting with serial No. 21,342. In 1957 Smith & Wesson switched to a numerical system of identification, and the Chief's Special became the Model 36, starting with serial No. 125,000.

Numerous minor external and internal changes have been made to the Chief's Special over the years, including the elimination of the front trigger guard screw in 1953, and changing the cylinder-unlocking thumbpiece from a flat to a more contoured style in 1966. But perhaps the most dramatic change occurred, in 1965, when a stainless steel version of the Model 36 was introduced, thus becoming the world's first stainless revolver. To differentiate it, the stainless gun became the Model 60.

Another notable variation of the Model 36 was a heavy-barreled three-inch version, available in 1967. And, beginning in 1955, there were limited runs of two- and three-inch barreled guns with adjustable target sights. (To make things confusing, from 1965 through 1975, these rarities, of which approximately 1,740 were made, were listed as the Model 50.) Other versions include the .38 Chief's Special

Airweight with an aluminum alloy cylinder and frame (do not shoot these guns without having them factory-checked for safety beforehand), and the highly popular stainless steel Lady Smith. Other offshoots of the basic Model 36 include the shrouded-hammer Model 49 Bodyguard and the hammerless Model 40 Centennial, with its squeeze-to-fire grip safety.

Years ago, I purchased a blued Model 36 for my wife. It easily fit her hand and, after some extended time at the range shooting Glaser self-defense loads and standard factory ammo (+P ammo should be avoided with these snubbies), she became uncannily proficient with it. In the meantime, I had fallen under the spell of that "cute little gun," so I went out and bought a Model 60 for myself.

The Model 60 and its variations have remained in the line, and though the original Model 36 was discontinued in 1999, it was brought back in 2008, as part of Smith & Wesson's Classic Series. It was a fitting return for a snub-nosed .38 that had won the praise of law enforcement veterans from its very first day on the job and, as such, deserves to be on my bucket list.

Below: The Model 36 owes its small size, in part, to the fact that it chambers only five rounds.

Below Middle: The rear sight is rudimentary and is all that is needed on a close-range self-defense gun, such as the Model 36.

WINCHESTER 9422

In the world of firearms manufacturing, there are few absolutes. However, one way to practically guarantee a new firearm will have marketing appeal is to make a .22 rimfire counterpart of a successful big-bore. Witness the Ruger 10/22, the Marlin 39, and the Ruger Single Six. Without a doubt, one of the most popular big-bore lever-actions is the Winchester Model 94. With more than nine million guns made from 1894 until the New Haven factory's closing in 2006, the Model 94 was the most popular deer rifle in America. But .30-30 shells are expensive, and deer season lasts only a few months each year—and a lookalike Winchester lever gun using inexpensive .22 rimfire ammunition could be shot all year 'round. That was the thought process that undoubtedly swept through the Winchester R&D department, over 40 years ago.

Aptly cataloged as the Model 9422, this well-built rimfire lever-action made its debut, in 1972. Like its big-bore big brother Model 94, the 9422 featured a full-sized straight-grip stock, a 20-inch barrel (actually it was 20½ inches, but few people noticed or cared), open rear sight that was drift-adjustable for windage with a traditional notched sliding bar for elevation, dove-tailed hooded front sight, and the same large, classic, glove-friendly trigger guard and lever. Tipping the scales at six

pounds, just a scant half-pound lighter than the Model 94, made it a perfect entry-level rifle for some lucky son, daughter, or grandchild. And fittingly, like the 94, it was initially designed as a basic working gun. In 1980, checkering was added to the previously plain black walnut stocks, but from there on, the 9422 was a different lever-action entirely.

For one thing, the Model 9422 featured a takedown action and—well before Winchester introduced its angle eject on the Model 94—the .22 version boasted side ejection and a solid-top receiver grooved to accept scope mounts. The tubular magazine was charged by withdrawing a spring-loaded brass plunger retained in a tube beneath the barrel—thus maintaining its Model 94 looks—and dropping the cartridges in one at a time through a cut-out loading port, *a lá* Winchester's older .22 pump rifles. The 9422 held 15 .22 Long Rifle cartridges or 17 Longs; the rifle was not chambered for .22 Shorts. There was also a version that held 11 .22 WMR rounds. A later variation, the Model 9217, was chambered for the .17 HMR and held 11 rounds. The gun came with a hammer spur extension and, best of all for purists, retained a half-cock safety throughout its entire production run, rather than the mushy "no-cock" hammer that eventually found its way onto later Model 94s with push-button and tang-mounted safeties.

One of the most unique functions of the Model 9422 was its takedown capability, a feature that many owners were either not aware of or never took advantage of, judging by the "unbuggered" condition of otherwise well-used 9422s encountered today. To take the gun apart, a single takedown screw on the left side of the receiver was backed out, thus permitting the buttstock assembly to be pulled down, back, and away from the receiver. Next, the bolt slid out of the receiver and the bolt and bolt slide could then be separated. With the rifle in two sections, the barrel could be cleaned from the breech. The barrel half also retained the scope (if one was mounted), so zero wasn't lost when the rifle was reassembled. When assembling the rifle, the hammer had to be brought to full cock before inserting the buttstock section into the receiver.

Winchester's 9422 serial No. 1 went to longtime Winchester employee Bill Kelly, upon his retirement in 1972. By 1991, more than 600,000 guns had been produced, an indication of the rifle's immense popularity. Winchester's 2003 manual called the Model 9422 "… the premier lever-action rimfire rifle."

Of course, nine years after the rifle's introduction, it was no longer made by Winchester *per se*, but, rather, by the U.S. Repeating Arms Company, as licensed by Olin Corp., owners of the Winchester name. Under USRAC's stewardship, a number of commemoratives were produced. One of the most notable was the Annie Oakley Commemorative in 1983, which featured fancy walnut stocks and a gold-plated and engraved receiver with a portrait of "Little Sure Shot," as Sitting Bull called her, on the right side of the receiver. The lever and barrel bands were gold-plated as well. Another unique offering was a special Boy Scout Commemorative 9422 carbine with French Grey receiver, lever, and barrel bands, issued in 1985. An even rarer Eagle Scout Limited Edition rifle was offered that same year, featuring an engraved and gold-plated receiver with a special Eagle Scout medallion stock inset. It was allegedly only available for purchase by Eagle Scouts. Also in 1985, an XTR version was produced, which featured a high-gloss, fancy checkered stock and forearm and a lustrous blued finish. Doing a complete about-face two years later, a .22 Magnum WinCam version was offered with synthetic stocks, and, in 1996, a 16½-inch barrel Trapper version was brought out. Both guns were evidence that the admirable accuracy of the 9422 made it a serious contender as a small-game getter. Indeed, in spite of its rising collectability, this lever-action rimfire has always been held in high esteem as a shooter.

"The 9422 is the perfect combination of function and history," I was once told by my good friend, firearms enthusiast and Hollywood screenwriter, the late John Fasano, whose motion picture and television credits include *Another 24 Hours, Tombstone, Saving Jessica Lynch*, and *Stone Cold* with Tom Selleck. "It's the ideal gun to introduce children to gun safety with a lever-action. I bought one for my three children the day each was born."

Indeed, in its 2005 catalog—the last year the 9422 was listed for sale—the company wrote, "More than just a rimfire rifle, it is a foundation for learning accuracy, safety, and building good memories … . The short, fluid action, special target crowns for improved accuracy and excellent fit and finish were all the evidence necessary to show that they were built to higher standards than other rimfire rifles. Now, after 33 years, production of the Model 9422 is ending. Tooling is being retired, and the production line at the New Haven, Connecticut facility will stop."

For its final run, a special limited edition of 9,244 guns were produced in four different variations of a special Tribute Series, with various engraving motifs and the Winchester horse and rider on the right side of the blued receivers. There were also 222 Custom Edition rifles, featuring hand-engraved, silver-plated receivers, with a gold inlaid Winchester horse and rider on one side and a gold inlaid banner, bearing the words "Model 9422 Tribute" on the other. Final prices ran from $549 up to $2,313 for the Custom Edition.

The demise of the Model 9422 was a precursor to the fate of Winchester itself. One year later, the New Haven plant where the 9422 had been made closed its doors. Shortly thereafter, a friend of mine sold his plain, no frills Model 9422 for $1,000. Today, although the 9422 is no longer in production, it seems its legend is just beginning. Thus, as a .22 that many of us Model 94 owners just never got around to getting, it belongs on our bucket

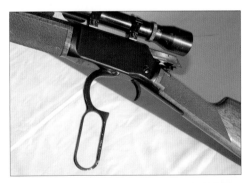

While differing mechanically, the action of the 9422 looks and feels like its big brother, the Model 94.

This 9422, made in 1980, has been fitted with a Weaver Marksman 4x scope, which, while adding to its usefulness, detracts from its value.

COLT FIRST, SECOND & THIRD
MODEL DRAGOONS

With endorsements from American Indian War heroes Captains Samuel Hamilton Walker and Jack C. Hayes, Samuel Colt finally got the military recognition—and orders for his 1847 Walker—that he craved. But although the Walker was a formidable weapon, it had its drawbacks, not the least of which was its 4½ pounds of weight. Additionally, recoil from its 60-grain powder charge often caused the loading lever to drop, plunging the rammer into the bottommost chamber and preventing the cylinder from rotating. Obviously, improvements would have to be made if Colt's was to remain in the arms race.

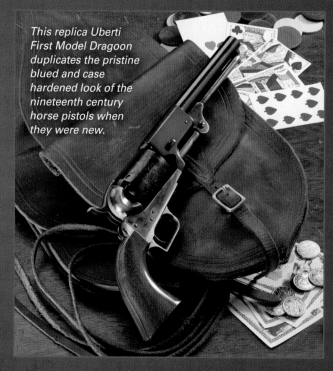

This replica Uberti First Model Dragoon duplicates the pristine blued and case hardened look of the nineteenth century horse pistols when they were new.

Back in those crude days of metallurgy, the only way to reduce the weight of a handgun was to reduce its size. Thus, in 1847, Colt's created a transition gun between the Walker and the subsequent First, Second, and Third Model Dragoons. This revolver, which used many leftover and modified Walker parts, was the Whitneyville-Hartford Dragoon, or Transition Walker, and it represents the very first gun to be made in Colt's new Hartford factory. But its life was short lived, because, in 1848, Sam Colt unveiled his First Model Dragoon (named after the U.S. Mounted Riflemen). Although still a hefty hunk of iron, the frame and cylinder had been slightly scaled down and the barrel shortened from the Walker's nine-inch tube to 7½ inches. Because of its smaller cylinder, the Dragoons carried a reduced powder charge of 40 grains.

These improvements trimmed the Dragoon's weight to four pounds, two ounces, still too large to qualify it as a belt or holster pistol. In fact, it was the Colt Dragoon that helped inspire the term "horse pistol," for the only way this behemoth could be conveniently carried was on horseback. The guns were typically issued in pairs to mounted troopers— the forerunners of the United States Cavalry—in elongated leather pommel holsters draped over both sides of the saddle.

The .44-caliber Dragoon was a handsome gun, with blued metal, and case hardened frame, loading lever, and hammer. The square-back trigger guard (a holdover from the Walker) and backstrap were polished brass, complemented by one-piece walnut grips. Military guns were stamped with a "U.S." on the frame and "WAT" on the grips (the latter for Ordnance Inspector W.A. Thornton). The large cylinder provided an ample canvas for an engraving by W.L. Ormsby, depicting Captain Hayes and his mounted riflemen in pursuit of Comanches.

Obviously, Sam Colt still had leftover parts in the bin, because the initial run of First Model Dragoons featured some Walker stampings and parts. This subvariation was discovered by John J. Fluck and reported by him in the September 1956 issue of *American Rifleman*. Today, these rare guns, which occur in the 2216 through 2515 serial number range, are known as Fluck Models.

This initial Dragoon, which was produced until 1850, also kept the Walker's oval bolt locking holes in the cylinder and the relatively weak "V" mainspring. These were changed, in 1850, with the appearance of the Second Model Dragoon. It is in this second generation that the flat, curved mainspring and squared-off cylinder bolt notches with their lead in-grooves first appeared, improvements that would stay with Colt revolvers into the 21st century. In addition, the loading lever latch was redesigned and a rolling wheel was added to the base of the hammer. The square-back trigger guard was retained, making the Second Model, in my opinion, the most attractive of the Dragoons.

Only 2,700 Second Models were produced, until 1851, when it was superseded by the Third Model Dragoon, of which 10,500 were manufactured, along with an additional 700 guns shipped to the British market between 1853 and 1857.

In the Third Model, the lever catch was again improved, but this time with a design that was to be incorporated in all subsequent cap-and-ball Colts, including the 1851 Navy and 1860 Army. The Third Model is also the only Dragoon produced in two barrel lengths, 7½ and eight inches. Some models also sported a folding leaf sight. Additional accuracy was obtained by the factory's enlarging of the loading grooves in the barrels. Finally, the trigger guard was rounded, thus losing the Dragoon's last vestige of its Walker heritage.

The Third Model was produced until 1861, but Colt's Dragoons continued to see action throughout the War Between the States and during the western expansion, when many were converted to cartridges. In addition, some Dragoons were factory cut for shoulder stocks, and a number of presentation guns were engraved by such notables as Gustave Young. Of the 22,000 Dragoons produced during its 13-year lifespan, approximately 10,000 were purchased by the government. The rest were eagerly sought by civilians, in spite of the substantial (for the time) $28 price tag. The civilian guns were usually better finished than military models and their brass backstraps and trigger guards were silver-plated.

Colt Dragoons remain popular not just among collectors, but also with shooters. As testimony to this, in 1974, Colt reissued its Third Model Dragoon, beginning with serial

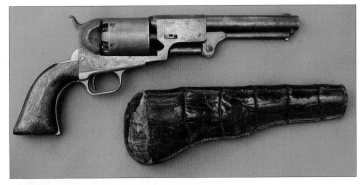

Although intended to be carried on horseback in a pair of pommel holsters, this rare Third Model was found with an original period holster made of alligator skin, lending credence to the speculation that this gun came from the South.

No. 20801—right where the originals left off. Starting in 1980, First and Second Models were also reissued. Although these Colt-produced guns are no longer made today, excellent replicas are offered by Uberti, Cimarron Fire Arms, and Dixie Gun Works.

Indeed, the cylinder scene on both originals and replicas are indicative of the Dragoon's place in history. It emerged when adventure waited anyone daring to venture into what maps of the time called "The Great American Desert". Although original specimens, such as the Third Model Dragoon shown here, are investments worthy of any collection, their lofty prices dictate acquisition of one of the better-made replicas for our bucket list. Besides, that way you can shoot it.

THE P08 LUGER

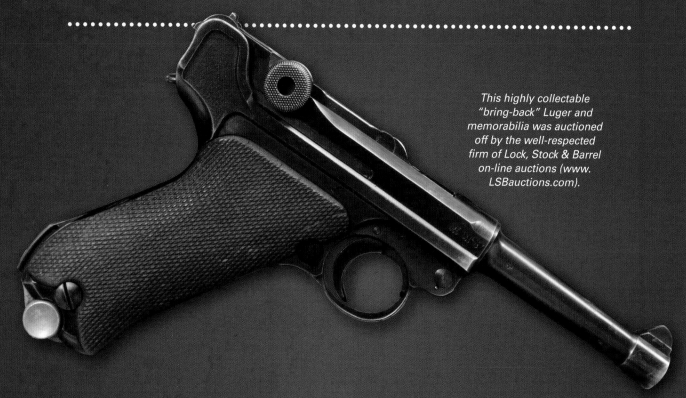

This highly collectable "bring-back" Luger and memorabilia was auctioned off by the well-respected firm of Lock, Stock & Barrel on-line auctions (www. LSBauctions.com).

Little did Georg Johann Luger realize, when he first patented his toggle-linked, recoil operated semi-automatic pistol, in 1898, that his surname would become synonymous with one of the most famous and collectable military handguns in the world. The Luger, as it commonly known today, was initially called "Pistole Parabellum," but, when the German Army adopted it, in 1908, they rechristened it the P08.

Luger was born in Austria, in 1849, and was destined for a career in business. But, at the age of 18, he volunteered as a Reserve Officer Cadet in the 78th Infantry Regiment, where his exceptional ability as a marksman caught the attention of his commanding officers, who enrolled him in the Austro-Hungarian Military Firearms School at Camp Bruckneudorf. Luger soon became an instructor and, eventually, was promoted to Lieutenant.

After his military service, he befriended Ferdinand Ritter von Mannlicher, a contemporary of Luger's who was soon to make his own mark in the firearms world. The two men collaborated on various rifle magazine designs, including a rotary device that would lead Mannlicher on his own road to fame. But Luger was intrigued with the concept of how magazines functioned in the overall gun. So, in 1891, he went to work as a designer for Ludwig Loewe & Company, which was soon to be reorganized as Deutsche Waffen und Munitionsfabriken Aktien-Gesellschaft—the German Weapons and Munitions company or, as it is better known, DWM. It's a familiar script that would be found on the receivers of many a Luger pistol.

While employed at DWM, Luger was sent to the United States to demonstrate the rather ungainly Borchardt C-93 semi-automatic pistol, which itself was based upon the Maxim machine gun, developed in 1884 by American-born British inventor Sir Hiram Stevens Maxim. The Maxim was one of the first weapons to be successfully operated by its own recoil, rather than by manual cranking. The U.S. government found favor with the Maxim and would, eventually, adopt it as the Maxim Machine Gun, Caliber .30, Model of 1904, but both the Army and Navy failed to be impressed with the C-93 pistol Luger showed them.

Luger, however, found something intriguing with the C-93's toggle-link system and the Maxim's recoil operation. He set about designing a pistol that would combine the best elements of both. What finally emerged was the Parabellum-Pistole (the two words are often inverted), one of the most innovative handguns the world had yet to see. After all, this was still the age of the single-action revolver; double-actions were just coming into their own, and semi-automatics were yet to be embraced by most shooters.

Central to the Luger's operation was its toggle-link action. Consisting of two ball-of-the-thumb-sized steel knobs on either side of a reciprocating, two-piece toggle (by which the bolt could be grasped and manually pulled back to either cock the gun, clear a jam, or chamber a round), the rearward force from the detonating cartridge drove the straightened link (which was attached to the barrel, which also briefly retracted with the breech), backwards, until it reached a "breaking point" where both pieces were joined. The two-piece link then arched and rode up against a curva-

ture in the frame, fully withdrawing the breechblock, which ejected the spent casing and picked up a fresh round as the toggle link was forced home again via a return spring.

In all, there were 37 parts to the Luger's mechanism, not counting the two-piece grips and eight-round magazine (a 32-round detachable drum was later offered). This included the trigger (slide) plate on the left side of the receiver, which was the key to disassembling the Luger. After insuring the gun is empty and locking the toggle bolt assembly in the "open" position, the locking bolt on the left side of the receiver is rotated down and the trigger plate removed by lifting it straight up. The toggle link assembly can then be lifted from the receiver by withdrawing the axle pin that holds it in place.

The grip was almost perfectly angled in relationship to the bore axis of the tapered barrel, designed to fire practically to point of aim by instinct. Many earlier semi-automatic pistols tended to shoot low, because the grip was angled less in relationship to the bore. In addition, the Luger's wide, fixed rear sight (milled into the rear portion of the toggle), and the blade front sight (which was drift-adjustable for windage) were surprisingly accurate out to 25 yards

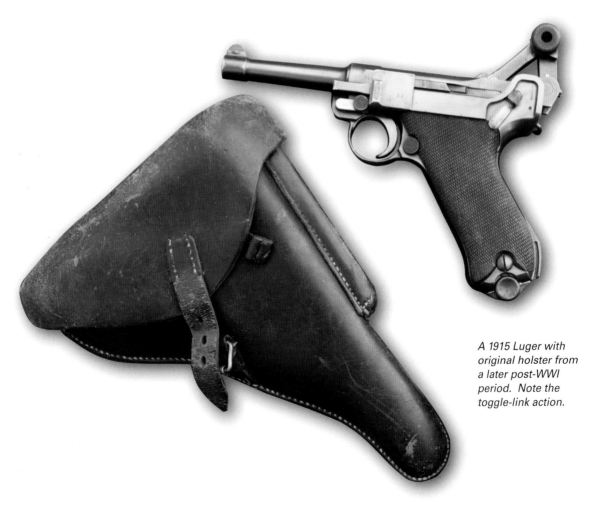

A 1915 Luger with original holster from a later post-WWI period. Note the toggle-link action.

at man-sized targets.

The Luger was originally chambered for the 7.65×21mm Parabellum, also known as the .30 Luger, which had previously been developed by Georg Luger as he worked with Hugo Borchardt in an attempt to find a better cartridge for Borchardt's C-93. In so doing, Luger created a shorter case that permitted the use of a correspondingly shorter toggle action and a narrower grip—thus setting the stage for the development of what would become the P08.

The Swiss Army was the first to see the advantages of the new Luger and placed an order with DWM, in May 1900. Through the years, other manufacturers, including W+F Bern, Krieghoff, Simson, Vickers, and Mauser, would all eventually add the P08 to their rosters, to meet demands. However, when the German government adopted the Luger, it was partly as a result of Georg Luger having developed a second cartridge, one specifically created for his gun, the 9x19mm Parabellum or, as it is more widely known, the 9mm Luger. As an aside, there were also two noticeably larger P08 pistols chambered in .45 ACP made by DWM under the personal supervision of Georg Luger—and stamped "GL" on their toggles to denote this fact—specifically for the U.S. Army trials of 1907. Numbered "1" and "2," the .45 Lugers fared well enough to cause the Army to ask for certain modifications for further testing, but, perhaps because of the looming specter of WWI, or maybe the cost of retooling for additional prototypes, Germany refused to participate further. One of the two known test guns has disappeared, but the other—briefly alluded to via a prop gun in Oliver Stone's 1987 movie, *Wall Street*—sold at auction for $1,000,000, in 1989, and, thus, became known as "the million dollar Luger." Unfortunately, the financial crash a few years ago resulted in that same gun selling for only $494,500 (including a 15-percent buyer's premium), in 2010, at Greg Martin Auctions in Anaheim, California.

Produced with a standard barrel length of four inches plus a six-inch Marine Model, an eight-inch barreled Lange Pistole 08 (long pistol) Artillery Model was also made. The Artillery Model was outfitted with tangent sights and a detachable shoulder stock with corresponding holster. It was often issued with a *Trommelmagazin 08* 32-round drum magazine. In addition, there was a rare carbine model with an 11¾-inch barrel that was also outfitted with a detachable stock. Needless to say, there are enough dates and stamping variances to keep Luger aficionados preoccupied for years, as the P08, in all its guises, was adopted by more than 15 countries, many with variations. Thankfully, most military models feature the dates of manufacture (not usually present on civilian models) and nationality stampings. And, while collectors covet Lugers with numerically matching magazines, the reality is that this was often the first part to get separated from its original gun.

On military models, it is far more important that all the parts are numbered to match, as the Luger is a very intricate, hand-fitted mechanism. Just as desirous for many is the color of the "straw"-finished small parts, such as trigger, thumb safety, and magazine release, as these deep-yellow parts (the shades will very) are simply the result of the heat treating methods that were used. It is an important factor to collectors, as the amount of color remaining is an indication of how much the gun was used, but it also adds a cosmetic beauty to the Luger.

Most of the WWI standard military and Artillery Lugers were produced by the Royal Arsenal of Efert, Germany, while approximately 10,000 post-WWI Lugers were made by the British firm of Vickers, Ltd., on contract for the Dutch government. One of the most desirable of Lugers is the "American Eagle," which was made for pre-war and post-war sales to the U.S. and bears The Great Seal of the United States stamped on the receiver. Also of interest is the fact that, in 1923, Stoeger, Inc., trademarked the Luger name and began importing these German-made guns—the first to bear the Luger name—into America. (Later, Stoeger and others actually began manufacturing Lugers in this country.)

In 1930, Mauser acquired DWM and produced most of the WWII-era Lugers, as well as non-military versions right up through the 1970s. And even though the Walther P38 officially replaced the Luger, in 1942, the P08 continued to be manufactured in Mauser's Oberndorf factory until the Armistice in 1945. Thus, the pre-WWI P08 ended up serving the German army and its allies throughout World War II and beyond, as a number of these refurbished guns were used to arm the East German police.

The P08 was an intricate design and, therefore, expensive to make. It was also prone to jamming if the slightest bit of mud interfered with the delicate toggle-link action. In addition, a number of wartime guns would malfunction if somehow the exact, originally numbered parts weren't used in reassembling the gun. Still, when functioning properly, it was an effective weapon, with the only real criticisms being the thumb-wrecking difficulty in loading its magazines, and its two chamberings, both of which were largely felt to be underpowered.

Nonetheless, while in a private collection, in 1960 the "million dollar Luger" was reportedly test fired 150 times without a single hiccup. In 1994, it was once again taken out of retirement and fired repeatedly without any malfunctions. But perhaps one of the greatest compliments to Georg Luger's original design was that the P08 served as the inspiration for Bill Ruger's first successful .22 semi-automatic pistol, the Standard.

MARLIN MODEL 39

Everyone enjoys meeting a celebrity, and when you pick up a Marlin Model 39, you are holding the oldest continuously produced rifle in firearms history. In a way, you are also connecting with Annie Oakley, one of the world's greatest trick shooters, and a woman who was dubbed "Little Sure Shot" by Chief Sitting Bull, when they were both appearing in Buffalo Bill Cody's Wild West shows around the turn of the last century. The diminutive shooter—she was only five-feet tall—repeatedly wowed audiences with her expertise at hitting targets with a Marlin 1897, the immediate predecessor to the Model 39.

The Model 39 is basically the same rifle Annie Oakley used in her trick shooting act with Buffalo Bill Cody's Wild West shows, around the turn of the last century.

Indeed, one cannot write about the Model 39 without bringing in the Model 97, the first repeater that could digest .22 Shorts, Longs, and Long Rifle cartridges interchangeably. The slim, lightweight lever-action also featured Marlin's new (at the time) takedown feature, which not only made for easy transportation, but also enabled shooters to clean the gun from the breech. To disassemble, all one had to do was cock the hammer, unscrew the large retaining screw on the right side of the receiver, and carefully lift the buttstock portion up to the right of the frame. The breech bolt then slides back, up, and out, as a separate piece from the action.

In 1922, after a brief manufacturing hiatus caused by World War I and a change in company ownership, the Model 1897 was brought back, only this time it carried a new designation as the Model 39. In all other respects, the new pistol-gripped .22 was nearly identical to the older Model 97, complete with casehardened receiver, octagon barrel, and its trademark .22 rimfire cartridge interchangeably and takedown features. Of course, being a Marlin lever-action, it also boasted a solid top

receiver and side ejection, just like the Model 97, although the new Model 39 loaded via a button-type magazine tube under the barrel, rather than the latch-type tube of the Model 97. Otherwise, this was basically the same gun as its predecessor. Initial cost was $26.50, which made the Marlin 39 one of the most expensive .22 rifles on the market. But quoting from Marlin's 1922 catalog:

The Marlin Model No. 39 lever action rifle is the most accurate .22 repeating rifle in the world, and is the choice of expert shooters for hunting small game such as rabbits, squirrels, crows, foxes, etc., and for target shooting up to 200 yards ... a great many big-game hunters prefer this lever action rifle, as it has the "feel" of a big game rifle and permits them to keep in practice at small expense.

Claims of 200-yard target accuracy and big-game rifle "feel" might have been a bit of a stretch for the slim, 5½-pound .22, but there was no denying that it could consistently pop tin cans at 100 yards and was fast handling enough for effective running shots at jackrab-

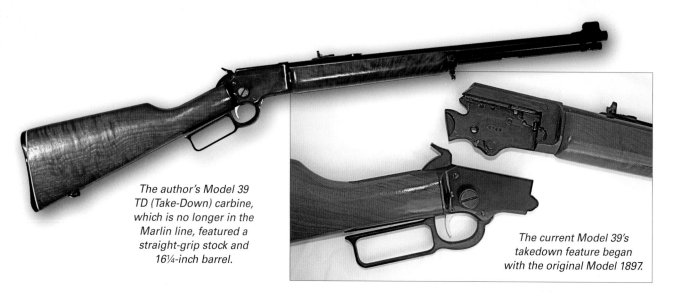

The author's Model 39 TD (Take-Down) carbine, which is no longer in the Marlin line, featured a straight-grip stock and 16¼-inch barrel.

The current Model 39's takedown feature began with the original Model 1897.

bits. For thousands of admirers, it seemed there was little that could be done to improve the Model 39. Nevertheless, somewhere around the early 1930s, the bolt was strengthened to permit use of the new, high-speed .22 ammo that was just coming onto the market. A retaining screw was also added to keep the internal frame-mounted ejector from hanging up on patches as the cleaning rod was pushed through the bore. (One thing to know with this model is that, if the ejector wasn't freed before reassembling the rifle, the gun would fail to eject.)

Although the Model 39 had neared mechanical perfection as the world's only lever-action .22, in 1939, it was reintroduced as the Model 39A. The changes were merely cosmetic. Gone was the old, octagon barrel, replaced by a round, semi-heavy barrel with Ballard-type rifling. The ivory bead front sight had been changed to a silver bead, but the tang was still drilled and tapped for a peep sight. More notable changes came a year later, when the slim stocks of the previous 1897 and Model 39 rifles were updated to a more hand-filling semi-beavertail forearm and a slightly thicker pistol grip buttstock.

In 1945, after a break in production prompted by WWII, the Model 39A returned, only this time with a ramped front sight and a blued receiver, which replaced the pre-war case hardened receiver. This is essentially the same rifle that remains in the Marlin line today, although, over the years, a number of minor variations have been made. The most notable was the 39A Mountie, a handsome, straight-stocked, 20-inch-barreled carbine that came out in 1953. In addition, the lever contour had been changed from square to round, and, in 1988, a cross-bolt safety and rebounding hammer was added, much to the chagrin of many who learned gun safety with the little .22 on half-cock.

Although Marlin did not normally offer custom options on its Model 39, a few notable exceptions exist. One I am personally familiar with is a pair of factory nickel-plated Model 39s that have a lasso-twirling cowgirl expertly relief-carved into the premium grade stocks. These guns were presented to the late Gail Davis, the actress (and expert trick shot) who played Annie Oakley on TV, from 1953 to 1956. In addition, Marlin has produced a number of commemorative models, including the 39ADL, a deluxe version manufactured in 1961, a Model 39 Article II, in 1971 (which paid tribute to the NRA's 100 years of dedication to America's gun owners), and, appropriately, an 1897 Annie Oakley Commemorative, in 1997.

My experience with the Model 39 goes back to the introduction of the Mountie, although, at the time, I was too young to harbor any realistic hopes of acquiring one. In the 1980s, I finally bought a used 39M and made the mistake of packing it as an extra camp gun on a big-game hunting trip. My guide couldn't take his eyes off that Marlin .22 from the minute I took the two halves from my bedroll. Later, when I "barked" a squirrel with that Model 39 (I was actually trying for a head shot and missed, but the effects were just as impressive to the guide, and who was I to tell him differently?), he offered me a ridiculous price for the little gun. I refused. After our hunt, the guide again approached me, this time with a wad of cash that far superseded his previous offer.

"I've got to have that rifle," he pleaded. "It's the best shootin' .22 I've ever seen."

I finally succumbed to temptation and have regretted it ever since. A few years later, right before the advent of the cross-bolt "safety," I did a shooting test with a then-current Marlin 39 TD (Take-Down) carbine, which featured a straight-grip stock and 16¼-inch barrel. The accuracy with copper plated bullets was so impressive (soft lead bullets tend to clog microgroove rifling), I bought the gun.

To date the Marlin 39 still remains in the line, with more than 2,200,000 having been produced—but, sadly, its days might be numbered. It is an expensive gun to manufacture (continuing its reputation as one of the most expensive .22s around), and other lever-action .22s now exist. But I've still got my 1980's Model 39. Needless to say, I'm hanging on to this one as a permanent part of my bucket list.

BROWNING HI-POWER

It can be argued that, for the first couple of decades of its life, the Colt Government Model of 1911 had no competition. After all, it helped win "The War To End All Wars," and, afterwards, continued to prove itself as a self-defense and law enforcement weapon, as well as one worth its salt on target ranges. In terms of reliability, ruggedness, and reputation, John M. Browning's slab-sided warhorse had no equal—that is, until 1935, when Fabrique Nationale (FN) of Herstal, Belgium, introduced the P-35, or the Browning Hi-Power, as it is more popularly known.

The Hi-Power, or HP nomenclature, was derived not from its caliber—the 9mm was hardly a qualifier in that respect—but for its improved magazine capacity of 13 rounds, compared to the 1911's seven-round stack. After all, it was only natural that the Hi-Power would be compared to John Browning's Government 1911, for the same man designed both guns.

Unfortunately, the Hi-Power was one of the last designs Browning worked on, for on November 26, 1929, this remarkable firearms genius died of a heart attack, while at his desk in his son Val's office at Liège. Browning's death came just two years after he had been granted two separate patents for a semi-automatic pistol the French government had commissioned him to produce. One was for a locked breech system, while the other was a blowback design, similar to the 1911. In spite of the fact that the locked-breech design was ultimately selected, the Hi-Power has often been referred to as an "improved 1911," the supposition being that Browning had taken his basic 1911 design and simply updated it. But such was not the case, for having sold all rights for the 1911 to Colt's, Browning was forced to, in essence, compete against himself by creating a gun that would circumvent his original patents. Of course, this situation became even more

complicated with his death.

Luckily for the future of the GP-35, or the *Grand Puissance*, as the gun was initially being called, Fabrique Nationale had another talented firearms designer, Dieudonné Joseph Saive, who became FN's head of firearms development, after Browning's demise. It was Saive who perfected the HP's double-stack magazine, thereby giving the gun its 13-plus-one capacity without dramatically thickening the grips. He also tweaked Browning's original grip contour, making it more comfortable in the hand. But proving the old adage that timing is everything, in 1928, the patents on the Colt 1911 expired, giving Saive an advantage that Browning did not have: he could now incorporate some of the 1911 elements into the Hi-Power including

This 9mm wartime Hi-Power Type II variant has desirable tangent sights, German "WaA 140" Waffenamt's (Weapons Office) inspector stamps, and matching serial numbers, with walnut grips (subsequent grips were Bakelite). It does not have Belgium's pre-war polish, but has yet to exhibit the roughness of later Nazi guns.

a simplified takedown system and a removable barrel bushing. Years later, Saive would also create an aluminum-alloy frame for the Hi-Power, as well as a short-lived double-action version, in 1952.

The Browning Hi-Power was well received when it was finally introduced in 1935. With its 4⅝-inch barrel, it was balanced and ergonomic, functioned flawlessly with military ball ammunition, was accurate enough to print 2½-inch groups at 25 yards (ideal for a military sidearm), and, being slightly smaller than the 1911, it weighed only two pounds. But it was less than perfect.

For one thing, the sights were small and difficult to align (the same critique given to the 1911). The safety on the left side of the frame was miniscule and "mushy," absent the defining "click" of the 1911. Most notoriously, the trigger pull was extremely heavy, and, when the gun went off, it had a nasty habit of biting the hand that held it—yet another trait the Hi-Power inherited from its inventor's Government 1911. Specifically, unless the pistol was held just right, the hammer spur could punch the web of the hand, between the thumb and the index finger, with each shot. This same anatomical area was also in danger of getting pinched as the slide cycled. Additionally, some shooters familiar with the 1911 objected that there was no grip safety, although like the 1911, the hammer did have a half-cock position. And then there was the magazine disconnect. This was even more disconcerting to many, for it prevented the gun from firing unless the magazine was fully inserted (in all fairness, it was a feature the French government required).

Nonetheless, these were finely crafted, superbly finished pistols exhibiting the best of Belgian manufacturing skills. Plus, with the Hi-Power's increased firepower, it quickly gained a reputation in the field, even though it was soon discovered that the 13-round mags were less prone to malfunction when only 12 rounds were loaded. Two versions were initially offered, a fixed sight Ordinary Model and an Adjustable Rear Sight Model. Some of the guns were fitted with backstraps that were cut for detachable shoulder stocks.

Ironically, France ended up *not* adopting the Hi-Power. But Belgium did, and, eventually, the gun ended up being used by both Allies and enemies during World War II. Germany took over manufacturing the Hi-Power, when it invaded Belgium, in 1940; the guns subsequently suffered a noticeable lack of refinement as the war progressed. As Joseph M. Cornell noted in his excellent *Standard Catalog of Browning Firearms* (Gun Digest Books, 2008), "The finish on these Nazi guns runs from as fine as the Pre-War Commercial series to downright crude, and it is possible to see how the war was progressing for Germany, by the finish on their weapons."

Before the Germans occupied the FN factory, Hi-Power drawings were sent to Canada and England and Allied wartime production relocated there. After VE Day, Hi-Power production in the FN factory regained its pre-war luster, and the pistol was eventually adopted by more than 50 armies throughout the world, including those of Belgium, Britain, Israel, Australia, and Singapore, to name but a few. In addition, ever since 1971, some Hi-Powers have been assembled in the FN Portuguese factory from Belgium-made parts (contrary to popular belief, they have never been *manufactured* in Portugal). The Hi-Power began arriving in the U.S. as a civilian arm in 1954, and has since enjoyed an admirable reputation as a self-defense and competition gun, as well as a collectable. At one time it was also chambered in .30 Luger, and a .40 S&W version was introduced in 1994. However, beginning in 2011, only the 9mm has been imported into the U.S.

Today, the Browning FN Hi-Power is actually a better gun than John Browning or Dieudonné Saive had originally conceived. The hammer, safety, and trigger pull (although still heavy) have all been improved, it now has an enlarged, ambidextrous safety, and it is available with fixed or adjustable sights. If there's a downside, due to U.S. import restrictions, the magazine now has a reduced capacity of 10 rounds. In addition, a number of limited edition versions, including the 1878-1978 Centennial Model, the highly desirable engraved Louis XVI Model (imported from 1980 to 1984), and the 75th Anniversary Model, with gold-accented and engraved silver nitride finish (a black oxide with thumbrest stocks, and polished blue steel versions are also available), make the Browning Hi-Power the ultimate testimony to John Browning's final vision of what a single-action semi-automatic pistol should be. As such, it deserves a place on our bucket list.

SPRINGFIELD
1873 TRAPDOOR CARBINE

It's easy to see how the Trapdoor got its name.

We tend to think of the Winchester lever-action and the Sharps buffalo rifle as the most prominent and effective firearms of the American West. But there was a third rifle that dramatically helped shape the history of the frontier, the 1873 Springfield Trapdoor .45-70 carbine. In fact, from 1874 until 1892, it was the standard issue shoulder arm for U.S. government mounted troops. Think of it as the MI Garand of the Indian Wars.

In sharp contrast to the muzzleloading muskets that preceded it in U.S. service, which required a soldier to load and fire five times a minute, a skilled cavalry trooper could fire an 1873 Trapdoor *13* times a minute, almost tripling the previous rate of fire; accuracy was probably not a factor in these rapid-fire endeavors. As a practical exercise, I have loaded, aimed, and fired an original Springfield Trapdoor Carbine seven times a minute from horseback, hitting a silhouette target each time. Needless to say, this single-shot cartridge-firing saddle gun was a formidable weapon in the hands of a trained soldier.

Given the limited but dramatic success of the breechloading Sharps and the cartridge-firing Henry during The Great Rebellion, the Army knew it had better start embracing this new technology, if it was going to accomplish its post-war mission of maintaining law in the east and establishing it in the west. Thus began an earnest search to replace its 1861 and 1863 muzzleloading Springfield rifle-muskets.

Ever distrustful of the newfangled repeating rifles, which were too complicated for in-the-field repairs, the Army decided to stick with what it knew best, the single-shot rifle. Much of the pressure to develop a new longarm fell upon Erskine S. Allin, master armorer at Springfield Armory. Drawing inspiration from a previous, reverse-hinged breechblock system invented in 1860 by George W. Morse, and a forward-hinged breechblock patented by William Mont Storm in 1856 at Harpers Ferry, Allin came up with a "quick fix" idea of converting the Armory's more than one million .58-caliber surplus muzzleloaders. He cut off the breech end of the barrels and installed a flip-up firing pin and bolt assembly that swung up on a hinge. In an attempt to identify with this new issue arm, troopers began calling it the Trap-Door Springfield. Allin also came up with a new .58 rimfire cartridge, known as the .58 Allin, a chunky round that featured a 500-grain bullet backed by 60 grains of powder.

Unfortunately, the Model 1865 First Allin rifle and cartridge conversion proved less than adequate in field trials and quickly led to the centerfire .50-caliber Model 1866, in which the .58 muskets had their barrels sleeved to accept the smaller .50 Government bullet. The new cartridge used a stepped-up charge of 70 grains of blackpowder, making the .50-70 the first centerfire cartridge to be officially adopted by the U.S. Army. Additional changes led to the Models 1868 and 1870 in this same caliber.

The .50-70 had limitations, as far as range was concerned. Consequently, the army conducted a series of tests and came up with a perfect combination of caliber, bullet weight, and powder: a .45-caliber, 405-grain lead bullet, backed by 70 grains of blackpowder. Subsequently, the list was whittled down to what would become one of the most famous rifle and cartridge combinations in firearms history, the 1873 Trapdoor Springfield and the .45-70 Government cartridge. Both were literally made for each other.

But it was the 1873 carbine, rather than the rifle, that was the ideal weapon for its time. In the wide-open spaces of the West, it was the cavalry, not the infantry, that was needed. Consequently, because of mounted warfare against the Indians, the 22-inch barreled 1873 saddle gun became the weapon of choice. Although muzzle velocity for the Army's new official cartridge was 1,350 fps when fired from a rifle, it soon became apparent that this was not a favored load for a seven-pound carbine. As a result, the .45-70's powder charge was reduced to 55 grains for the carbine, which produced a muzzle velocity of 1,100 fps, a concession to the saddle gun's lighter weight and resultant increased recoil.

Like the rifle, the carbine featured three-groove rifling with a 1:22 twist, case hardened receiver, and rear sights stamped on the left side with a "C" (rifle sights were stamped with an "R").

All carbines were fitted with a stock-mounted bar and saddle ring, which was hooked to a leather sling worn diagonally across the trooper's body, thus preventing the carbine from being accidently dropped. Unlike subsequent models, the 1873 carbine had no buttplate provision for carrying a detachable cleaning rod. In addition, the first carbines had a stacking swivel affixed to the barrel band; this feature was eliminated in later models.

There were numerous changes made to the 1873 carbine throughout its 20-year lifespan. A few of the more readily identifiable variations include: the Model 1877, with a thicker stock, low-arched breechblock, and hinged buttplate for carrying a three-piece cleaning rod; the Model 1879 with its slightly wider receiver and buckhorn rear sight; and the Model 1884 with its Buffington rear sight.

Like all military guns, parts were readily interchangeable, and it is rare to find a trapdoor in "as issued" condition. Even today, parts are replaced by collectors to upgrade specimens. In addition, because of its romantic image and subsequent desirability, many "carbines" have been made from cut-down rifles. (A filled-in ramrod hole is your first clue.) The most desirable Model 1873 carbines are those with serial numbers below 43,700. These pre-1876 trapdoors are known as "Custer Guns," as there is a chance they saw action on June 25, 1876, at the Little Big Horn. However, as Al Frasca, author of *The .45-70 Springfield*, mentioned to me in an e-mail some years back, "There are so very few [authentic] Custer guns around ... I have not seen one I can say is right, for many years."

Although the 1873 carbine was an enlisted man's weapon, it was quickly embraced by officers, who began ordering customized sporting versions from Springfield Armory. Due to the popularity of these Officer's Models and the disruption they caused to the regular production run of service guns, their features were standardized by the Armory, in 1875. This included a 26-inch barrel, checkered stock, pewter fore-end, and a cleaning rod affixed under the barrel. In all, 477 Model 1873 Officer's Models were produced. Although originally priced at $36, today their costs are in the five-figure range.

The standard 1873 carbine served gallantly in the Indian Wars, as well as the Spanish American War. It was also issued to Apache scouts in Arizona, and, as late as the 1920s was still in use by many National Guard units. In the 1880s and '90s, many carbines were altered for civilian use by firms such as Hartley and Graham of New York, who dressed up these warhorses with buffalo horn fore-ends and checkered stocks. In all, there were 60,912 carbines made from 1873 to 1893, of which approximately 20,000 were actual first issue Model 1873s.

Although once sold as surplus for as little as $3.50 apiece and touted by the Philadelphia firm of W. Stokes Kirk in a 1922 ad as being a "Handy, strong knock-about gun for boys on ranch," it has always been a rugged and reliable firearm. That fact was not lost on Harrington & Richardson, which produced replicas of the trapdoor carbine, in the 1970s. Today, firms such as Dixie Gun Works and Uberti import excellent Pedersoli-made recreations of this famous Indian Wars gun, and original guns can still be readily found at most good-sized gun shows. I still shoot my Model 1879 carbine, which was manufactured in 1881. A five-pointed star stamped after the serial number indicates that this gun was an arsenal rebuild, and further research revealed that, in 1898, this carbine was reissued to the 13th Colorado Volunteers. In addition, I occasionally hunt with my Dixie Gun Works replica and my Pedersoli Officer's Model. So I can tell you from personal experience that the trapdoor carbine, whether original or replica, still can hold its own on my bucket list.

COLT FRONTIER SCOUT .22

Inspired by the popularity of TV westerns such as Gunsmoke and Maverick coupled with the burgeoning sport of fast draw, and no doubt spurred on by the success of Ruger's Single Six, in 1957, Colt Industries brought out a .22-caliber version of its famed Single Action Army, which they had reintroduced two years earlier. This new, scaled-down sixgun was appropriately christened the Colt Frontier Scout.

Initially, the Scout was offered with a polished aluminum "duo-tone" frame that contrasted nicely with the rest of the blued gun, somewhat akin to the aluminum-framed Lightweight Single Six that Ruger had brought out in 1955. Also like the Ruger, the Scout featured a one-piece backstrap and trigger guard, which made production less costly than hand fitting a two-piece trigger guard and backstrap to the frame.

Actually, the Scout was machined to such close tolerances and so well finished, very little hand fitting was necessary. Each gun went through a five-man team of inspectors and assemblers. Moreover, according to the late Don Wilkerson in his excellent and now out-of-print book *Scouts, Peacemakers and New Frontiers*, the same machinery used for the top-of-the-line Colt Python was used to machine and polish the barrels of the Scout, which justifiably became known for its accuracy.

Initially, the Scout was fitted with black composition grips similar to those on the Model P, but walnut grips were offered as an extra-cost option a year later. Barrel length was 4¾ inches, but, due to its smaller size, this gave the little .22 the same look as its big brother with a 5½-inch barrel, as the muzzle poked slightly past the ejector rod housing.

Even though the Frontier Scout resembled the Model P externally, internally it was a different gun. The post-war spring-loaded push

Although the Colt .22 Scout Buntline only has a 9½-inch barrel, its smaller scale puts it in proportion to the 12-inch barrel of the larger .45 Colt Buntline. This gun is courtesy of American Gun Works (www. AmericanGun Works .net)

pin that held the cylinder base pin was replaced by a lookalike screw, which required a screwdriver (included with each gun), for removal. The action was simplified by having only two screws—one for the hammer, the other for the bolt and trigger—instead of the Peacemaker's three. Finally, the firing pin was inset into the frame, rather than allowed to protrude from the hammer.

Because ads announcing the new Colt Frontier Scout began appearing in 1956—almost a full year before the first guns were shipped from the factory, on November 27, 1957—demand had built. Priced at only $49.50 (later at $54.50, for walnut stocks), the Colt Scout proved immensely popular right out of the starting gate. Now owners of the full-sized SAA could have an economical seven-eighths scale version to shoot, and for those who couldn't afford the $125 price of the big SAA, they could still buy a genuine Colt single-action for less than half the price. By the end of 1958, more than 36,500 Frontier Scouts had been shipped from the factory.

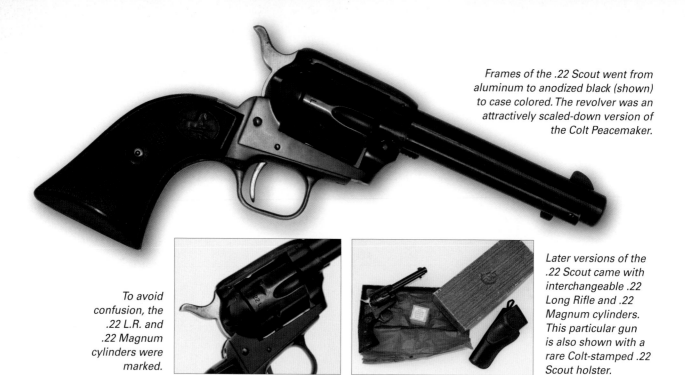

Frames of the .22 Scout went from aluminum to anodized black (shown) to case colored. The revolver was an attractively scaled-down version of the Colt Peacemaker.

To avoid confusion, the .22 L.R. and .22 Magnum cylinders were marked.

Later versions of the .22 Scout came with interchangeable .22 Long Rifle and .22 Magnum cylinders. This particular gun is also shown with a rare Colt-stamped .22 Scout holster.

In September 1958, an all-blued (actually a black anodized aluminum frame) Frontier Scout was added for $57.50, and, in November of that year, a Buntline Scout was introduced. Priced at $59.50, the Buntline's 9½-inch barrel gave it a profile that closely followed Colt's full-sized 12-inch barreled version introduced a year earlier.

In 1959, a .22 Winchester Magnum chambering for both the Frontier Scout and Buntline Scout was offered, and it was only a matter of time—1964, actually—that dual cylinder Scouts were introduced. A dual cylinder Buntline Scout was added, in 1969. These guns were also offered in two-gun cased sets. Because the rifling differed for the .22 Magnum barrel (which would also stabilize a .22 Long Rifle bullet, but a barrel rifled for the .22 Long Rifle would not give acceptable accuracy with a .22 Magnum), factory assemblers had to know which barrel to fit onto a frame, especially if it was for a dual-caliber gun. Thus, .22 Magnum barrels featured a crowned muzzle, while .22 Long Rifle barrels were finished flat at the muzzles. In addition, .22 Long Rifle cylinders were recessed on the back, while the rear of .22 Magnum cylinders were flush.

Collectors tend to classify Frontier Scouts by the suffix letter designation of their serial numbers, with the "Q" series denoting the first two years of production, after which it was changed to an "F" series, as the "Q" looked too much like an "O" and could be misconstrued as part of the numerical serial number. The "F" series lasted until 1971, when the lightweight-framed Frontier Scout was discontinued in favor of the "K" series, which denotes a heavier "Zamac" (zinc-aluminum) frame. The "K" series also introduced a nickel finish option.

A "P" series ran concurrently with the "F" series and lasted from 1962 until 1971. It was used for the Scout's deeper "Midnight Blue" finish (actually an epoxy coating) on its Zamac frame, and the addition of composite "stag" stocks. There were also a few special-order nickel Scouts in the "P" series. The final Scouts were produced in the "G" Series, which featured a case hardened steel frame and ebony "eagle" rampant colt stocks. This was the closest the Frontier Scout came to duplicating the physical look of the Model P. Subsequently, the name was changed to the Peacemaker .22. Barrel lengths were 4.4 inches (approximating the 4¾-inch barrel "look" of the full-sized Colt), six inches, and a 7½-inch Buntline. There was also a New Frontier Scout with adjustable sights, introduced in 1971. The "G" series was produced from 1970 to 1977, when production was temporarily halted due to manufacturing problems. After a four-year hiatus, the Peacemaker .22 and New Frontier Scout reappeared with a cross-bolt safety and the "G" series became the "GS." In 1985, a fully blued version was offered.

The Frontier Scout also accounted for more than seventy different commemoratives, starting, in 1961, with the Pony Express Centennial Scout and the Kansas Statehood Scout, and ending, in 1984, with a "G"-framed Kit Carson New Frontier. Most of the commemoratives were produced on the "K" frame.

Production of the Frontier Scout in all its forms came to an end, in 1986. As far as consumer interest was concerned, a *Star Wars* mentality had taken over, and the Frontier Scout slowly rode off into the sunset. Today, it is a much sought-after .22 single-action, and, like the Old West itself, a reminder of days gone by.

This was one of the guns I always wanted as a kid, but, of course, could never afford and, consequently, never got. When I finally did get old enough and had saved enough, I bought a full-sized, used, first generation Single Action Army .45 instead. But now that I am older and, perhaps, wiser than I ever have been, this is definitely a gun I am adding to my bucket list.

THE L.C. SMITH

By all accounts, the sidelock double-barreled shotgun belongs to the British. Indeed, "best guns" such as Purdey and Holland & Holland set the tone for the classic gentleman's sidelock of the nineteenth and twentieth centuries. In America, names like Parker and Remington were giving the Union Jack a run for its money, but the hammerless versions were boxlocks, which became the norm. Only one firearms manufacturer emerged with the mechanical skills to produce an American hammerless sidelock, an elegant, sturdy shotgun that took the name of its creator, L.C. Smith—or "Elsie," as this well-designed side-by-side was affectionately called.

Hacker's 16-gauge L.C. Smith Ideal Grade was completely refurbished and brought back to life by Briley Manufacturing of Houston, Texas.

Lyman Cornelius Smith had been in partnership with his brother, Leroy, and a neighbor, W.H. Baker, manufacturing and marketing Baker's unique three-barreled drilling, which consisted of two side-by-side 12- or 10-gauge smoothbores over a .44-40 barrel. But this European-styled design wasn't popular in America, and, by 1880, L.C. Smith found himself the sole proprietor of W.H. Baker & Co.

Having married into a prosperous family, money wasn't a problem for Smith—but success was. Sales lagged. Fortunately, the entrepreneurial Smith had an inventive employee named Alexander T. Brown (who went on to develop the Dunlop tire and other automotive inventions in later years). Brown designed an exposed hammer sidelock double, which involved a sturdy "double cross-locking" rotary bolt, a strengthened barrel hinge, and hammer ears that dropped below the shooter's line of sight when cocked. Produced in 10- and

12-gauge, the new "L.C. Smith Hammer Gun" was introduced, in 1884, with much fanfare and success.

This greatly improved smoothbore was offered in a number of grades, or "Qualities," as the company initially called them, ranging from 2 through 7 (or A to F and AA in subsequent catalogs) and priced from $55 up to $450, princely sums in the days of an average $16 weekly paycheck. For escalating Qualities and prices, you got progressively better grades of Damascus and, later, fluid steel barrels, more engraving, and better, more finely checkered wood. In 1913, the L.C. Smith grading system changed to reflect names like Field, Ideal, Olympic, Trap, Specialty, Eagle, Crown, Mono-

A double on ducks, taken with the Italian-made L.C. Smith, which performs extremely well in the field, but doesn't have the collectability of the original side lock.

gram, Premier, and De Luxe. In addition, a 12-gauge single-barreled trap gun was produced between 1917 and World War II.

Clearly, the L.C. Smith shotgun was geared towards sportsmen who wanted the best and were willing to pay for it. But, while the shotgun attracted well-heeled hunters, it failed to hold L.C. Smith's attention; he had become enthralled with developing a new-fangled device called the typewriter. Thus, in 1888, Smith sold his company to a Fulton, New York, railroad builder named John Hunter, Sr. Hunter was looking for new ventures at the time and was planning to invest in a shotgun a neighbor named Harry Comstock was de-

veloping. Indeed, had Leroy Smith not learned about Hunter's gunmaking interests, you might have been reading about the Comstock shotgun instead of those by L.C. Smith. Alas, for poor Harry, his patents and a pending partnership were scrapped once Hunter met Smith. After all, here was a quality shotgun, already established and with machinery and workers in place. Consequently, L.C. Smith went on to create what would become the famous Smith-Corona typewriter, and Hunter Arms Company was established to manufacture the equally famous L.C. Smith shotgun. And so it was under the Hunter Arms banner, which flew from 1889 until 1945, that the L.C. Smith legacy was established. This was America's golden age of shotgunning, and we now had our very own sidelock with which to break records and bag birds.

In 1889, the Hunter Arms Company built a factory in Fulton, New York, a location that—under the leadership of John Sr. and, over the years, with his six sons—was to become revered in the annals of shotgunning. The guns were stamped "L.C. Smith" on the lockplates, while the barrels were marked, "HUNTER ARMS CO.–MAKERS–FULTON, N.Y." In 1891, a 16-gauge was added to the line, and, in 1896, a few 8-gauges were produced; the 8-bores were discontinued one year later and today are extremely rare. In 1908, the first L.C. Smith 20-gauge made its appearance. Only one 28-gauge was made, serial No. 100, while the .410 was introduced in 1926, with a scant 2,665 of these smallbores known to exist.

In 1892, L.C. Smith became the first U.S.-made shotgun to offer automatic ejectors, especially featured, in 1895, on the company's top-of-the-line A3 Automatic Ejector Gun. Additionally, in 1904, the company catalog touted its new Hunter One-Trigger, a non-selective system that fired the right barrel first. The Hunter One-Trigger could be ordered in any of three fixed positions: forward, middle of the trigger guard, or to the rear. It was extremely fast, yet was guaranteed against doubling. Later, in 1935, a selective single trigger was offered.

Every L.C. Smith exuded quality, from the "workhorse" blued and case hardened 00 Field Grade to the elaborately engraved and checkered A3 Monogram. Internally, all guns exhibited the same excellent workmanship. Barrels were imported rough-bored, then reamed and polished at the factory. Initially there were varying grades of Damascus, ranging from English Stub Twist to the finest qualities and patterns. Later, only the best steel tubes were used, escalating in quality from Armour Steel on the Field Grade to Nitro and Royal Steel on the higher grades. Each tube was hand straightened, and the pairs of tubes were brazed together, rather than soldered. All internal parts were mirror-polished and hand fitted. Higher grades had internal parts damascened, like a fine pocketwatch. Stocks were American, English, or French walnut, shaped at the factory and hand rubbed with linseed oil; the higher the grade, the more coats the stock received. The completed guns were then test fired for patterning perfection at the company's indoor range.

Unfortunately, the reoccurring gremlins of financial woes and mismanagement plagued this family-owned operation and, in 1917, the Hunter Arms Company filed for bankruptcy. The reins were quickly picked up by a small cadre of Fulton businessmen who didn't want to lose L.C. Smith, which was the town's claim to fame. Nonetheless, in 1920, the company was sold to the Simmons family of Massachusetts, who, unfortunately, also did a less than stellar job of management. On one occasion, Hunter Arms was contracted to make a bolt-action shotgun for Sears Roebuck & Company, but a miscalculation of costs resulted in financial catastrophe. Then, in 1939, the company was put up for sale, but World War II halted negotiations. After continuing shotgun making for both civilians and the government, Hunter Arms again went into bankruptcy.

This time to its rescue rode the Marlin Firearms Company, which, on November 20, 1945, purchased the assets. The plant was reopened as the L.C. Smith Gun Company—the first time "Smith" was included as part of the company name. It was a perfect match, as Marlin, led by Frank Kenna, was also family owned. Unfortunately, after only five years, in which a total of 57,929 guns were made, a floor in the factory collapsed, putting L.C. Smith out of business.

In 1967, Frank Kenna, Jr., who'd become president of Marlin in 1959, resurrected L.C. Smith as a limited production gun. This time it was made in Marlin's New Haven, Connecticut, factory. Offered only in 12-gauge, it differed from the original in that it featured a ventilated rib. But the demands of producing a labor-intensive sidelock, plus competition from imports and the popularity of pumps and semi-automatics doomed the "Elsie." A scant 2,539 Marlin-made L.C. Smiths were all that remained of this classic double, before production was finally halted, in 1971.

Interestingly, Marlin resurrected the L.C. Smith once again, but this time it was in name only. The new side-by-side was, in reality, a boxlock made in Italy, one that featured false sideplates to make it look like a sidelock. It was offered in 12- and 20-gauge, and there was an Italian-made L.C. Smith over-and-under as well. Both were made for Marlin by the well-known firm of Fausti Stefano, cataloged only from 2005 through 2009. I took one of the new 12 bore side-by-sides on a Canadian goose hunt and found that the gun, with its single selective trigger and screw-in chokes, performed admirably. But though it was well made, I was bothered by the false sideplates over a boxlock action. Why not just call it as it is—a boxlock—rather than trying to make it look like something it isn't—a sidelock? Still, unlike my original 16-gauge L C Smith Ideal Grade, I wasn't afraid to get this one wet and muddy. You can still find those Fausti-made guns in used condition and fairly affordable but, of course, they have no collector's value. Personally, I would much rather have an original, as made by the Hunter family, or a post-war gun made by Marlin.

It is interesting to note that L.C. Smith, the man who gave his name to this legendary American sidelock, was involved with it only for a brief four-year period. Yet his namesake shotgun continues to endure as both a highly desirable hunting companion and a collectable, while the typewriter he invented has become obsolete.

MODEL 1903 SPRINGFIELD

Once the .30-06 cartridge was adopted for the Model 1903, the flip-up rear battle sights were optimistically calibrated for 2,850 yards. With the leaf folded down, the sights were set for a slightly more realistic 525 yards.

Originally designed in 1900, revised in 1901 and 1902, and formally drafted into the service in 1903, the '03 Springfield—or more officially, United States Rifle, Caliber .30, Model 1903—marked a turning point in the way the Army viewed the infantry rifle.

For one thing, unlike previous individual shoulder weapons such as the 1892-99 Krag-Jorgensen and the trapdoor Springfield, which were issued in both rifle and carbine versions, the 1903 Springfield existed only as a rifle. Moreover, it was a bolt-action that fired a new high-pressure smokeless powder cartridge with a spitzer bullet. The rifle's development was given additional emphasis when Theodore Roosevelt—who had battlefield experience in the Spanish American War with the slow-loading .30-40 Krag—became president after McKinley's assassination. Specifically developed as an improvement over the Krag, the 1903 Springfield was approved on June 20, 1903, and manufacturing was undertaken by both Springfield Armory and Rock Island Arsenal.

The milled trigger guard of the WWI 1903 would eventually be changed to a stamped steel version on the 1903A3, during WWII. Note the O.G.E.K. Elmer Keith inspector's mark, showing this rifle was inspected by the well-known late gun writer during his stint at the Ogden, Utah, arsenal in the 1930s.

The 1903 Springfield weighed 8½ pounds, had a 24-inch barrel, and featured a full-length wooden stock with elongated finger-groove forearm and a "humped" handguard to protect the rear sight. Its internal, five-round magazine was loaded via a stripper clip, with cartridges thumb-pressed into the magazine through the opened receiver. The rifle also incorporated a unique "rod bayonet" that slid out from the stock underneath the barrel, providing a comparatively flimsy means of close-quarters combat. Soldiers were thankful when the much sturdier Model 1905 bayonet, with its 16-inch blade, was adopted, largely due to the insistence of Roosevelt, who called the rod bayonet, "about as poor an invention as I ever saw."

The '03 Springfield incorporated many features, including safety and extractor modifications and stripper clip, from the 1893 Mauser. In fact, royalties were paid by the U.S. government to the Mauser factory, which was rather ironic, considering an impending World War with the Kaiser was on the not-too-distant horizon. But, among the 1903 Springfield's other attributes was a non-rotary extractor that prevented the double feeding of cartridges, and a bolt-cocking plunger, which permitted the rifle to be de-cocked by pulling the trigger while holding back and manually releasing the plunger, thus without having to fire the rifle.

Bordering on the "What were they thinking?" syndrome was the M1903's magazine "Cut Off Lever," a thick steel tab located on the left side of the receiver and incorporated to allay governmental fears of a wanton waste of ammo by trigger-happy troops armed with this new "repeater." It was no doubt prompted by some of the Old Guard, who may have still remembered doing battle with the single-shot Trapdoor Springfield. When placed in the middle position, the Cut Off Lever permitted the bolt to be withdrawn from the receiver and, when in the upward "On" position, the rifle functioned like a bolt-action should, ejecting and feeding rounds as the bolt was operated. However, when in its "Off" or downward position, which nestled the tab into an inlet in the stock, the Cut Off Lever disengaged the magazine follower. Thus, cartridges would not feed into the chamber from the fixed magazine when the bolt went forward. This effectively turned the rifle from a bolt-action repeater with a cycling rate of 15 to 20 shots per minute into a bolt-action single-shot.

During basic training, recruits were instructed to employ the magazine Cut Off Lever in the "Off" position and to load each round manually, keeping the cartridges in the internal magazine as a reserve. These instructions were no doubt immediately forgotten as soon as a doughboy got into his first firefight.

Originally, the 1903 Springfield was chambered for a round that almost immediately became obsolete, the .30-03, even though, at the time, it was heralded as an improvement over the .30-40 Krag. But it used the same 200-grain round-nosed bullet, which resulted in a rainbow trajectory that sacrificed range and accuracy. The .30-03 also built up excessive chamber pressures and, hence, recoil.

Consequently, in 1906, the Springfield's caliber was changed to what has become one of the most famous cartridges of all time, the .30-06 Government. Designated "Cartridge, Ball, Caliber .30, Model of 1906," it fired a 150-grain spitzer bullet (changed to a 172-grain boat-tail, in 1926), which left the barrel at 2,800 fps. This revolutionary new cartridge necessitated a slight redesign of the rifle, which included changing the rear sight to compensate for the flatter trajectory of the .30-06. The government optimistically calibrated the flip-up battle sights for 2,850 yards. With the leaf folded down, the sight was set for 525 yards. Rifles already chambered for the .30-03 were altered by having their barrels turned back slightly and their chambers recut. Today, any early 1903 Springfield in original .30-03 configuration is a rarity.

One such gun that retained its .30-03 chambering was serial No. 6000, which was ordered by President Roosevelt soon after the 1903's adoption. Roosevelt heartedly embraced the new bolt-action, and had No. 6000 made into a customized sporter, the first such "sporterized" '03 on record. Following Roosevelt's lead, a budding group of custom riflemakers, including Griffin & Howe, Fred Adolph, and R.F. Sedgley, transformed these surplus workhorse military rifles into classic sporting arms, during the first part of the twentieth century.

By the time the U.S. entered World War I, in 1917, 843,239 rifles were already in service and production quickly ramped up. After the Armistice, manufacturing was halted at Rock Island, but the 1903 continued to be made at Springfield Armory, until 1927. The rifle was again brought into battle during World War II, with Remington and Smith-Corona joining in its production.

There were numerous variants of the Model 1903, including the 1903A1 with semi-pistol grip stock, the WWII–era 1903A3 with stamped metal parts, and the 1903A4 sniper rifle. It should be noted that early heat treating problems have resulted in a small number of rifles wearing serial numbers below 800,000 (Springfield Armory) and under 286,506 (Rock Island Arsenal) malfunctioning and causing damage to both gun and shooter. These guns are generally considered unsafe to fire without extensive examination of the metallurgy.

Manufacturing of the Springfield 1903, which had become the 1903A3, was halted, in 1945, when it was overshadowed by the M1 Garand. However, the Springfield's excellent accuracy and superb balance kept it in the service, until 1957. In fact, it was this superb balance that first brought the 1903 to my attention years later, for it was not on the firing line, but in ROTC, as a member of the Pershing Rifles Drill Team at Arizona State University. Using military surplus nickeled rifles with white leather slings, we executed complex maneuvers with the 1903, such as twirls, spins, and the Queen Anne Salute. Today, as a shooter and collector, I have come to fully appreciate the 1903 Springfield as one of the finest and most versatile military rifles of the twentieth century, and well deserving to be on my bucket list.

COLT
1903-1908 POCKET
HAMMERLESS

In 1900, as the world rounded the bend heading into the twentieth century, Colt's Patent Firearms Manufacturing took the lead in the race for American handgun superiority. The company had already made the transition from single-action to double-action revolvers, and now, with what would prove to be a legendary link with firearms genius John Moses Browning, Colt's had just introduced its first semi-automatic pistol, a gun that Browning had been developing since 1894.

The Colt 1903 Pocket Hammerless came boxed with a set of instructions that reminded the owner the trigger had to be pulled once for each shot fired, in spite of the pistol's "automatic" nomenclature. Remember, this was before The National Firearms Act of 1934, which prohibited private ownership of fully automatic weapons.

Years before, while duck hunting in a Utah marsh, Browning became fascinated by the way the blasts from his shotgun would sway the reeds surrounding the muzzle. Realizing this was an indication of energy, the young gunsmith began wondering how he could harness these escaping gases and trap them into operating the action of a pistol. The result was Colt's first successful semi-auto, the Model 1900, although, at that early stage of its development, it was simply stamped, "Automatic Colt—Browning's Patent." Chambered in .38 Colt Automatic (.38 ACP), a semi-rimless round developed by Browning specifically for this gun—the magazine held seven rounds. With a six-inch barrel and a less-than-ergonomic grip, the Model 1900 did not balance well, although it can lay claim to being the first-ever "long slide" semi-automatic. Its high, thin hammer spur aided in cocking the single-action, blowback design, which had the unusual feature of a rear sight that doubled as a safety; when pushed down, it blocked the hammer from striking the primer.

Approximately 3,500 Model 1900s were manufactured (including about 350 military marked versions for the Army and the Navy). But, obviously, there was room for improvement. In 1902, a Sporting Model was introduced, which eliminated the rear sight/safety combination and, instead, had the gun rely upon a shorter firing pin to prevent accidental discharge; a full blow from the hammer was required to provide enough inertia to fire the chambered cartridge. At the same time, and inexplicably, a much more cumbersome rounded hammer spur replaced the previous thinner profile. A military version of the 1902 was also produced that featured a slide stop and lanyard ring, plus a longer grip and a correspondingly larger magazine that held eight rounds instead of seven.

The success of the Model 1902 was evident by the appearance, one year later, of a similar version, dubbed the Pocket Model of 1903, which sported a shorter 4½-inch barrel. But that gun was quickly eclipsed by the Colt 1903 Pocket Hammerless, or the Model M, as it was factory designated, which had an even shorter four-inch barrel. This made the Pocket Hammerless a much more compact and practical pistol. In fact, it proved so popular, it remained in the Colt line until 1945.

The gun wasn't actually hammerless at all, but the breech end of its closed, rounded slide concealed the hammer. The result was a snag-proof handgun that could easily be carried in pocket or purse and quickly drawn with little to hinder a fast presentation. Moreover, the Pocket Hammerless featured the first of Colt's grip safeties, which was located under the rear arch of the backstrap. Unless the pistol was firmly grasped with the web of the thumb depressing this safety, the gun couldn't fire. In addition, a newly incorporated "Slide Lock" on the left side of the frame prevented the cocked hammer from falling when the slide lock lever was pushed up. "This allows the arm to be carried cocked, without danger of accidental discharge," stated Colt's literature. In essence, this was the first instance of what is today known as "cocked and locked," or the Condition One carry.

The Colt Hammerless Pocket Model of 1903 was chambered for the Browning-designed .32 ACP (Automatic Colt Pistol) cartridge, which had already achieved a fair amount of popularity in Europe, where it was known as the 7.65mm. Although considered a bare minimum for self-defense, its small size enabled eight rounds to be stacked in the 1903's magazine, which had its release located on the heel of the grip frame. In 1908, a nearly identical variation, the Model 1908, was chambered for .380 ACP, another Browning-designed round that was slightly more potent as a man-stopper. Only seven rounds could be carried in its magazine, but the .380 packed a slightly bigger punch.

The guns were charcoal blued, with nickeled versions available, but noticeably scarcer. Grips were originally checkered hard rubber embossed with a rampant Colt; checkered walnut with an inset Colt medallion became standard, in 1924. Factory ivory or pearl grips were available at extra cost, as was engraving, although such guns are rare. Collectors categorize the 1903-1908 Hammerless into four distinct types, though with some overlapping features: Type I (1903-1910) has a four-inch barrel and barrel bushing; Type II (1908-1910) has a 3¾-inch barrel; Type III (1910-1926) retains the shorter 3¾-inch barrel, but no longer has a barrel bushing; and Type IV (1926-1945)

The Colt 1908 (top) and the 1903 (bottom), were outwardly identical, except for the caliber, which was stamped on the right side of the slide.

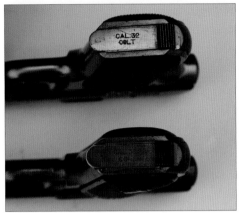

The magazines of the 1908 and the 1903 Pocket Hammerless were stamped with their respective calibers and, of course, were not interchangeable between the two different guns.

has an added magazine safety.

With its fast action, easy pointability, and a weight of just 24 ounces, the Hammerless Pocket Model of 1903-1908 was a favorite of many notable personalities, including the infamous Al Capone and popular cowboy movie star Tom Mix. In addition, Humphrey Bogart, as Detective Phillip Marlowe, brandished one in *The Big Sleep*. More recently, Johnny Depp—a gun guy in real life—packed one as John Dillinger in *Public Enemies*. There was also a rare variant (sometimes referred to as a Type V version), known as General Officer pistols, which were issued to U.S. Army and Air Force officers, including Generals Patton, Bradley, and Eisenhower. Prior to 1942, these "U.S. Property" marked guns were blued. After that, and up until 1970, when these General Officer pistols were replaced with a 1911 version (the M15), the guns were Parkerized. Several thousand hammerless pocket pistols were also sent to the British Home Guard, during WWII.

In all, more than 572,000 of these little guns, in both civilian and military guises, were produced, making it one of the most prolific Colts to ever leave the Hartford stables. Today, it is both a collectable and a classic self-defense arm, the purpose for which it was originally designed over a century ago. In either caliber, although my preference would be for the 1908 version in .380 ACP, it belongs on our bucket list.

WINCHESTER
1885 HIGH WALL

While the 1860 Henry Repeating Rifle can rightfully be credited as the gun that started the Winchester lever-action legacy, it was actually a single-shot invented 19 years later that paved the way for the company's continued success and profitability well into the smokeless powder era.

On May 12, 1879, John Moses Browning, just 24 years of age, and his younger half-brother Ed, received a patent for a single-shot, falling breech rifle they had invented. The Browning brothers soon began manufacturing and selling their Model 1878 Single Shot from their modest shop in Ogden, Utah. The octagon barreled guns were stamped "Browning Bros, Ogden Utah, USA" across the top barrel flat and are now exceedingly rare, with the few surviving specimens commanding figures well into five-digit ranges.

By 1883, with slightly less than 600 of the hand-built Browning single-shots sold, word of the rifle's existence reached T.G. Bennett, Oliver Winchester's son-in-law, who was also vice president of the company. Bennett knew Winchester was losing out to the Marlin 1881 lever-action, especially in its .45-70 chambering, as a large segment of the hunting market was demanding heavier bullets for dangerous game. Winchester's Model 1873 and 1876 repeaters, with their short actions and toggle link systems, could not handle these longer,

more powerful cartridges. Bennett also knew his father-in-law's company had to expand its line, if it was to remain competitive, and back then, just as it is today, one of the great debates was whether a rapid-fire repeater was more effective than one well-placed and more powerful bullet from a single-shot.

The collapse of the Sharps Rifle Company, in 1881, left the field open for a new sporting rifle that could handle the more popular big-game rounds of the day. Thus, Bennett decided to make the long, dusty train trip from New Haven to Ogden and, after arriving in town and doing some diligent searching, he strode into the Browning gun shop. Bennett was surprised to discover that the two "workmen" he saw huddled over their benches intently building rifles were actually John and Ed Browning. He promptly offered them $8,000 for their patent and all their single-shot inventory. The Browning brothers agreed, and Winchester soon began tooling up for what would become one of the most versatile single-shot rifles in firearms history.

First, Winchester set about slightly revamping the stock and receiver dimensions, ending up with a more graceful looking gun. The company also renamed it the Winchester Model 1885, although it was initially referred to as simply the Winchester Single Shot in catalogs, a notable departure from the famous Winchester Repeating Rifles moniker. This first Browning-designed Winchester rifle made its debut in November 1885. It incorporated an open-curved finger lever similar to that of the Maynard No. 16 Target Rifle. When the lever was thrown forward, a solid breechblock dropped, which withdrew the floating firing pin and exposed the breech for loading and cleaning. Closing the breech automatically cocked the hammer, readying it for the next shot. Of course, the exposed hammer could be manually cocked or lowered, as well. Unlike the Sharps, which featured a large, heavy side hammer and an angled firing pin, the Model 1885 sported a much lighter, centrally mounted hammer and a firing pin that was in line with the bore. It consequently had a fast lock time and accuracy was superb. Small wonder the rifle was embraced by hunters and target shooters alike.

But then, why shouldn't it have been? From the onset, buyers had a choice of single or double set triggers, no less than five different barrel weights, four different frame sizes, straight or pistol grip stocks, checkered or plain stocks in different grades of walnut, and an almost limitless choice of front and rear sights. During the course of its production, the Model 1885 encompassed Sporting Rifles (with straight gripped stock), Special Sporting Rifles (with pistol grip), Military Muskets, spur lever Schuetzens with adjustable palm rests and extended butt plates, and an ultra-rare baby carbine. All came with a wooden (later brass) cleaning rod. Takedown options and engraving could be special ordered on any of these versions.

Most impressive was the incredible number of calibers offered for the Winchester Model 1885. During its lifetime, no less than 65 chamberings were available, ranging from .22 Short all the way up to the .50-140 Winchester Express (basically the same as the .50-140 Sharps, but reintroduced in the late 1880s to take advantage of the Model 1885's popularity). Sandwiched in between were such versatile rounds as the .405 Winchester and even the .30-06. Because of these vast and varied caliber designations, two versions of the Model 1885 were eventually created. The original configuration is now known as the High Wall, as its receiver frame concealed all of the breechblock, with just the hammer spur exposed for cocking. For smaller-sized cartridges, a Low Wall design emerged right around the 5,000 serial number range. This variation featured a slightly scaled-down receiver in which all of the breechblock and hammer were exposed. Both High Wall and Low Wall rifles were numbered in the same Model 1885 serial range. Generally, Low Walls had barrel lengths of 24 or 26 inches, while High Walls sported 30-inch barrels, but there were numerous variations, depending on the customer's desires.

Initially all single-shots came with case hardened receivers, but right around 1910, in the 90,000 serial range, blued receivers became standard. Somewhere between the 100,000 to 110,000 range, the flat mainspring was changed to coil and the hammer was redesigned so that it was brought to half cock, rather than full, when the lever was closed.

With 139,725 Model 1885 Single Shots produced, production was finally halted, in 1920. By that time, Winchester had become legendary with Browning-designed lever-actions that included Models 1886, '92, '94, and '95—none of which might have been possible had it not been for the Model 1885, a single-shot rifle that introduced John M. Browning to Winchester, thereby launching one of the most successful collaborations in firearms history.

Many years ago, I purchased a brand new Browning 78, which was basically an updated reintroduction of the older Hi Wall, in .30-06. I outfitted this graceful, tapered octagon-barreled rifle with a Leopold Vari-X scope and with that combination went on to make some respectable long-range one-shot kills, including a 375-yard shot on a Wyoming antelope. I had failed earlier in that day with my muzzleloader at 60 yards—go figure! But now I think it is time to do some hunting with the real deal, so the Winchester 1885 High Wall goes on my bucket list. I'll know the right caliber when I find the right gun.

REMINGTON
MODEL 95 DOUBLE DERRINGER

Like Levi jeans and Stetson hats, the term "derringer" has become a lexicon of frontier Americana. Originally, the name was derived from the popularity of the small percussion pistols made by Henry Deringer, Jr., beginning around the 1830s. But one of the many guns that generically took this gunmaker's name has outlived the manufacturing span of any other "derringer" created before it or since.

Fittingly, it was America's oldest gunmaker, E. Remington & Sons, that produced the Model 95—more popularly known as the Remington Double Derringer—a palm-sized, close-range defense gun that remained in production from 1866 until 1935. More than 150,000 Model 95s were produced in a remarkable 69-year span that saw the emergence of post-Civil War frontier America, the settling of the West, a World War, the roaring twenties, and the Great Depression, which indirectly had a hand in the eventual demise of the graceful over-and-under pocket pistol.

In a way, this is really the story about a brilliant dentist from Plattsburgh, New York, named William H. Elliott. By the 1850s, Dr. Elliott had already invented numerous dental devices, when he decided to focus his visionary genius on firearms. Before his career was over, he would hold the patents to no less than 50 different firearms, one of which would be the famous Colt Lightning slide-action rifle. The other notable gun would be the Remington double derringer.

Dr. Elliott launched his gun inventing career by setting up shop as Elliott Arms Co., with offices located at 404 Broadway, in New York City. However, being a firearms' visionary rather than a manufacturer, he contracted with Remington to make his guns for him. On December 12, 1865, Elliott was issued a patent for a unique "over under" double-barreled derringer with a spur trigger and graceful bird's head grip. The barrels

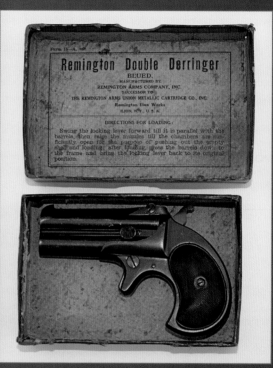

Remington's Model 95 came in a cardboard box, although presentation cases were offered for engraved and plated guns.

pivoted upwards on a hinge and, when closed, were secured to the frame by a rotating lever on the right-hand side. The real key to this little gun's design was a single oscillating firing pin built into the hammer. This fired one of the barrels with the first cocking of the gun, and then automatically positioned itself up or down, as the case may be, when the hammer was cocked again to fire the other barrel. Remington's earliest catalogs listed it as its "Double Repeating Derringer Pistol," a name notably longer than the 4⅞-inch, 11-ounce gun. Later, Remington UMC box labels simply described it as a "Double Derringer," with two "r's" in the spelling to fend off any possible lawsuits by Henry Deringer, Jr., who was adamant about protecting his name.

Unlike his earlier .22- and .32-caliber pepperboxstyle guns, Elliott's double derringer was chambered for the bigger-bored .41 Short, a rimfire cartridge that had been introduced, in 1863, by the National Firearms Company. The stubby little round contained 13 grains of black powder topped off by a 130-grain soft lead bullet. All of this combined to produce a muzzle velocity of 425 fps and a muzzle energy of 52 ft-lbs, or approximately one-tenth that of the soon-to-be developed .44-40. And although the Remington derringer boasted three-inch barrels, much of that length was taken up by the cartridge inside the tube. Still, there was just enough five-grooved rifling to give the bullet stabilization, if not accuracy.

In addition to its large caliber and small size, another factor in the tiny gun's popularity was its equally small price tag. It initially listed for $8 blued; a fully nickeled version could be had for $.50 more. Engraved guns, although rare, were offered for $11, and rosewood, ivory or pearl grips were also extra cost options. The first guns were made without an extractor, but this was soon remedied with a push-type double extractor on the left side of the barrels. In all, there were three basic variations, with numerous sub-variations and barrel rib stampings, as well as hammer and extractor checkering differences.

The double derringer's sights, befitting its low-powered chambering, were rudimentary at best, consisting of a token shallow notch over the hinge and a front sight that was part of the top barrel's rib—then again, this was strictly a close-in self-defense weapon, with a practical shooting range that wasn't expected to exceed the width of a Faro table.

Indeed, the little gun was immediately embraced by soiled doves, gamblers, and all manner of nefarious individuals who haunted the smoke-filled saloons and dark alleyways of eastern cities and frontier towns. Clandestinely carried in garter belts, vests, and armband holsters, the derringer could instantly turn a losing streak into a winning one.

Of course, not everyone who carried a double derringer was on the shady side of the law. Businessmen, sutlers, and folks who didn't want to openly flaunt a large-framed revolver often opted for the vest pocket-sized Remington. In addition, William F. "Buffalo Bill" Cody found that the Remington derringer made handy and relatively inexpensive presentation gifts. He gave one such gun, factory engraved on the butt, to dime novel writer Colonel Prentiss Ingraham. Another derringer, suitably engraved and silver-plated, was presented by Cody to a William Fieldmer. And there are tales of double derringers being used by officers

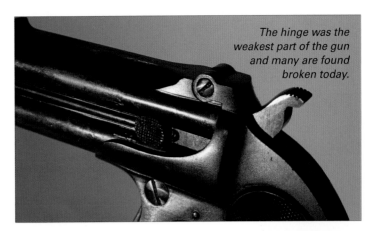

The hinge was the weakest part of the gun and many are found broken today.

during World War I, as backup weapons.

Although the derringer could be deadly at point blank range, from a practical standpoint, its use was psychological at best. During one gunfight chronicled from the late nineteenth century, a gambler was shot in the forehead with a double derringer. Rather than penetrating the skull, the chunky bullet merely knocked the culprit unconscious. It is therefore worth quoting the late Frank C. Barnes in his Cartridges of the World, in which he writes, "The .41 rimfire Short is so underpowered as to be worthless for anything but rats, mice, or sparrows at short range. Fired from the average deringer [sic] at a tree or hard object 15 to 25 yards away, the bullet will usually bounce back and land at your feet."

In addition to its underpowered cartridge, the double derringer's weakest link was just that: The barrel hinges often cracked and today, buyers of original guns should check carefully for breaks or welds. Still, the derringer's design remains timeless. Back in 1956, California gun dealer Hy Hunter reintroduced a Great Western double derringer chambered in .38 S&W. And a few years ago, the late Val Forgett, Jr., of Navy Arms produced a limited run of .41 rimfire ammo, some of which, I am told, was a bit too hot for the original guns to handle. Today, anyone wanting to recapture the wrist-snapping thrill of firing a double barreled handful of firepower can find double derringer-style guns by Bond and Cobra chambered for cartridges that include 9mm Luger, .38 Special/.357 Magnum, and .45 Colt and which are often effectively used for Cowboy Action side matches, as well as for concealed carry.

Throughout its colorful lifetime, the compact double derringer provided an unobtrusive feeling of security for its owners and its presence no doubt made many an antagonist back away. After all, no one likes looking down the open end of stacked .41-caliber muzzles, no matter how underpowered its cartridge may be.

A rotating lever on the right side of the frame unlocked the barrels, which could then be swung up for loading and unloading.

RUGER 10/22 CARBINE

Photo courtesy Sturm Ruger & Co.

Yes, this is a Ruger 10/22, only dressed up in a Scottwerx Thompson sub-machine gun drop-in kit. The author also installed a Volquartsen trigger assembly to speed up the trigger action, although it still is a semi-automatic rifle—but what fast-firing fun!

Ever since the advent of the .22 Long Rifle cartridge, in 1887, it has been a rite of passage for many good (and responsible) little boys to receive a .22 rifle for Christmas. In the past, those rifles have included the Stevens No. 14½ Little Scout single-shot, Winchester 1890 pump, and Remington 511 Scoremaster bolt-action. But, beginning in 1964, that enticingly long, brightly wrapped package under the tree was likely to contain a Ruger 10/22 Carbine, which has become one of the most popular .22 autoloaders in firearms history.

Although the concept of Ruger's first .22 rifle began in the 1950s, the final design took its inspiration from the success of the Ruger .44 Magnum Carbine, which was introduced in 1960. An obvious hint can be found in this line from Ruger's 1964 catalog describing the 10/22 as a rimfire rifle "built to high-power rifle standards … ." In fact, anyone comparing the two rifles will notice a not-so-coincidental similarity in design, including their carbine-style barrel bands, basic pistol grip stock configurations, and semi-curved, carbine-style buttplates.

The 10/22 was the result of a collaboration between Bill Ruger, Harry Sefried (a firearms engineer who worked on the M2 carbine at Winchester and then went on to revamp many of High Standard's semi-automatic pistols), and Doug McClenahan (a gun designer who had previously worked at Colt's and High Standard and, later, founded the original Charter Arms company). Like everything the meticulous Bill Ruger conceived, the 10/22 was over-engineered, yet, due to its well thought-out mechanics, was eminently affordable; it carried an initial price tag of just $54.50. As Bill Ruger wrote to Jack O'Connor a few months before the 10/22 was introduced, "From a technological point of view, the new 10/22 is one of the best things we have done."

On March 24, 1964, Bill Ruger sent proofs from his upcoming catalog, announcing the new .22 rifle, to gun writers. At that time, though, only three pre-production prototypes existed. At the 1964 National Rifle Association Annual Meetings, attendees got to see and handle the actual rifle in Ruger's booth, even though it wasn't officially announced in the *American Rifleman* and other gun magazines until June of that year. "The New Ruger 10/22

The 10/22's push button safety. This early rifle features the aluminum trigger housing.

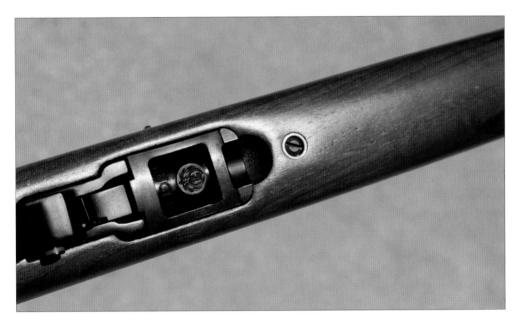

The 10/22's rotary 10-shot magazine was inspired by the Savage 99's rotary magazine.

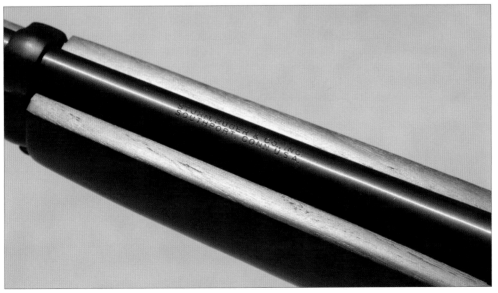

This is an early pre-warning barrel.

No matter what type of wood and metal it's wearing, the 10/22 is accurate, which is one of the reasons it's so popular.

.22 Caliber R.F. Self-Loader" that first advertising headline proclaimed, was "the ultimate in logical design."

And indeed it was. The trigger housing group could be easily dropped out of the gun for cleaning, and disassembly was simple enough to require only a screwdriver and a punch. The barrel screwed in, making subsequent replacements and upgrades easy. The receiver was investment cast of aircraft grade aluminum, as were the trigger guard and buttplate. Metal parts were either blued or anodized blue/black, and the stocks were walnut. The 18½-inch barrel was topped with a simple but effective sporting, fold-down leaf rear sight and a gold bead front post. Lock time was fast and, combined with twin anchoring points for the six-grove 1:16 barrel twist, resulted in exceptional accuracy. But, perhaps most revolutionary—an apropos word in this case—was the 10/22's 10-shot rotary magazine, a concept that took its inspiration from Bill Ruger's admiration of the rotary magazine in the Savage 99 (another gun that made our bucket list).

As it was with so many others in this book, the 10/22 proved extremely popular, especially for shooters who already owned a Ruger .44 Magnum Carbine, for here was the perfect companion piece. With its easy to carry weight of only 5¼ pounds, the rifle also found immediate favor as an economical plinker and a fast-handling small-game rifle. A more sleekly styled Sporter—sans barrel band and with a rubber recoil pad—was introduced, in 1966, with a hand-checkered variant coming out a year later. There was also a version with a Monte Carlo comb, plus a fully stocked Mannlicher-style, which, unfortunately, did not have the staying power of some of the other stock configurations.

In 1980, with the cost of walnut escalating, Ruger switched to birch stocks. Still later, stocks were changed again, this time to maple. As a sign of the times, laminated stocks were introduced, in 1986, and a stainless steel barrel was offered, in 1992. Recently, the trigger housing has been changed from aluminum to polymer.

Today, the 10/22 exists in six basic configurations. The Carbine is still made in the same style of the original 1960s version, although with an improved extended magazine release (one of the few distractions—along with a sluggish trigger pull—of the earlier 10/22s), which has become standard on all models. Plus, in addition to hardwood stocks, there are options for synthetic stocks and a stainless steel barrel and receiver. The Sporter is also a continuation of the original 10/22 version,

complete with a checkered American walnut stock outfitted with sling swivels.

The Compact features an uncheckered hardwood stock, a fiber optic front sight, and a 16¼-inch barrel. Capitalizing on the 10/22's penchant for accuracy, the Target sports a crisply tuned trigger and a 20-inch bull barrel without sights, but drilled and tapped for a scope; its laminate stock sports sling swivels. Today there is a new, highly popular takedown model, and, finally, the Tactical is based on the Carbine configuration, but is actually a tricked-out Target model with a 16¼-inch crowned bull barrel. This rifle comes without sights, but has a combination scope base adapter and offers a choice of either black Hogue Over-molded or black synthetic stocks, along with an adjustable bi-pod.

It is this latter version that has now extended the 10/22's popularity far beyond the target ranges and hunting fields. A number of these rifles have been equipped with silencers and supplied to various law enforcement organizations, as well as military units, for use in covert operations. In its camo guise, it is a favorite for commando operatives and has been issued to such elite groups as the Navy S.E.A.L.S.

Along the way, a few commemorative 10/22s have been produced, including the Canadian Centennial commemorative, in 1976, and, more recently, the officially licensed Ruger Boy Scout 10/22 Rifle. The 10/22 has also spawned the SR-22, a .22 rimfire version of Ruger's SR-556, which is built on an AR platform. Add to these the .22 Charger, with its 10/22 action, synthetic stock, and built-in bi-pod, which has put an entirely new spin on rimfire pistol target and varmint shooting. With all these, its' small wonder the 10/22 is now one of the most accessorized and customized rimfires in the aftermarket world. Competition kits abound from firms such as Cabela's, Midway USA, Power Custom, and Volquartsen, just to name a few. Completely tricked-out competition guns (often used for side matches at many of the major shoots) are available from firms such as Clark Custom Guns. Heck, just for fun plinking, I turned my standard 10/22 into a .22 rimfire semi-auto version of the Thompson sub-machine gun, with a drop-in kit from Scottwerx. (Please turn to pages 53 through 55 for the Thompson submachine gun story.)

To date, more than six million 10/22 rifles, in all its variations, have been sold, a number that no doubt would have pleased the late Bill Ruger. Indeed, the 10/22 has taken the traditional Christmas "boy's rifle" to places where no .22 rimfire rifle has gone before. And that's why it's on our bucket list.

Not-A-Thompson. No, it's a Ruger 10/22 in Scottwerx disguise. There are numerous drop-in kits for the 10/22, but this is my favorite. The stick magazine is a dummy.

COLT 1860 ARMY

Most nineteenth century cap-and-ball revolvers are emblematic of the era in which they were created. The straight, regimented lines of Colt's Model 1849 and 1851 Navy, and the fanciful complexities of the Whitney and Spiller & Burr, were designs evoking the Victorian age.

Not so with the 1860 Army. With the smooth, streamlined curvatures of its rounded barrel and an underlug that flowed into the frame and cascaded out on the other side into an unusually elongated grip, the graceful .44 could easily have come from the Art-Deco period of the 1920s. In fact, judging this sixgun solely as a work of art, some might have a difficult time realizing it was the principal sidearm of the Union Army in the War Between The States.

The 1860 wasn't just a Yankee gun. Many were sent to Confederate forces through agents like H.D. Norton & Brothers of San Antonio, Texas, and Peter Williams & Co. of Richmond, Virginia, before the blockades were in force. Afterwards, numerous 1860s were confiscated by Rebel forces. Quantrill's Raiders were said to have been armed with four 1860s per man—two carried in holsters and

two more in pommel scabbards. Yet this was one Yankee gun that was never copied by the Confederacy; it was just too difficult to make.

Of course, Samuel Colt didn't think so. He knew he had to do something to satisfy the military's growing demand. With the ever-increasing rumblings of an impending Civil War, he was selling all the 1851 Navies he could manufacture, but the army wanted something harder hitting than .36-caliber. On the other hand, Colt's mighty four-plus- pound .44 Dragoon was deemed too heavy for dismounted combat, and shortening the barrel length and cutting cylinder flutes in the bulky Dragoon to shave weight just didn't work. Sam had already tried that. Too, the cylinder of the 1851 Navy was too small to safely handle six chambers of the larger .44-caliber that the army favored. By 1860, Colt had found the answer.

He started with an 1851 Navy frame, then milled and lowered the front two-thirds of its profile slightly, which enabled it to clear the larger forward portion of a newly designed, rebated cylinder. This cylinder featured six slightly tapered blackpowder cavities that opened out to .44-caliber chambers, thereby permitting a .44-caliber cylinder on what was essentially a .36-caliber frame. The result was a two-pound, 11-ounce belt gun capable of

The author's original 1860 Army, which he purchased years ago from the late Turner Kirkland, of Dixie Gun Works, looks like it has gone through the Civil War, but was actually made in 1867.

launching a heavier .44 projectile previously associated only with the horse pistol.

Another innovation was the under-barrel rammer. Rather that retain the hinged rammer used in most of his previous revolvers, Colt adapted a "Patent Creeping Lever" that had been designed by his chief engineer, Elisha King Root, in 1849. It had already been used successfully on Colt's 1855 Sidehammer Model, but was to find even greater acceptance with the new 1860 Army. Basically a steel knobuled rack-and-pinion system, it provided a smooth, jam-free movement that did away with the friction of a single screw binding against a steel hole, such as in the 1851 Navy. Adding to the 1860s sleek appearance, the under-barrel lug was gracefully rounded to encase and protect the ratchet.

Finally, and perhaps most notably, the New Model Holster Pistol, as it was officially called, sported a dramatically elongated grip, one unlike any Colt before it. Initially, the first few thousand revolvers featured a standard 1851 Navy grip and a 7½-inch barrel. That made the gun, with its heftier .44-caliber cylinder and lightened frame, feel awkward. I have handled one of the earliest of these 7½-inch barreled guns and it had none of the pointability inherent with the 1851 Navy or the improved 1860 Army. The difference was the elongated grip, which was added to balance the gun and to, allegedly, help absorb recoil of the stouter .44-caliber charge. However, as anyone who has ever fired an original or replica 1860 can attest, the grip does more for settling the gun in the hand than it does for taming recoil, for what it does is reduce muzzle flip, thereby enabling the shooter to cock the hammer and get back on target quicker. This same principle was later applied to the underswept grips of the Colt Bisley and, more recently, on Ruger's earliest .44 Magnum Super Blackhawk. In ad-

dition, per the Army's request, the barrel was lengthened to eight inches, which helped balance the gun even more.

Interestingly, the 1851 Navy's Ormsby-engraved May 1843 naval battle scene between Texas and Mexico also was used for the rebated cylinder of the 1860 Army. And just so you know, the "Sept 10, 1850" patent date on the cylinder refers to changing the cylinder bolt slots from oval to rectangular. The 1860s trigger guard was brass, but the backstrap was blued steel. The frame, rammer, and hammer were case hardened, while the rest of the gun was highly polished and blued. After 1862, this lustrous finish was omitted on military guns, due to wartime pressures and Colt's desire to keep prices low in the face of competition. Initially, the 1860 cost the government $24.14 apiece, compared to $14.95 for the 1858 Remington, Colt's nearest competitor. Obviously the Army was willing to pay extra for Colt's name and reputation. Later, Colt's dropped its price to $14 per gun, but as they only cost $8 to $10 apiece to manufacture, the company still made a hefty profit.

At last the army had the gun it wanted, a lightweight, hard-hitting, and well-balanced .44 revolver. The report from the first U.S. Ordnance trial, dated May 19, 1860, stated, "The improvement, as claimed by Mr. Colt, consists of diminishing the weight of his revolver known as the Dragoon or Holster Pistol, and retaining the same caliber, thereby securing the same efficiency of fire without the disadvantages of heretofore found in handling the heavier pistol ... there are a few minor points requiring modification ... with these modifications the Board will be satisfied that the New Model Revolvers, with 8-inch barrel, will make the most superior cavalry arm we have ever had, and they recommend its issue to all the mounted troops." Not surprisingly, the govern-

Left: The "creeping ratchet" loading lever of the 1860 Army was a big improvement over Colt's previous cap-and-ball designs, as it prevented binding.

Right: That little notch on the top of the hammer is actually the rear sight.

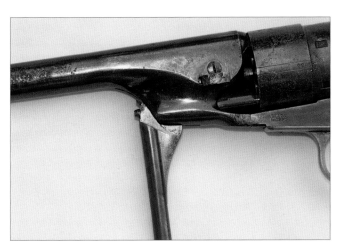

The author enjoys regularly shooting his original 1860 Army.

The originals, while fairly accurate at 25 yards, shot high and to the left, although the force with which the wedge was driven in could alter the point of impact somewhat.

ment ended up ordering 119,300 Model 1860 Armies between 1861 and 1863.

Some of the earliest guns, called Cavalry models, featured full fluted cylinders. Many of them, along with later, non-fluted guns referred to as Military Models, were offered with detachable "carbine" buttstocks. These popular variations featured a "carbine breech" cutaway in the bottom of each recoil shield, plus a projecting screw on both sides of the frame (thus making them "four-screw models") for affixing a detachable buttstock. Approximately 1,900 of these separate buttstocks did double duty as hollowed-out canteens—rarities that often bring more on today's collector's markets than the guns themselves. By comparison, the less plentiful but better finished Civilian Models had no provisions for detachable buttstocks.

In all, a total of 200,500 New Model Holster Pistols were made between 1860 and 1872, when the 1860 was superseded by the Colt 1872 Open Top and, subsequently, the Single

Action Army. But the gun was so revered, many made the transition into the cartridge era via Thuer, Richards, and Richards-Mason conversions. Consequently, they played an important role in the settling of the post-Civil War west.

Fortunately for collectors, factory records for more than two-thirds of all 1860 Army revolvers survived a disastrous fire in Colt's Old Armory in 1864, so many of these guns, including those assembled in the London factory, can be authenticated. Like all of Col. Colt's guns, a number of 1860 Armies were engraved and used for special presentations. While visiting the Frederick VII Foundation in Jaegerspris, Denmarkm with my friend, pipemaker Erik Nørding, I was permitted to actually handle an elaborate cased pair of gold mounted, Gustave Young-engraved 1860s that had been presented to King Frederick VII of Denmark, by President Abraham Lincoln, in 1863.

All I could think was, "Boy, it would be fun to shoot these!"

REMINGTON
MODEL 700

· ·

Above: This Remington 700 BDL is fitted with a Bushnell Banner 4-12x scope and was manufactured in 1980.

Given its classic styling, calibers, model variations, and widespread use by civilians, law enforcement, and the military, one would think the Remington 700 had been around since the days of Colonel Townsend Whelan. But it is definitely a post-war gun, having been designed in 1962, though this bolt-action has its roots in the latter half of the 1930s.

Back then, two of Remington's designers, Oliver H. Loomis and A.L. Lowe, had developed a new bolt-action, the Model 720, which was based on the Pattern 14 Enfield action that had proven itself in World War I. The Remington 720 was launched, in 1941, just in time to see the United States enter World War II. This bolt-action was initially positioned as a sporting rifle. However, the war changed all that, and the initial run was purchased by the Navy, after which production was put on hold.

Nonetheless, the Model 720 set the stage for a new generation of bolt-actions that would ultimately lead to the Model 700.

After the war, the short-lived Model 720 was replaced with two improved yet almost-identical bolt-action sporters, the Models 721 and 722, the only differences being the length of their receivers. The 721 had a longer action and was initially chambered for .270 Winchester, .30-06, and .300 H&H Magnum cartridges. Its sister rifle, the Model 722, had a short action and was chambered for the .257 Roberts and the .300 Savage. Subsequent chamberings were added to the 721 and 722 over the years. Both guns enjoyed moderate success during their production run, which lasted from 1948 until 1962, when they were replaced with what would become, to many, the best bolt-action sporter ever produced—the Remington 700.

Remington engineers Merle "Mike" Walker and Homer W. Young and their team had created the Models 721 and 722, yet they always wanted to do more with that basic rifle. This was especially true of Walker, an avowed competitive benchrest shooter, who saw in the

700 series the potential for a mass-produced rifle that would combine strength with superb out-of-the-box accuracy. In 1962, that goal was achieved with the Remington Model 700. To quote from Roy Marcot's excellent book, *Remington – America's Oldest Gunmaker* (Primedia, 1998):

Considerable debate has occurred over the years on the reason for the Model 700's accuracy reputation. It appears there is not one factor, but a combination of several: the greater stiffness of the Model 700 cylindrical receiver; the unique bedding system of a free-floated barrel except for twin, V-shaped contact points at the front of the fore-end; fast lock time (3.2 milliseconds) from the rifle's bolt and trigger design; sharp, crisp-breaking action of the single-stage trigger; a snug barrel chamber with relatively short lead; tight barrel-manufacturing tolerances for bore and groove diameters; straightness and uniformity of crown; and consistent, uniform cartridge positioning by the recessed bolt face.

In addition to its physical design and shootability, another factor that made the Remington 700 an immediate success was the fact that this rifle was offered in both long and short actions and, consequently, was available in a wide variety of calibers, including .222 Remington and Remington Magnum, .243 Winchester, .270 Winchester, .280 Remington, .30-06, .308 Winchester, and the .264 Winchester Magnum. The .375 H&H and .458 Winchester Magnum Safari Grades were also available through Remington's Custom Shop. In addition, the new Model 700 was also chambered for the 7mm Remington Magnum, which became one of the hottest big-game cartridges in America. In short, the Remington 700 had something for every hunter.

Two versions of the 700 were initially offered: a 700 ADL (A Deluxe Grade) with checkered Monte Carlo stock, hooded ramp front sight, and without a hinged floor plate (also known as a "blind magazine," so that the gun could only be unloaded from the top of the open receiver); and a 700 BDL (B Deluxe Grade), which featured *fleur de lis* checkering, black composite pistol grip cap and fore-end tip, hinged floorplate (thereby permitting the gun to be quickly unloaded from the bottom by springing open the hinge lock), detachable swivels and sling, and a higher blued steel polish. In 1969, the rifle went through a series of internal and external changes, including a stock redesign and a revamped bolt that prompted Remington to tout it as the world's strongest.

Since then, the Model 700 has been produced in a multiplicity of calibers and a bewildering plethora of models. Some of the more notable variations were the introduction of the Model 700 C Custom Shop special order rifle with upgraded wood and metal finish, in 1965; a left-handed model, brought out in 1973; the six-pound, 12-ounce Mountain Rifle, introduced in 1986;

a fiberglass-stocked ADL, in 1987; stainless and camo varmint models, in 1992; the synthetically-stocked Model 700 Sendero Special, introduced in 1993; and detachable magazines offered on select models, in 1994. In addition, beginning in 1981, a limited edition Model 700 Classic Rifle series debuted, available in one specially selected caliber per year, starting with the 7mm Mauser and including such stalwarts as the .257 Roberts (1982), the .35 Whelen (1988), and the .25-06 Remington (1990).

Launching a variant that has taken the Model 700 into the tactical arena, as early as 1966 Remington developed the Model 40 Marine Corps Sniper Rifle. In 1986, a Model 700 SWS (Sniper Weapons System) Rifle was introduced in 7.62 NATO, and 2008 saw the XCR Tactical Long Range Model 700, with black stainless barrel, externally adjustable trigger, and Bell & Carlson synthetic stock. Model 700 Police Rifles in .223 Remington featured Kevlar stocks with aircraft-grade aluminum bedding, while the DM version of this model was chambered in .308 and had a detachable box magazine. All are available with a Tactical Weapons System (TWS) package, which includes telescopic sights, bipod, and carrying case.

Although other specialty rifles are now entering the scene, the Marine Corps M40 and the Army's thick-barreled, synthetically-stocked M24 SWS were the mainstay of our snipers in Iraq and Afghanistan. The Special Forces troops at Fort Bragg had nothing but praise for their M24A2 rifles, which were outfitted with detachable Leupold 10x42 Ultra M3A scope, HS Precision adjustable stock, detachable 10-round magazine, Remington MARS (Modular Accessory Rail System) Picatinny rail, and a suppressor-equipped barrel. These rifles can fire more than 10,000 rounds without requiring major repairs and easily punch out 1.30-inch groups or less at 200 yards. Thus, although the Remington 700 remains the quintessential hunting rifle, in its various military and law enforcement guises, it has proven to be extremely versatile.

To celebrate the fiftieth anniversary of this classic rifle, in 2012, the Remington 700 returned to its roots with a recreation of the BDL in its first chambering, the 7mm Remington Magnum, and embellished with a laser-engraved commemorative floor plate, a "B" grade walnut stock adorned with *fleur de lis* checkering, and satin bluing on the receiver and barrel. Then, taking a giant step backwards and forwards at the same time, in 2014, Remington introduced the Model 700 Ultimate Muzzleloader, an inline (the company's second; the first was introduced in 1996 and is now discontinued), that uses a proprietary shell and primer casing. Frankly, I'm more of a traditionalist, when it comes to front stuffers, but the Remington 700—specifically the cartridge-firing versions—deserves a place in our hunting camp, on our battlefield, and on my bucket list.

BUNTLINE SPECIAL

The Buntline Special is kind of like a unicorn. It's a mythical entity that exists in literature and has been brought to life in films. After all, if there is one thing that Hollywood does well, it is create legends and, in so doing, make them real.

Cimarron Fire Arm's replica of the 10-inch barreled Buntline Special used by Kurt Russell starring as Wyatt Earp in the motion picture, Tombstone. It is shown with an original first edition of Stuart Lake's book that started the Buntline legend.

By common definition, a Buntline Special is an otherwise standard .45 caliber Colt Single Action Army that has a longer than average barrel, usually 12 inches, but also sometimes seen as 10 inches. However, a few Buntline Specials—primarily commemoratives—have been made with 16- and 18-inch tubes, which qualifies them, under modern gun laws, to be outfitted with detachable skeleton shoulder stocks, as were some of the "originals."

The legend of the Buntline Special was first brought to the public's attention, in 1931, with the publication of author Stuart N. Lake's widely-read book *Wyatt Earp: Frontier Marshal*, a biography that Lake wrote after interviewing the aging ex-lawman shortly before his death in Los Angeles, California. In his book, Lake recounts Earp telling him that, back in the 1880s, a flamboyant writer of dime novel adventures named Edward Zane Carroll Judson, who used the pen name Ned Buntline, presented Earp and four other Dodge City lawmen—Bat Masterson, Bill Tilghman, Charlie Bassett and Neal Brown—with identical, specially ordered Peacemakers, all of which bore walnut grips and were fitted with foot-long barrels.

Unfortunately, the facts don't quite substantiate the story. While it is true that customers could pay a dollar an inch for any Colt Model P barrel length over 7½ inches, and approximately 31 such guns with barrels ranging from 10 to 16 inches were produced by the factory from 1876 through 1884, there is no record nor evidence that Earp or any of the other four lawmen were recipients of these "Buntline Specials," as they have come to be called. Moreover, historical facts suggest that not all four of these individuals were in Dodge City at the same time, which would have made such a group presentation impossible.

Nonetheless, the story was too good to ignore. It was during the golden years of television Westerns, with back-to-back nightly showdowns on various networks between the likes of Cheyenne, Sugarfoot, and Maverick that the legend of the Buntline Special was revived. Specifically, it was with an extremely popular TV series, *The Life and Legend of Wyatt Earp,* which aired from 1955 until 1961 and starred Hugh O'Brian as Marshal Earp. In one of the episodes during the second year of the series, the marshal is presented with a special 12-inch barreled Colt single-action by Judson, played by actor, writer, and director Lloyd Corrigan.

By the next episode, Earp's double buscadero rig, in which O'Brian had previously packed two 4¾-inch Colt .45s, now featured a highly exaggerated drop on an elongated right-hand

Colt's made Buntline Specials with 12-inch barrels in both second (shown) and third generation guns.

holster to accommodate clearing leather in a timely manner with the elongated hogleg.

Marshall Earp wasn't the only one who had to have a Buntline Special. We all wanted to be like Wyatt Earp—or at least own the same stretch-barreled sixgun Hugh O'Brian was able to draw with amazing dexterity on the show. Thus, just as the TV Westerns and the resultant sport of fast draw had corralled Colt's into bringing back its Model P, in 1955, the Earp-mania phenomenon caused by *The Life and Legend of Wyatt Earp* had created a growing market for the Buntline Special. After all, there were already Buntline Special cap guns for kids—why shouldn't adults have something to play with, too?

Finally, in 1958, Colt's again yielded to demand and brought out the Buntline Special, a .45-caliber Single Action Army fitted with a 12-inch barrel that was roll marked "Colt Buntline Special .45." The guns were serial numbered in the same SA suffix range as standard second generation Peacemakers, but, up through the late 1960s, the underside of the barrels had a three- or four-digit special BB (Buntline Barrel) assembly number on the underside of their

Hugh O'Brian shows off one of the few Buntline Colts produced, in 2010, as a very limited edition Hugh O'Brian-Wyatt Earp Tribute Buntline cased set, which came with a matching 4¾-inch Peacemaker. John Bianchi made an equally limited run of special two-gun holsters.

barrels; this has no relation to the Buntline's serial number. Most of these guns were blued and case hardened with rubber stocks, but some had two-piece walnut grips, and 65 of the guns were nickeled. The Buntline Special remained in the line until 1975, with a total of 4,060 second generation Buntlines produced. It continued to be made as third generation guns, finally being discontinued in 1988.

Later on, a few commemoratives were produced to use up leftover parts, and some Buntlines were also chambered in .44-40. During the 1980s and '90s, a number of Buntlines had their barrels swapped out to become lengths of 4¾, or 7½ inches, as, at that time, those barrel lengths were bringing more money on the used gun market. Of course, that makes finding original Buntlines a little more difficult nowadays.

Although Colt's is not currently producing the third generation Buntline Special, in 2010, it made a very limited edition Hugh O'Brian-Wyatt Earp Tribute Buntline cased set, which came with a matching 4¾-inch Peacemaker. Then, inspired by the 1993 film Tombstone, starring Kurt Russell, Cimarron brought out a 10-inch barreled .45-caliber Wyatt Earp Buntline, complete with sterling silver-inlaid grip presentation plaque. Interestingly, the 10-inch version used in the movie sported a brass plaque engraved by craftsman John Ennis, and there were actually three, consecutively numbered Buntlines used in the movie, one of which is now owned by Kurt Russell, who played Wyatt Earp. Like the movie guns, Cimarron's Buntline is made by Uberti (the movie guns used Colt's barrels).

Whether Cimarron or Colt's, everyone should have a Buntline Special, just for the nostalgic fun of it. Admittedly, it's not a six-shooter you'll be packing around a lot, and, if you do, you'll have to get a custom holster made for it. But even though there is a bit of a perceived "whip" to the barrel when you pull the trigger, they are accurate plinkers, definite conversation starters, and help us relive the glory days of the TV West.

WINCHESTER MODEL 1897 RIOT GUN

Whether brandished by Lee Marvin in *The Professionals* or wielded by William Holden in *The Wild Bunch*, the Winchester Model 97 Riot Gun is the bad boy of smoothbores, but, paradoxically, was also a favorite of early twentieth century law enforcement agencies, including the Texas Rangers, the Los Angeles Police Department, Alcatraz prison guards, and the Union Pacific Railroad, to name just a few of the authenticated guns I have examined over the years. In fact, a rather pristine Model 97 Riot Gun that I have in my collection was purchased by the Pasadena Police Department in 1924, during the heyday of the "Roarin' '20s." It is nothing short of fascinating that, with all these historical links, one *wouldn't* want to own one.

Because of its rugged yet fast-shooting action, the Model 97 Riot Gun is a favorite among Cowboy Action Shooters, and yet, due to those very attributes, its short, easy-to-swing 20-inch barrel, an Improved Cylinder open choke that makes it hard to miss in tight quarters, and an exposed hammer for easy cocking in times of stress, make it perfect for home-defense,

as well. Still, it is hardly surprising that, in its standard 30-inch barreled configuration, the 12-gauge version of John Browning's pump design was one of the most popular sporting shotguns in America, around the turn of the last century. In more modern times, I remember rabbit hunting with a friend of a friend, many years ago, who was using his granddad's old Model 97 riot gun as a brush clearing device with the first couple of shots, thereby exposing any cottontail stupid enough to still remain in the vicinity.

The Model 1897 was a much-needed evolution of Browning's Model 1893, a weaker gun that was designed for blackpowder and, consequently, was plagued by fouling problems and a resultant poor reputation. It was one of Browning's least successful inventions, bad enough to the point that, after approximately 31,000 guns had been sold, Winchester of-

fered dealers a trade of any unsold Model 93 for a brand new Model 97. Fortunately, by the time Browning's improved 1897 slide-action came on the scene, not only was it mechanically more proficient, but, by then, smokeless powder was in vogue and the new firearm's metallurgy was ready for it.

With its solid-topped receiver and side ejection, the Model 1897 was a marked improvement over the Model 1893. In fact, the Model 97 stayed in the line until 1957, with 1,024,700 guns made. Initially chambered for the new 2¾-inch smokeless 12-gauge shells, the Winchester 97, like its 1893 predecessor, featured a tubular magazine that held five rounds. A forward movement of the automatic slide lock—usually recoil was enough—freed the pump handle for fast cycling of the action. First offered as a solid-frame model with a 30-inch barrel, a number of variations were eventually cataloged, including Field, Trap, and Pigeon Grades. However, the most dramatic of the Model 97's configurations was the Riot Gun, which featured a 20-inch Cylinder-choked barrel. By 1898, a takedown version was also being produced. A note of warning: Riot Guns are so popular that many standard-length barrels have been cut down over the years, so, if buying the gun as an original or for investment, be sure the choke is marked CYL (Cylinder), the only authentic choke on a Riot Gun.

Another fascinating variation of the Model 97 Riot Gun is the Model 97 Trench Gun, which was given a military countenance via a distinctive, ventilated "heat shield." Normally in a hunting situation, a sporting arm such as the standard Model 97 isn't fired enough to become too hot to hold—in a wartime firefight, that 20-inch tube can become sizzling. To prevent scorched hands, a perforated steel heat shield was affixed to the barrel, along with a bayonet lug. This lug was meant for the standard military M-1917 bayonet, but the bay-

onet's 16½-inch blade interfered with the otherwise excellent balance of the Trench Gun and was cumbersome in close quarters, especially during the trench warfare of WWI. The bayonet looked menacing when affixed to the Trench Gun, but it hampered movement and, obviously, was only useful in last-ditch operations. The sling swivels that were often fitted onto the Trench Gun, on the other hand, were much more practical. Early WWI guns were unmarked, but a "U.S." and Army ordnance "flaming bomb" stamped on the receiver completed the identity for WWII guns that were called back into service.

Military loads often consisted of 00 buckshot, and an extra round in the chamber gave the Trench Gun a formidable capacity of six fast shots (in fact, sporting versions of the Model 97 were often advertised has having "six shots" even though their magazines only held five shells). Plus, the lack of a detent or trigger disconnect on the Model 97 meant a soldier could keep the trigger of his Trench Gun depressed and fire as fast as he could work the slide. The Trench Gun became so effective that it was soon nicknamed the "Trench Sweeper," and soldiers who had been skilled trap and skeet shooters in civilian life often used their Model 97s to blast enemy hand grenades in mid-air before they landed. So devastating were these smoothbores that Germany tried unsuccessfully to get them outlawed from The Great War, declaring that "Every prisoner found to have in his possession such guns or ammunition belonging thereto forfeits his life." Naturally, our troops continued to use their Trench Guns to blast their way to victory. And even though Trench Gun production was halted in 1945, this sawed-off shotgun continued to see action throughout Vietnam and the Gulf War.

Of course, the standard Model 97, including Riot Guns, remained in production for slightly more than a decade after that. When encountered today, most Trench Guns are quite worn, showing hard battlefield use, while the Riot Guns used by various police departments are usually in better shape, having spent much of their time in station gun racks and patrol cars. Whichever way, whether in civilian, law enforcement, or military dress, the Winchester Model 97 Trench and Riot Guns played important roles in keeping America not only safe, but free, which more than qualifies them to be included on my bucket list.

COLT 1871-1872 OPEN TOP

It's a shame Sam Colt never got to see his company's legendary revolver, the Single Action Army. Colonel Colt died in 1862, 11 years before the Model P made its appearance. As unfortunate as that was, he did give the shooting world its most famous handguns of the era, the 1851 Navy and the 1860 Army. In turn, both of these cap-and-ball sixguns formed the basis for the first cartridge revolver ever completely designed and produced by Colt's Patent Fire Arms Manufacturing Company (cap-and-ball conversions obviously notwithstanding), the Open Top Model of 1871-'72—and it was the Open Top that evolved into the SAA.

This exquisite 1871-1872 Open Top was made for the author by Cimarron Fire Arms and features charcoal bluing, fancy burl walnut one-piece grips, and elegant period-style engraving. The matching belt and holster were custom made for this gun by El Paso Saddlery.

With the end of the American Civil War, in 1865, and the expiration of Rollin White's patent four years later, the field was wide open for the development of pistols with bored-through cylinders that could chamber the new-fangled, self-contained metallic cartridge. But a surplus of parts for both the 1851 Navy and 1860 Army—the two most prominent handguns of The Great Rebellion—inspired a Colt's employee, Charles B. Richards, to alter the cylinder and hammer of the 1860 Army so that a centerfire .44 cartridge could be loaded from the rear of the cylinder, rather than have loose powder and ball rammed in from the front. This was accomplished by milling off the back portion of the percussion cylinder and affixing the frame with a conversion ring. This ring contained a shallow fixed rear sight and a surprisingly modern-looking spring-plunger firing pin, which was struck by the flat surface of a filed-off percussion hammer. In addition, the under-barrel rammer hole was plugged with a round ejector rod assembly that angled to the right of the barrel, to facilitate punching out empty cases when the gun was put on half-cock, which would align one of the cylinder bores with the ejector rod.

As successful as the Richards Conversion was, blackpowder fouling often plugged the spring-loaded firing pin. Plus, the supply of surplus 1860 barrels was dwindling. So it was, in 1872, that another Colt employee, one named William Mason, designed a new barrel with a solid contour underneath, which did away with the rammer hole, thereby alleviating the need for a plug. Mason also replaced the spring-loaded arrangement on the frame with a modified conversion ring containing a

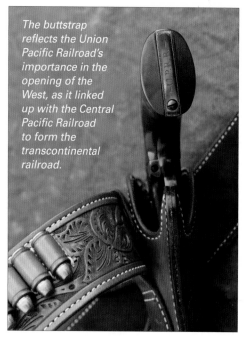

The buttstrap reflects the Union Pacific Railroad's importance in the opening of the West, as it linked up with the Central Pacific Railroad to form the transcontinental railroad.

Even the backstrap was period-engraved for the author.

hole for a fixed firing pin riveted onto an 1860 percussion hammer. In addition, he lengthened the ejector rod tube.

The Richards and Richards-Mason systems were notable but interim transitions into the era of fixed ammunition. But surplus cap-and-ball parts were being used up, and it was clear a new cartridge gun was needed, especially in light of the upcoming Army trials scheduled to select a large-bore handgun. Thus, in 1872, a new Colt galloped onto the scene, the 1871-'72 Open Top (at the time it was referred to as the New Model Holster Pistol). The twin dates refer to the "Pat. July 25, 1871" and "Pat. July 2, 1872" stamps on the left side of the frame, which covered an improved method of attaching the ejector rod to the barrel. Except for the

The ejector rod button of the Open Top was a precursor to the bull's-eye ejector rod of the 1873 Colt Single Action Army.

grip frames, none of the parts interchanged with any previous Colt, making the Open Top the company's first factory-built cartridge gun.

Interestingly, the Open Top was chambered for .44 rimfire, as it was more familiar to frontiersmen than any centerfire cartridge of the time. It was basically the same cartridge used in the Henry and Winchester 1866 rifles, but sported a more elongated 200-grain bullet and packed 23 grains of Blackpowder—the equivalent of the older cap-and-ball charges. For the first time, it offered the convenience of using the same cartridge for both rifle and pistol, thus pre-dating the more oft-touted Winchester-Colt calibers of .44-40, .38-40, and .32-20, all of which came later.

At first glance, the Open Top appeared to be a Richards-Mason conversion, but there were notable differences. For one thing, there was no separate "conversion ring" on the frame. In addition, the cylinder was newly manufactured, although still roll-engraved with the same W.L. Ormsby 1843 Naval scene previously used on both the 1851 Navy and 1860 Army (the Colt's factory certainly got their money's worth out of those dies!). Also, the fixed notch rear sight was not on the hammer, but, rather, was an integral part of the barrel, near the breech. Finally, the six-shot .44 caliber cylinder was not rebated, as it had been on the 1860 Army (which had enabled it to be fitted onto the smaller .36 caliber 1851 Navy frame). Instead, the straight-sided cylinder was matched to a larger .44-caliber frame.

The Open Top was offered in two versions, with the distinctive, elongated grip of the

1860 Army, or with the plow-handled grip of the 1851 Navy (which would, eventually, be adapted to the Single Action Army). The backstrap and trigger guard initially were brass (and sometimes nickel plated), with iron being used on later models. Grips were one-piece varnished walnut, although special order ivory was available. The hammer and frame were case hardened, while the rest of the gun was blued, and, as on all Colts, nickel-plating and engraving were options. Barrel length was 7½ inches, but some rare eight-inch versions are known to exist.

The 1871-1872 Open Top met with immediate acceptance, hampered only by the availability of .44 rimfire ammunition in some of the more remote regions of the frontier. However, Colt's new cartridge revolver still utilized the old cap-and-ball system of using a wedge to affix the barrel to the frame and, so, without a rammer to facilitate leveraging the barrel off so the cylinder could be removed, disassembly was a bit tricky. That and its lack of a topstrap doomed the Open Top in the Army trials of 1872. Undaunted, Colt's designers added a topstrap with an elongated groove for a rear sight, strengthened the ejector rod and loading gate, and took note of the Army's last-minute request for a .45-caliber chambering, rather than .44. Instead of calling it the Improved Open Top, Colt's named its new gun the Single Action Army.

The appearance of the SAA, in 1873, spelled the end of the Open Top, with only 7,000 produced during its short lifespan. Many of these guns were shipped to Mexico and South America, where they saw rugged use. Even most Open Tops found in the U.S. show much wear, testimony to the importance this little-

known cartridge and revolver played in blazing a trail in the West.

Most of the original Open Tops I have encountered have been either too worn or, if not, were then too expensive for any serious consideration, even though this pre-Peacemaker single-action has long been on my bucket list. But a few years ago, Mike Harvey, head honcho of Cimarron Fire Arms, brought out an excellent Uberti-made 1871-'72 Open Top replica chambered in .44 Colt, a centerfire cartridge that was originally developed for the Army's use in the Richards-Mason 1860 Army cartridge conversions.

Interestingly, the .44 Colt was available as a factory loading, from 1871 until just prior to World War II, although the Army's use of this cartridge lasted only until 1873, when they replaced it with the .45 Long Colt and the Single

The author has found the Open Top to be highly accurate in .44 Colt, a comfortable caliber to shoot—plus it's authentic to the gun!

Cimarron can bore its 1871-1872 Open Tops to accept .44 Specials, as well as .44 Colt.

The Open Top's loading gate predated that of the Colt Single Action Army.

The Open Top disassembles in the same manner as the open top Colt-style cap-and-ball revolvers.

Action Army. However, thanks to the revived interest in replica cartridge conversions and, now, with the availability of Cimarron's 1871-'72 Open Top, the .44 Colt is once again obtainable from firms such as Black Hills Ammunition and Ten-X. In addition, on special order, Cimarron will bore out the .44 Colt chambers of the Open Top so that they will also accept .44 Specials, although I should caution you that this is at the extreme end of what this nineteenth century handgun design can take, so I suggest having a competent gunsmith check out your Open Top before shucking in the slightly elongated .44 Specials—even then, I would only recommend cowboy loads.

As for me, yes, I had my Open Top bored out to .44 Special, but, so far, I have only fired it with .44 Colt ammo. Somehow, it seems more in keeping with this little known but historic gun from my bucket list.

The standard Open Top from Cimarron Fire Arms is a thing of beauty and bridges the gap between cap-and-ball and cartridge pistols.

THOMPSON
SUBMACHINE GUN

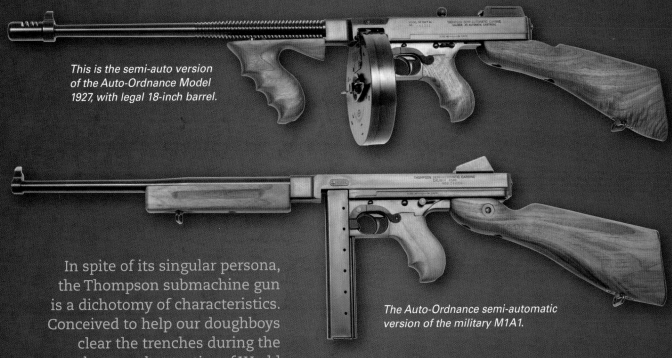

This is the semi-auto version of the Auto-Ordnance Model 1927, with legal 18-inch barrel.

The Auto-Ordnance semi-automatic version of the military M1A1.

In spite of its singular persona, the Thompson submachine gun is a dichotomy of characteristics. Conceived to help our doughboys clear the trenches during the close combat tactics of World War I, unfortunately, it wasn't perfected until after the armistice. Consequently, the Thompson was repositioned as a Roaring '20s peacekeeper. However, its greatest imagery was as a gangster weapon, during the crime-ridden Prohibition years. Movies like James Cagney's Public Enemy, and Little Caesar with Edward G. Robinson, heightened this image, making the finned-barreled, pistol-gripped M1921A1 famous as "The Gun that Made the Twenties Roar." Other Thompson monikers were "The Chicago Typewriter," and "Chopper," both inspired by its 800 rounds-per-minute rate of fire.

The Thompson Submachine Gun was the inspiration of U.S. Army Brigadier General John Taliaferro Thompson. As a respected firearms expert and the youngest colonel in the U.S. Army during the Spanish American War, Thompson realized the need for what he called, "a one man, handheld machine gun." Later, as chief of the Small Arms Division for the Ordnance Department, Thompson was involved with the government's adoption of John Browning's Model 1911 pistol. He was impressed with Browning's .45 ACP cartridge and ordered extensive testing of the round on human cadavers and cattle. He became convinced the .45 ACP would be ideal for what he had come to refer to as a submachine gun—a fully automatic weapon chambered for a pistol round, rather than a rifle cartridge.

The Army was slow to take up his cause. Frustrated with President Woodrow Wilson's hesitation to enter the First World War, Thompson resigned his commission and

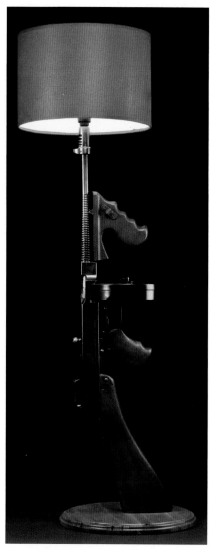

*This Thompson could literally light up the room. It was offered as a limited edition a few years ago by WETA, the imaginative workshop created by Peter Jackson, award-winning New Zealand director of films such as **The Hobbit** and **Lord of the Rings**. Conceived in WETA's prop department by John Harvey and Callum Lingard, it completely sold out within a few weeks.*

joined Remington as its Chief Arms Engineer, while continuing his sub-machine gun research. He discovered a patent for a unique, delayed-action blowback receiver designed by a retired U.S. Navy captain named John Bell Blish. Realizing this could be the key to his handheld machine gun, in 1916, Thompson sought the financial help of a Wall Street investor appropriately named Thomas Fortune Ryan. Thompson then con-tacted Blish and offered him a partnership is his fledgling New York firm, the Auto-Ordnance Cor-poration. Blish assigned his patent to Auto-Ord-nance in exchange for company stock. When the U.S. finally entered WWI, in 1917, Thompson rejoined the army, was promoted to Brigadier General, and made Direc-tor of Arsenals.

By 1919, with the war over, Thompson returned as president of Auto-Ord-nance. Working with two other talented individu-als, Theodore Eickhoff and Oscar Payne, their first product, the Model of 1919, was aptly dubbed The Annihilator. Equipped with either 20 or 30-round stick magazines, or optional 50 or 100-round drum magazines, it was capable of firing 1,500 rounds per minute. The initial Annihilator was actually an automatic pistol, as it had no buttstock, but featured a pistol grip trigger and fore-end, along with a finned barrel. Later, a detachable stock was added.

This, in turn, evolved into the most recog-nized Thompson today, the Model of 1921, which soon became known as the "Tommy Gun." It was initially produced for Auto-Ord-nance by Colt's and featured extremely well-finished and -fitted parts. Outfitted with a 10½-inch barrel and a Cutts Compensator, a rounded charging knob on top of the receiver, adjustable rear sights, and a fixed blade front sight, it was capable of semi-automatic or fully automatic fire, the latter of which could eat up rounds at a rate of 800 shots per minute. It has been reported that General Thompson had his personal Model 1921 fine-tuned to fire bursts in cadence to one of his favorite mili-tary marches.

More than 15,000 Model 1921s were pro-duced for the U.S. Post Office, the Navy and Coast Guard, the U.S. Treasury Department, the Northwest Mounted Police, and law enforce-ment organizations as diverse as the New York and San Francisco Police Departments and the Texas Rangers. "Here's the Gun that Bandits Fear Most!" proclaimed one 1920s ad, "That's why bandits surrender to the man with the Thompson Gun … they know, 'There's no get-away against a Thompson!'"

Indeed there wasn't. Uncannily accurate, even in full auto, a trained marksman could write his name with a Tommy gun. Moreover, the .45 ACP round was capable of 100-yard knockdown accuracy on man-sized targets, and, with its hefty 13 pounds of weight, recoil was practically nonexistent. Speaking from ex-perience, the gun rarely jams when using ball ammunition (hollowpoint .45 ACPs did not exist during the Thompson's era, and, conse-quently, the gun was not designed for them).

Unfortunately, for all its attributes, the Thompson was a prohibitively expensive gun, retailing for $225, a lofty price at the time. As desirable as the Thompson was, many law en-forcement agencies simply could not afford one. Sales soon dropped to a point where, in 1928, Thompson was ousted as president of the company that bore his name.

A semi-automatic-only version, the Model of 1927, was produced to increase sales, but nothing really happened until December 7, 1941, when the Japanese bombed Pearl Har-bor, thus catapulting the U.S. into World War II. The Thompson, now under ownership of an entrepreneur named Russell Maguire, was sud-denly in demand and its production was sub-contracted out to Savage Arms. Thus evolved the Model of 1928 and 1928A1, which were really nothing more than the Model of 1921 outfitted with a wooden horizontal fore-end instead of a pistol grip, a change of sights, omission of the compensator, and fitted with sling swivels. This then became the M1, with a reduced 650-rpm rate of fire, a simplified "L"-shaped rear peep sight, and a side-mounted charging handle. The M1A1 was even more simplified, omitting the finned barrel. With a war-time manufacturing price of $45 each, the M1A1 went on to win acclaim in WWII and numerous other conflicts, including Korea and Vietnam.

Do Not Handle!!

Today, more than 1,700,000 Tommy Guns have been built, with originals now costing more than most mid-range automobiles. In 1951, Auto-Ordnance was purchased by George Numrich, of Numrich Arms, and, in 1999, was bought by Kahr Arms. Unfortunately, John Thompson died on June 21, 1940, seven months before the U.S. entered World War II. He never got to see his Tommy Gun finally get to play the role for which it was created.

Of course, as spelled out in The National Firearms Act of 1934 and as further defined by the more recent Firearms Owners' Protection Act of May 19, 1986, it is illegal for private citizens to own a fully automatic weapon (that is, one that fires multiple shots with a single pull of the trigger), unless one has a Class III license, pays a registration fee per gun, and is able to jump through a maze of background checks and legal hoops. However, Kahr's Auto-Ordnance Corporation does offer semi-automatic versions of the .45 ACP Thompson

1927A and the M1. That is, these guns can only fire a single shot with each pull of the trigger. But even they are expensive, and, in some states like California, are illegal to own simply because they "look bad." Their high-capacity magazines bar them from many other states, as well.

If you really must have a Tommy gun—or at least a gun that looks like a Tommy—another alternative is to buy one of the aircraft-grade aluminum and steel drop-in kits from Scottwerx (www.1022fungun.com) that transforms your Ruger 10/22 rifle into a semi-automatic .22 rimfire look-alike Thompson. The Squad Leader kit makes a 10/22 look like an M1, while the Chicago gives it a Thompson 1927A appearance. Both guns are still semi-automatic Ruger 10/22 and can only fire .22 rimfire ammunition, but that's a lot cheaper than .45 ACP. Either way, the Tommy gun belongs on our bucket list, as a tribute to the gun that kept gangsters at bay and helped win a war.

The ultimate Tommy Gun, as seen at the 2014 Shooting Hunting Outdoor Trade (SHOT) show, in Las Vegas. What better city to sport a golden Tommy?

KIMBER
SUPER MATCH II

Although designed for match-grade accuracy, the author feels a high-end gun such as the Super Match more than qualifies it for home-defense and personal protection.

Just as John Browning's original "perfected" design of the 1911 (which is on our bucket list), subsequently evolved into the even more refined 1911A1, that improved 1911 platform has since been enhanced even further by numerous skilled gunsmiths such as Ed Brown, Bill Wilson, and Les Baer, to name but a few. These and others have put their individual, indelible marks on what was once a workhorse pistol and turned it into a sophisticated shooting machine. Of course, very often these upgrades come with equally lofty price tags and lengthy delivery schedules—and, occasionally, they are not improvements at all, such as checkering so sharp it painfully grates the hand under recoil, or guns tuned so tightly they do not always function reliably. Add to this the fact that, by the very nature of some of the best custom guns, they are often not readily available.

And then there's Kimber, which, beginning in 1996, emerged upon the handgun scene by filling in the gap between mass-produced and customized 1911s with an ever-expanding line of semi-custom and highly tuned custom 1911-style pistols, all of which feature match grade barrels, beavertail grip safeties, loaded shell indicators, and polished feed ramps as standard equipment and regularly cataloged. Indeed, while Ruger and Colt's may have been one of the first to incorporate aluminum frames on their early .22 single-actions, it was Kimber that was pretty much single handedly responsible for changing shooter's views on the practicality of cast aluminum frames for the harder-hitting .45 ACPs. In addition, Kimber keep costs competitive and tolerances tight on its highly accurate handguns by using metal injection molding (MIM) for many of its small parts, as well as computer-aided design (CAD) coupled with computer-aided manufacturing (CAM) technologies. It should also be noted that Kimber makes every major component of its guns in America.

Virtually every Kimber I have tested over the years has shot "photographable groups," right out of the box. So it's hardly surprising that, in the relatively short time that its handgun division has existed, Kimber has become the world's largest manufacturer of 1911-styled pistols. Kimber catalogs more than 25 variations of the 1911 at last count, including models with both fixed and adjustable sights and barrel lengths ranging from three to five inches. But the one that goes into my bucket is the top-of-the-line Super Match II. Here's why.

First, it's a handsome, two-toned, all-stainless steel pistol, with diamond checkered rosewood grips, a non-glare satin silver-finished frame, and black KimPro II protective finish on the slide, which features both front and rear cocking serrations. Frontstrap and under-the-trigger-guard checkering (one of the few production guns to offer this feature) is a comfortable and anchoring 30 lines per inch. Mag well, ambi safety, and beavertail grip safety are standard, of course, as would be expected on a handgun of this stature. A micro-adjustable rear sight and eight-round magazine capacity enhances shooting performance, as does the match grade barrel teamed with a match grade bushing and a four-pound trigger pull. Consequently, the Super Match II is guaranteed to shoot a five-shot, 25-yard group that will measure one inch or less.

All of this doesn't come cheaply, as the Super Match II lists for a little bit north of $2,000. It is worth it? Beautifully printed catalogs and advertising claims aside, I had to find out for myself, and there is no better proving ground for a handgun or its owner than the 250 Defensive Pistol Class at Gunsite Academy (www.gunsite.com), located in Paulden, Arizona, just a short drive from Prescott. This five-day event, which is held on a regularly scheduled basis, is essentially a boot camp that teaches defensive shooting. The 250 is an intensive class, in which each student burns 800 to 1,000 rounds of ammunition within a week's time and fires double tap, failure drills, night fire, and "playhouse" hostage/bad guy scenarios at ranges from three to 25 yards. It was the perfect scenario to see how the Super Match II would hold up under a variety of situations.

The Kimber wasn't the only gun I used (I always bring spares to grueling events like these), but without going into details (that's a story for another book), I can tell you that

Extended beavertail grip safety, skeletonized hammer, ambidextrous safety, and a serrated anti-glare rear sight are just some of the upscale features of the Super Match.

For his Kimber Super Match shootout at Gunsite Academy, the author used a Bianchi El Paso No. 1911 speed rig and, of course, Kimber stainless steel TacMags.

I put more than 500 rounds through the Super Match II without cleaning it once; I merely wiped it down at the end of each day. By the end of the week, the gun had not suffered a single malfunction. Ammo used consisted of both 230-grain ball and hollowpoints from Hornady, Winchester, and Federal. I should also mention that the only magazines I used were Kimber's eight-round stainless steel TacMags that came with the gun, plus two additional TacMags that I purchased to get me through the 250 course. Cheat on the quality of the magazines you use and you cheat on yourself.

The end result? The Super Match II works. And it looks elegant. It is reliable enough for self-defense, accurate enough for match shooting, and sophisticated enough to put in the desk drawer of a multi-million dollar condominium penthouse along Billionaire's Row on Wilshire Boulevard in West Los Angeles. And that definitely qualifies it for my bucket list.

COLT
DETECTIVE SPECIAL

In the surreal world of Hollywood, one of the greatest accolades for an actor is when a toy company produces a doll in his or her likeness, usually based upon a character they've played. By that same token, I've always thought that one of the hallmarks of a classic firearm was when a toy manufacturer deemed it worthy enough to design a cap gun after it. At least, this is the way it was with the Dick Special, a compact, pot metal snubbie made by Hubley, I believe, that fired a red-paper roll of caps in the hands of many a would-be childhood detective, back in the 1940s and '50s.

Of course, back then, "Dick" was synonymous with "detective," those trench coat-clad sleuths who lurked in the back alleys and shadowy lairs of the city streets. It was the urban answer to the wide-open spaces of the Wild West, and the snub-nosed revolver was the citified counterpart to the Colt Single Action Army.

The role model for all those pocket-sized snubbies—indeed, the first of the twentieth century's eventual long line of compact, swing-out cylinder revolvers—was the aptly named Colt Detective Special. First introduced in 1927, it was really a short-barreled Colt Police Positive Special, a double-action handgun that had been introduced in 1907 and remained in the line until 1946. It proved to be an extremely popular sidearm for law enforcement personnel; among its .32- and .38-caliber chamberings, the .38 Special version was most in demand. This all-around self-defense round had been developed by Smith & Wesson for its Military & Police revolver back in 1902, but, soon, any handgun manufacturer worthy of the name was chambering revolvers for it. That, of course, included Colt's and its Police Positive Special.

The six-shot Police Positive Special was normally outfitted with either a four-, five-, or six-inch barrel on Colt's .38 caliber D frame. However, there was obviously a need among lawmen and undercover cops for an easier to conceal "pocket pistol" with a shorter barrel. As evidence of this, in my collection I have a Colt Police Positive Special made in the early '20s and issued to a detective working for the Union Pacific Railroad. That lawman had taken his Police Positive Special to the railroad's machine shop and had its original four-inch barrel shortened to two inches. This may very well have been one of the first "non-factory" versions of Colt's ubiquitous snubbie, although John Henry FitzGerald, a Colt's firearms tester and exhibition shooter, had been lopping the ends off of his Colt's revolvers for years and, in fact, is credited with convincing Colt's to come out with the first regularly cataloged snub-nosed revolver.

In any case, evidently there was sufficient demand for a snub-nosed .38 Special revolver like my UPRR pocket pistol, because, in 1926, Colt's began producing a small number of Police Positive Specials with two-inch tubes. But by 1927, demand was such that the little gun received its own apropos designation, although it continued to share serial numbers with its longer-barreled brother. And, thus, the Detective Special was born.

Initially, it was only chambered in .38 Special, but, after 1946, less effective self-defense cartridges—the .38 Colt New Police, .38 S&W, .32 Colt, and .32 S&W—were added. No doubt this was done to boost sales and reduce recoil in the little 21-ounce gun. In addition, a very scarce variation with a three-inch barrel was made for a short period after World War II. Stocks were checkered walnut with an inset gold-colored rampant Colt medallion. The gun was primarily offered with a blued finish; a scarcer nickel finish was an option, though it was not favored by lawmen due to its reflective qualities. Let's face it, the Detective Special was strictly a hideout gun, and Colt's marketed it as such. Quoting from its 1936 centennial catalog:

More power is packed into the snub-nosed Colt Detective Special, than in any other arm of its size. This model is especially popular among Plain Clothes Detectives, Police Officers off duty, Bank Messengers and Payroll Clerks. The small size of the Detective Special—it is but 6¼ inches overall—makes it possible to carry it ready for instant action, in the pocket or shoulder holster … . The Detective Special handles all .38 Special ammunition, including the High Speed. Although primarily for "close quarters" service, the Detective Special is surprisingly accurate at distances of 25 yards and more.

And indeed it is. Using Federal's 110-grain .38 Special Hydra-Shoks, my 1950s-era Detective Special prints 3½-inch groups at 25 yards, exhibiting deadly accuracy for a self-defense snub-nosed revolver in which most shots would likely be fired at substantially closer distances. But an even more dramatic demonstration of the Detective Special's capabilities was performed many years ago by the crack exhibition shooting of J. Henry FitzGerald. "Fitz" worked as a ballistician and trick shooter for Colt's for 27 years, first joining the company in 1918. He was known for shooting tiny wafers and blocks of wood out of the air with amazing speed, using a pair of Colt Detective Specials that he had modified by bobbing the hammers and cutting away the front half of the trigger guards for gaining easier access to the triggers and thus, being able to draw the guns from his leather-lined pants pockets with lighting speed without snagging. Although FitzGerald personally made approximately 35 of these special guns, many more were subsequently copied by numerous gunsmiths and have since become known as "Fitz Specials."

Even without alteration, the Detective Special was emblematic of the almost-custom quality that was the hallmark of all pre-war Colt's handguns. Parts were polished and hand fitted, and the flat mainspring offered much less resistance than many of the coil springs that would come later. In addition, and like the Police Positive Special, the gun featured a Colt Positive Safety Lock, which in essence was a $\frac{1}{10}$-inch steel finger that kept the hammer from touching the frame unless the trigger was pulled. Finally, and no doubt inspired by FitzGerald's bobbed hammers, an optional detachable hammer shroud was offered later in production.

There are four distinct variations of the Colt Detective Special. The first had a sharply defined square butt that was changed to a more ergonomic butt and grip combination with slightly rounded corners, in 1933. The second issue, which ran from 1947 through 1972, saw the replacement of wood grips with plastic and the addition of the lesser-powered post-war .32- and .38-caliber choices mentioned earlier. Wood grips were brought back in 1954. The third issue, which ran from 1973 until 1986, saw a tweaking of the lock work, the addition of wraparound grips, a front sight with an elongated ramp that ran the length of the two-inch barrel, and a more practical but less attractive shrouded ejector rod. A short-lived fourth series, which lasted from 1993 until 1995, included a last gasp for the little gun by its being offered in stainless steel, as well as with an alloy frame, plus in a double action-only mode with bobbed hammer.

Clearly, it is the pre-1972 guns—the ones without the shrouded ejector rod—and, more specifically, those from the 1950s and earlier, that are now capturing collectors' attention. They invoke not only an era of high-quality belly guns, but a period of film noir and images of tough-talking guys like Mickey Spillane, Robert Mitchum, and Richard Widmark, regular Joes who didn't know where their next check or their next meal was coming from, but who could crank off six well-placed shots in a darkened room, thus striking a winning blow for law and order with their Colt Detective Specials.

M1 GARAND

It is somewhat ironic that the primary shoulder arm of U.S. troops during World War II—in fact, the rifle that's credited with winning the war for America and her Allies—was invented by a Canadian.

Fortunately for the future of world peace, Jean Cantius Garand was born in Quebec in January 1888, and developed an innate curiosity and mechanical ability to determine what made things work. An interest in firearms coupled with a proficiency in marksmanship eventually directed his talents towards trying to convert a WWI surplus bolt-action 1903 Springfield into a semi-automatic.

The activities of the young inventor (who by then had Anglicized his first name to John), eventually caught the attention of a senior military officer named Douglas MacArthur, who arranged for Garand to bring his talents to the Springfield National Armory. There the young inventor began work on what would eventually become known as "U.S. Rifle, Caliber .30, M1." These descriptively memorized words fairly tap danced out of the mouths of any G.I. who went through basic training with the slightly unorthodox yet extremely effective weapon. This mantra was almost always followed by the phrase, "...a gas operated, clip fed, semi-automatic shoulder weapon," quoting right from the tan, soft-cover field training manual.

Although Garand's initial test rifles were chambered for the government .30 cartridge,

A three-part firing, ejecting, and final round (with the empty clip being ejected at the last shot).

This is the proper way to load the M1 Garand, pressing down on the en bloc clip while the fleshy part of the hand holds the operating rod back. No M1 thumb here!

at one point in its development, the inventor was forced to rechamber his semi-automatic in .276-caliber, to make it compatible with the Pedersen rifle, which was also being tested at the time. Fortunately, General MacArthur intervened, and the .30-caliber remained the official cartridge of the M1. After a series of minor changes, the M1 Garand was officially adopted in 1936. It was a fortuitous stroke of timing, for five years later we would be at war.

The M1 nomenclature was the result of the government's then-new system of classifying weapons as "models," and the Garand was the first to receive this designation. Thus, it became known as the M1 (i.e., Model 1), a name that has come to be used concurrently with the inventor's own "Garand" surname.

By today's standards, the M1, with its Parkerized finish and muscular wooden stock, was somewhat bulky-looking. As a matter of fact, it tipped the scales at 9.5 pounds. It held eight rounds in a sheet metal *en bloc* clip that was forcibly ejected out of the receiver with a loud "ping" when the last shot was fired. (It is a somewhat debatable point that WWII combat veterans cringed at this sound, as it supposedly signaled the enemy that the rifle was out of ammunition.) The bolt then automatically locked open, ready for the soldier to press down another loaded clip with

his thumb, while using the fleshy edge of his hand to hold back the tab-eared operating rod handle. Once the clip was fully inserted, the hand was quickly raised, permitting the spring-driven bolt to slam home, chambering a round on the way. Unfortunately, many troopers forgot to lift their thumbs out of the receiver before releasing the bolt. The result was the all-too-familiar "M1 thumb," embarrassingly painful, and easily identified by a blood-blackened thumbnail.

In spite of this and a few other shortcomings, the M1 was an extremely practical battlefield weapon. It was rugged, accurate, and rapid-firing. A steel peep sight, click-adjustable for windage and elevation, was paired with a thick, post front sight protected by two steel "ears." A safety was mounted on the front of the trigger guard, easily snapped back to lock the trigger and just as easily pushed "off" with the thumb.

Throughout its 24 years of production, there were numerous variations made to practically every component of the M1. Perhaps one of the most notable was changing the gas trap system to a gas port in 1940, which eliminated the M1's tendency to hang up after the sixth round was fired. Other changes were more subtle. One of the most visible was the trigger guard. The earliest rifles, those produced up until 1941, featured a milled trigger guard, with a thick hole as part of the rear trigger guard profile. But due to the expense of manufacture, a flat, stamped trigger guard was incorporated by Springfield Armory in 1943. However, in 1939, with a European war looming on the horizon, Winchester was contracted to produce the M1 along with Springfield Armory. Eschewing the stamped trigger guard, Winchester retained the milled trigger guard throughout its entire production of 513,880 rifles, which ended in 1945. (By comparison, Springfield Armory produced slightly more than three and a half million rifles during that same period.) Later, in 1952, during the Korean conflict, Harrington & Richardson and International Harvester were also contracted to make M1 Garands. These were the only four authorized manufacturers of the government-issued M1.

Another variation on the earliest Garands is the solid buttplate. In 1940, this was changed to a hinged buttplate, with a door covering two cylindrical compartments that held an oiler and grease containers, a detachable cleaning rod, and a collapsible maintenance tool with chamber brush. A stacking swivel just forward of the upper handguard was used to hook three rifles together, forming a stacked tripod of rifles for storage during bivouac. Pre-WWII Garands were issued with surplus 1903 leather slings, but a surprisingly large number of post-1941 rifles were outfitted with surplus 1917 and 1918 leather slings, which were still in great abundance at the time. Shortly after the U.S. entered WWII, a webbed M1 sling was officially adopted.

The M1 proved to be eminently adaptable to a number of accessories, including the M2 flash hider, M7 and M7A3 grenade launchers, and various evolutions of bayonets. In addition, highly accurized National Match versions were produced, along with far more lethal sniper models, which were outfitted with telescopic sights and leather cheek rests.

By the end of WWII, there were slightly more than four million M1 rifles in the government's inventory, and most were destined for refurbishing. Thus, the chance of obtaining an unaltered M1 Garand today pretty much dictates that it be unissued and coated in original cosmoline.

Not wishing to date myself, I remember training with the M1 Garand during my Junior ROTC (Reserve Officer Training Corps) years at West High School in Phoenix, Arizona. By then, the old army veteran had been relegated to such status with fuzzy-faced teenagers. By the time my class had gone on to graduate college and was commissioned, standard issue was the M-16, which was light years away from the Garand, although I still trained in boot camp with the Garand, as M-16s were in such short supply. So, not surprisingly, the U.S. Rifle, Caliber .30, M1 was resurrected for active duty in Vietnam, where it served as an infantryman's favorite sniper rifle. I don't want to say my training was faultless, but I can still take an M1 apart in the dark: simply pull back on the trigger guard, swing it up, lift out the trigger housing group, then lift off the stock. Pull back on the follower rod, a spitzer bullet pushes out the retaining pin, and … well, the rest just comes naturally.

In all, over six million Garands were produced, and although most are now "rebuilds," many are extremely collectable and, considering that most have been rebarreled, they remain eminently shootable. No wonder General George S. Patton, Jr., called the M1 Garand, "The greatest battle implement ever devised." As such, and an old friend besides, it's definitely on my bucket list.

M1 CARBINE

This IBM carbine was made in 1944 and was completely restored to its former glory by Miltech (www.
MiltechArms.com), which returns each M1 Carbine in a protective, appropriately-marked pine ches

It seems that the smallest guys are sometimes the toughest. Think Edward G. Robinson, James Cagney, and Alan Ladd. And that's pretty much the case with the 5½-pound M1 Carbine, a welterweight, compared with its heftier 9½-pound sidekick, the M1 Garand, but still able to blast its way to victory in World War II, the Korean conflict, and Vietnam. And, like all three of those actors, the M1 Carbine had impeccable timing.

On November 24, 1941, the United States Army signed a contract to have Winchester Repeating Arms Company and General Motors' Inland Manufacturing Division start producing a newly designed rifle to be used by military support personnel. Two weeks later, the Japanese bombed Pearl Harbor. As a result, the M1 Carbine, like a new recruit fresh out of boot camp, went directly from the assembly lines into battle. In the process, it became the most prolific weapon of WWII, with 6,221,220

carbines made between 1941 and 1943 alone

Initially, the impetus for the M1 Carbine wasn't the threat of a global conflict. Rather, i was the fact that many of our soldiers couldn' hit the broad side of a tank with the 191 Government pistol. Specifically, it was battle field support personnel, including medics, ar tillery and mortar crews, radio operators and NCOs and officers—soldiers whose efficiency would be encumbered by a weighty Garanc slung across their backs—who were typically issued a 1911A1. But their effectiveness, no to mention their survival, was compromisec by a pistol that far too few could shoot with any degree of accuracy. So, under orders from General Douglas MacArthur to modernize the Army, in 1938, a directive was issued by the Chief of Infantry to develop for rear line per sonnel a "light rifle" that would provide a lon ger sighting radius than the five-inch barrel o the 1911A1.

Interestingly, the M1 Carbine began with a concept by Jonathon Edmund Browning, the half-brother of John Browning, who had de signed the 1911. However, the carbine's fina design was the result of concentrated efforts

by a team of top Winchester engineers, including William C. Roemer and Fred Humeston, and supervised by Edwin Pugsley.

Hollywood dramatically altered these facts in a 1952 movie entitled *Carbine Williams*, which starred James Stewart in the title role as David Marshall Williams. In that motion picture, Williams is credited with inventing the M1 Carbine almost single handedly. But, as Bruce Canfield points out in *The Complete Guide To The M1 Garand and M1 Carbine* (Mowbray Publishing), Williams' sole contribution to the project was the carbine's short-stroke gas piston system, which the convicted bootlegger and murderer invented while in prison and which he had initially adapted to the Colt .22 Service Model Ace five years earlier. That is not to belittle his genius, but, as a cantankerous iconoclast, "Marsh" Williams created dissension while working on the M1 Carbine at Winchester. He eventually broke away from the group to perfect his own version of the gun, which was not adopted, even though Pugsley admitted it had some advantages over the Winchester-approved design. But it was too late. The war was under way and production had been started.

The finalized version was known as United States Carbine, Caliber .30, M1, a sleek, pointable, and portable rapid-fire, gas-operated, magazine fed, semi-automatic shoulder weapon. It featured an 18-inch barrel that fired a .30-caliber straight-walled cartridge loosely based on the then-obsolete .32 Winchester Self-Loading round of 1906. Its 110-grain round-nosed bullet exited the barrel at about 1,975 fps, putting it on a par with the Winchester .32-30. Hardly a halftrack-stopper, but certainly adequate to keep the enemy at bay, should the possessor of such a weapon come under attack. Given the carbine's 15-round magazine,

Even after all these years, Hacker finds his WWII-vintage M1 carbine still performs flawlessly.

A later-style WWII carbine with milled trigger guard and safety lever.

Firing the new/old Rock-Ola carbine from James River Armory (www.jamesriverarmory.com), which is made with new Rock-Ola receiver forgings and a combination of USGI and Mil Spec parts.

Post-WWII carbines were outfitted with bayonet sleeves for the M4 bayonet.

plenty of firepower could be laid down, plus, its sights were quick to line up. Those sights initially consisted of an L-shaped, folding peep, but that was changed, around 1944, to an adjustable milled (later stamped) aperture. That same year, a bayonet lug sleeve, designed for the M4 bayonet, was added, although these accessories were only used after WWII, Hollywood depictions notwithstanding.

To meet wartime demands, Winchester and Inland (both of which produced the majority of guns) were assisted by (in order of quantity: Hartford, Connecticut, typewriter manufacturer Underwood-Elliot-Fisher; the Saginaw Steering Gear Division of General Motors, which assembled carbines from parts made by the Irwin-Petersen Arms Company of Grand Rapids, Michigan; National Postal Meter, which

had previously only made postal meters and scales; International Business Machines of Poughkeepsie, New York, the famous office equipment and computer corporation; automotive parts maker Standard Products, of Port Clinton, Ohio; and Rock-ola Manufacturing Company of Chicago, which silenced its juke box business for the war effort. Extra receivers were produced by the Quality Hardware Machine Company, of Chicago.

In addition to the standard M1 carbine, there were four variations. The M1A1 with its folding wire stock was a paratrooper's favorite. The M2, with fish-belly stock and selective-fire lever on the left side of the receiver could go fully automatic, spewing out 850 rounds per minute. With two of its 30-round banana clips taped together, it was a formidable weapon. Equipped with a night scope, it became the M3, while the T3 featured an integral scope base for sniper use.

In 1963, about 240,000 M1 carbines were decommissioned and sold to NRA members for a mouth-watering $20 apiece. Later, during the 1990s, numerous "import" carbines also became available. Back in the '60s I was working my way through school at the A. J. Bayless grocery store in Phoenix, Arizona, and didn't have $20. But my buddy Jim did and bought one of the NRA carbines. I subsequently bought it from him and still have it today. It consistently shoots 1⅛-inch groups, making it ideal for coyotes or plinking. All of which proves the M1 carbine can still accomplish any mission to which it is assigned.

COLT .38 SUPER AUTOMATIC

This highly desirable National Match Super .38, with original box, papers, and sales receipt, was sold by Lock, Stock & Barrel on-line auctions. Photo courtesy Lock, Stock & Barrel (www.LSBauctions.com)

Without a doubt, one of the world's greatest pistol-cartridge combinations is the Colt Government Model 1911 and its .45 ACP chambering. At the time of its adoption as the official handgun and pistol cartridge of the United States military, on March 29, 1911, it was felt no one could improve upon either. However, Colt's Patent Firearms Manufacturing Company updated its warhorse in 1925 and rechristened it the Colt Government Model 1911A1, thereby setting the stage for the Colt .38 Super four years later.

The "A1" improvements included changing the flat mainspring housing to a more palm-filling arched design, shortening the trigger for easier access, and lengthening the gun's grip safety spur to prevent it from "biting" the hand that shot it. The revised .45 Government remained a best seller throughout the Roaring Twenties, but there was trouble looming on the horizon.

On "Black Thursday"—October 24, 1929—the stock market crashed, plunging the country into The Great Depression. Along with everything else, gun sales toppled. Colt's took a long, hard look at its .45 automatic and de-

The .38 Super has proven itself in the field. The author's 1930s-style buscadero rig was made by Jim Lockwood of Legends In Leather. (www.legendsinleather.com).

cided something must be done to breathe new life into the slab-sided shooter. In so doing, it was reminded of the fact that the Model 1911 had descended from the Colt Sporting Model of 1900, a highly successful design collaboration between Colt's and legendary gun designer John Moses Browning.

Hoping for a lucrative government contract, Colt's chambered this revolutionary semi-auto loader for a new, Browning-designed .38 Automatic Colt Pistol (ACP) cartridge to appeal to the Army's then-current penchant for .38-cali-

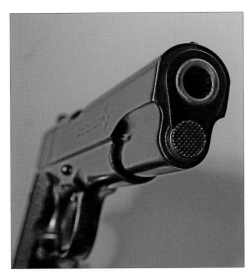

ber. With a magazine holding seven semi-rimmed cartridges, the Colt Sporting Model fired a 130-grain FMJ bullet with a muzzle velocity (MV) of 1,040 fps and a muzzle energy (ME) of 310 ft-lbs, putting it on a par with the old .44-40 blackpowder pistol load, even though the new .38 Auto (as it was commonly called), was loaded with smokeless powder.

Unfortunately, the government purchased only a few hundred guns for testing. Colt's and Browning went back to the drawing boards and subsequently came up with the Sporting Model of 1902, the 1902 Military Model (basically the same gun, but with a lanyard and larger grip to accommodate an eight-round magazine), and, finally, the Military Model of 1905; all were chambered for the .38 Auto. It

Thanks in large part to International Practical Shooting Confederation (IPSC) competition shooters, .38 Super ammunition is still available.

was the Military Model of 1905, with its seven-round magazine, angled grip, five-inch barrel, and grip safety that finally evolved into the Automatic Pistol, Caliber .45 Model of 1911. But even though the Army had shunned all the previous semi-automatics, Colt's .38 Autos proved extremely popular for both self-defense and sporting purposes with the civilian market. As a result, these guns remained in the Colt lineup.

Because of the ongoing popularity of the .38 Auto pistols, as well as the success of its .45 ACP Model 1911A1, Colt's now considered discontinuing its older .38 Autos and replacing them with a Model 1911 chambered for a beefed-up .38 cartridge. The 1911A1 was eminently adaptable to a smaller bore, but it needed a powerful round to take advantage of the gun's potential. The obvious solution was an amped-up .38 Automatic, a cartridge that was already familiar to shooters. Thus evolved the .38 Super Automatic, later shortened to .38 Super.

The .38 Super used the same case and 130-grain FMJ bullet as the old .38 Automatic, but the brass held a heftier powder charge, zinging the bullet past the muzzle at 1,215 feet per second (fps) and 426 ft-lbs of muzzle energy, making the .38 Super, at the time of its introduction, the most powerful semi-automatic pistol cartridge in the world—and the only gun chambered for it was the Colt Government Model 1911A1. This had an additional benefit on the law enforcement front, as many police officers still remembered the 1911 as the handgun that helped win World War I. Now, with an increased rash of gangsterism caused first by the Roaring Twenties and then the Great Depression, the .38 Super had the potential of punching through bulletproof vests and steel-bodied cars, both of which were favored by mobsters and bootleggers.

Although most references give 1929 as the date of the .38 Super's introduction, manufacturing didn't really gear up until 1930. The new .38 Super semi-automatic carried the same $27 price tag as its .45 ACP big brother, but had its own set of serial numbers and the distinctive ".38 Super Automatic" stamped on the slide. The pistol came with a nine-round, two-toned magazine and initially was only offered in blued finish, though nickel was available for an extra charge. Just 32 pre-war .38 Supers were factory engraved, with the first such gun being serial No. 25, which was also fitted with Mexican Eagle ivory stocks and shipped to Wolf & Klar, in Fort Worth, Texas on March 1, 1929, the first year of production.

In spite of the Depression, the .38 Super met with enthusiastic reception, especially among target shooters and hunters, the latter of whom no doubt were encouraged by Colt's somewhat optimistic ads proclaiming it would "… stop any animal on the American continent," with one such ad showing an illustration of an outdoorsman taking aim at a cougar with his .38 Super.

Interestingly, the gun was initially faulted for a lack of accuracy, but gunsmith and writer George Nonte hit upon the idea of rechambering the barrel so that the .38 Super case headspaced on the case mouth, rather than the rim. That changed everything, and, today, the .38 Super, with its lighter recoil and two extra rounds (compared to the .45 ACP), is the choice for many top contenders in International Practical Shooting Confederation (IPSC) events.

As testimony to the hard-hitting, flat-shooting cartridge, many pre-war .38 Supers were carried by Texas Rangers, some of whom wrapped the grips with rawhide or electrical tape to disconnect the grip safety. The gun also saw wide use in Mexico, where military cartridges were banned for use by civilians, but nothing prohibited them from using a military gun chambered for a non-military caliber. In fact, the .38 Super is so closely associated with south of the border adventure, it inspired a somewhat obscure 1969 movie entitled, *Super Colt 38*, starring Jeffrey Hunter and Rosa Maria Vazquez.

During its first 39 years of production, a total of 202,188 Colt Super Automatics were produced. After that, and with the passage of the Gun Control Act of 1968, the .38 Super was given a new set of serial numbers, starting with CS001001. This was used until 1970-'71, when the Model 1911A1 became the MK IV Series 70 Government, which then encompassed the .38 Super chambering.

Although it was not always cataloged, Colt's officials have told me that their .38 Super semi-automatic has never been out of production. In fact, it can still be ordered today. Factory ammunition remains available from Federal (American Eagle), Remington (UMC), and Winchester (USA). However, I have found that pre-MK IV Series 70 pistols have proven to be extremely elusive. Of course, these are the guns that are most in demand, especially among shooter-collectors. I've unintentionally let a couple of them slip through my fingers. One of the most recent occurrences happened a few years ago, when I was high bidder in an on-line auction for a 1957-era .38 Super—nickeled, of course—that came with its original box. But, as fate would have it, I was scheduled to attend a business dinner that evening, and would be unable to be there for the auction's conclusion. I upped my bid by a hundred dollars and left for my appointment.

When I returned—you guessed it—I had been out-bid. And, so, the Colt .38 Super still remains an unfulfilled item on my bucket list.

COLT 1911

This WWII veteran still does active duty as a personal-defense weapon. It is shown here in the "cocked and locked" position.

By now it's no secret that 2011 marked the hundredth anniversary of the Colt Automatic Pistol, Caliber .45, Model of 1911. Numerous gun writers, myself included, heaped well-deserved and glowing praise about this slab-sided warhorse that rode across the Mexican border with General "Black Jack" Pershing in pursuit of Pancho Villa. Later, this same seven-shot semi-automatic helped blaze America's victory through two World Wars and Korea, and then continued to fight in the jungles of Vietnam. And, in spite of the fact that it was replaced as the Army's official sidearm by the Beretta M9 in 1985, the Model 1911A1 is still used by many of our Special Forces and other military personnel in combat zones, fighting alongside M4s and SAWs. Not bad for a gun that had its beginnings before the turn of the twentieth century.

The Model 1911 Civilian Model (as denoted by the "C" prefix of its serial number) was a favorite sidearm of many law enforcement agencies.

Back then, while the United States Army was grappling with the changeover from small-bore double-action revolvers to big-bore single-action semi-automatics, firearms genius John Moses Browning had "seen the future," so to speak. During the 1890s, Browning began working on a pistol that, in his words, incorporated a "moveable breech block or bolt carrier mounted to slide upon [the] frame." Patent No. 580,924, issued to Browning on April 20, 1897, established the design that would eventually become the .38-caliber Colt Automatic Pistol of 1900. Ungainly as it was, it was Colt's first successful semi-auto, and set the stage for the 1911.

The Model 1900 (although it was never officially called that) evolved into the 1902 Model Colt Automatic Pistol in both a civilian Sporting Model and a military version, the latter of which featured a slide stop, a longer grip to accommodate an eight-round magazine, and a lanyard ring. Like the Model 1900, it was chambered for the .38 ACP (Automatic Colt Pistol), a cartridge Browning had designed specifically for these two pistols.

Meanwhile, the Army was having second thoughts about the .38 Long Colt chambering in its official handgun, the New Army and Navy Model of 1892-1903. This cartridge had proved to be woefully incapable of stopping the drug-and-adrenalin-crazed Moros during the Philippine Insurrection, with many warriors taking multiple body hits while still advancing upon U.S. troops. In desperation, the Army returned to an old ally, the Single Action Army, which

was chambered in .45 Colt, a proven man-stopper during the Indian wars on our own U.S. soil. However, even though the cartridge was adequate, the 1873 design of the SAA was clearly outdated. Semi-automatics such as the Borchart C-96, Mauser "Broomhandle" C96, and the P08 Luger were already being adopted by other nations.

Browning was aware of all this and had been meticulously improving his Colt .38 ACP Military Model into what would become the Model 1905, adding an angled grip with built-in safety, a 5¼-inch barrel, and a seven-round magazine—features that would eventually find their way into the 1911. Nor did Browning ignore the Army's revitalized penchant for the .45-caliber. Just as he had developed a proprietary cartridge for his Models 1900 and 1902 semi-automatics, working with Colt's and Brigadier General John Taliaferro Thompson of the Army Ordnance Corps, a 230-grain, full metal jacketed cartridge was developed that was ballistically similar to the .45 Colt. It would become known as Cal .45 Automatic Pistol Ball Cartridge, Model of 1911 or, more popularly, the .45 ACP (Automatic Colt Pistol). Later, impressed by the bullet's stopping power, which was tested on cattle and cadavers, General Thompson would chamber his famous Thompson Sub-Machine Gun for this same cartridge.

Although the Army had previously conducted tests in 1899 and 1900 to select a semi-automatic pistol, at that time the samples from Colt's, Mauser, Steyr Mannlicher, and Luger

The author enjoys the nostalgia of regularly shooting his WWII vintage Government 1911A1, even though these guns are increasing in value almost daily.

Recoil of the ACP, while distinctive, is controllable.

were all sub-.45-caliber and, thus, deemed ineffective. (Interestingly, the Army did purchase 1,000 Deutsche Waffen und Munitionsfabriken (DWM) Lugers for further testing, but found them ineffective). Now, with the Army's new .45 ACP caliber dictum in place, in early 1906 invitations were again sent out to manufacturers. There were eight respondents: Colt's (with Browning's 1905 design), experimental Knoble and White-Merrill self-cocking pistols, Bergmann-Bayard, Webley Fosbery, plus Smith & Wesson, Savage, and Luger (which entered two specially chambered P08s in .45-caliber and serial numbered No. 1 and No. 2). Design flaws eliminated every gun except the Colt,

Savage, and Luger. Subsequent testing saw Luger No. 1 blow up and, for reasons never revealed, serial No. 2 was withdrawn from competition. That left Colt and Savage in the finals.

Determined to have his gun the winner, Browning began improving the Model 1905 with Models 1907, 1909, and 1910, with many being issued to cavalry units in New Mexico, Iowa, and Georgia for extensive field-testing. Ironically, with the mechanized warfare of World War I on the horizon, the earliest design criteria nonetheless came from the mounted cavalry. Hence, the addition of a lanyard loop on both gun and magazine to prevent dropping them from the saddle, and not just one,

The classic World War II Model 1911A1, with its Parkerized finish, arched mainspring housing, and shortened, serrated trigger.

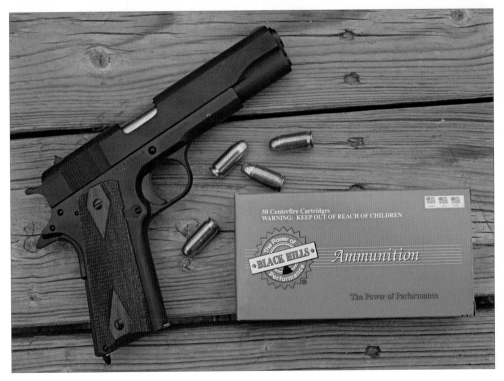

In 2011, as part of the hundredth anniversary celebration of the Government Model 1911, Colt reissued its G.I. 1918 "Black Colt," which was available only until December 31, 2011. Note the flat mainspring housing and wider trigger, two distinctive characteristics of the early guns.

but three safeties—grip, thumb-operated slide/hammer lock, and half-cock—to keep the gun from going off and accidentally incapacitating a trooper's horse at a full gallop. The result was the Model 1911.

For the final Army field trials of March 15, 1911, Browning personally supervised the assembly of every part of his pistol at the Colt's factory. Its only competition? An improved version of the Savage 1907, chambered in .45 ACP. After a grueling 6,000-round test for each gun, the Savage had suffered numerous broken parts and malfunctions, while the Colt hadn't incurred a single failure to function. Thus, on March 29, 1911, the Colt Model 1911 became the United States Army's official handgun, beginning a legacy that continues to this day.

Soon a nearly identical civilian version was

There are wide varieties of ammo for the owner of a 1911 (shown) or a 1911A1.

In spite of what others may say, Hacker finds as-issued G.I. 1911A1s to be accurate, when used with the right ammunition.

Firing his 1911 Colt reissue, the author experienced no malfunctions with factory ball ammunition.

produced, easily identified by the "C" prefix of its serial number, a more polished finish, and the lack of a lanyard ring on its magazine. It wasn't long before the 1911 was enthusiastically adopted for law enforcement, self-defense, and even as a much-advertised hunting arm. The U.S. Border Patrol and the Texas Rangers were some of its most enthusiastic users, with many of the Texas DPS boys turning their sidearms into "barbeque guns," with nickel plating, engraving, and fancy grips.

In 1924 the 1911 got a minor makeover, with an arched mainspring housing, a shorter trigger, longer grip safety spur, wider hammer spur, and improved sights. In addition, on military models, the original Carbona blue was changed to a more durable Parkerized finish. This, then, became the 1911A1. Over the years, other variations evolved, including the .38 Super, in 1929, the adjustable-sighted National Match, in 1933 (reintroduced, in 1957, as the Gold Cup), and, in 1931, a full-sized .22 called the Ace, followed by a more refined Service Model Ace, in 1936. There have since been countless 1911 variations encompassing lowered ejection ports, extended ambidextrous thumb safeties, accessory rails, night sights, beavertail grip safeties—refinements even John Browning may not have envisioned.

It was as a battle weapon that the Colt 1911 is best revered. Counting both Models 1911 and 1911A1, more than 2,695,000 government pistols were produced, comprising the longest continuous run of any Colt's firearm. Today, more than 100 years after its adoption by the Army, the 1911 is still very much with us, as a collectable, a shooter, and as various models still produced by the same company that first gave it life.

1874 SHARPS

Certain rifles transcend their time, and one of the most enduring is the 1874 Sharps. Known by monikers such as "Old Reliable," "Buffler Rifle," and "The Big 50" (referring to its popular .50-100 chambering), it was praised by such nineteenth century luminaries as John C. Fremont, Buffalo Bill Cody, and Theodore Roosevelt. Quick to reload and having both a solid, drop-block action and superbly rifled barrel, the 1874 Sharps was not only the choice for serious big-game hunters, it played a major role in disseminating the West's vast buffalo herds—a dubious distinction, to be sure.

The evolution of events leading up to the single-shot that tamed the west began on September 12, 1848, when a young inventor named Christian Sharps patented a breech-loading rifle that utilized a lever-operated drop-down breechblock. In the era of the muzzleloader, where one had to stand in order to ram a charge down the barrel, the Sharps had an enticing military appeal, as it enabled soldiers to reload without exposing themselves to enemy fire. They merely opened the lever, which exposed the breech, put in a lead bullet, and then seated it against the rifling with a powder charge. Closing the breech and placing a percussion cap on the nipple readied the gun for firing. Unfortunately, America was not at war in 1848, and, consequently, the government had little interest in the unique breech-loader. This lack of interest and, subsequently, a lack of funds, forced Sharps to subcontract his first 700 rifles; they weren't even stamped with his name.

A few years later, Sharps convinced the firm of Robbins & Lawrence to manufacture his Im-

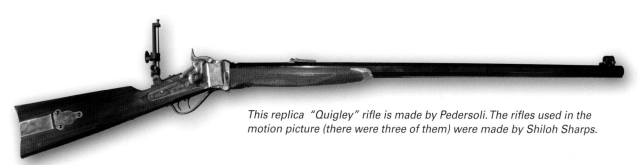

This replica "Quigley" rifle is made by Pedersoli. The rifles used in the motion picture (there were three of them) were made by Shiloh Sharps.

This Dixie Gun Works "Quigley" long-range rifle by Pedersoli is shown with a limited edition silver .45-110 commemorative bullet offered by the National Rifle Association and embossed with actor Tom Selleck's signature.

proved Model of 1851. Thus, the Sharps Rifle Manufacturing Company was formed in Hartford, Connecticut. Shortly thereafter, a series of personality clashes caused Christian Sharps to leave the firm. Although Sharps continued to receive royalties on his rifles, it was Richard S. Lawrence, the company's armorer, who continued to make improvements on the original patent and kept the rifle in production.

Subsequent versions, including the slant-breech Model of 1852 and the more efficient vertical breechblock of the New Model 1859, eventually brought the Sharps rifle to the attention of the U.S. government. But it was The War Between The States that finally brought orders and much needed Yankee dollars to the struggling Sharps company. During The Great Rebellion, the Sharps became a favored weapon for snipers, who found it convenient to reload while concealed in treetop perches. The rifle's reputation also resulted in Colonel Berden's 2nd Regiment of Sharpshooters threatening mutiny when they were shipped 2,000 of Colt's revolving rifles, instead of the Sharps rifles they had been promised—they quickly got their Sharps. By the end of hostilities in 1865, a total of 80,512 carbines and 9,141 full-stocked military rifles had been shipped to Union troops. The Model of 1865 was the last percussion Sharps made, with

5,000 carbines manufactured shortly after the war.

With such sizable orders, a great reputation, and thousands of ex-Rebels and Yanks heading west and in need of a reliable rifle, one would think that the ill-fated fortunes of the Sharps Rifle Manufacturing Company were over. But, in 1874, right on the eve of America's great frontier expansion, Christian Sharps and Richard Lawrence died within months of each other. With the passing of the rifle's inventor and its chief proponent, the company shuttered its doors. Indeed, the Model 1874 might never have been a reality had it not been for a group of investors, who reorganized the firm as the Sharps Rifle Company.

The rifle that launched this second venture was the Model 1874, an updated version of the older percussion models and designed for the new era of the self-contained metallic cartridge. While lever-actions of the day such as the Henry and Winchester's Models 1866 and 1873 were boasting repeat-fire capabilities, their slim and relatively weak actions simply could not contain nor sustain heavy loads—certainly not cartridges packing enough power to anchor tenacious western big game such as grizzlies and elk.

The new 1874 Sharps had no such problems. It was a handsome, solid, and hefty rifle,

The heavy weight of many Sharps hunting rifles necessitates the use of shooting sticks.

The author replicates the bison hunter's technique of keeping an extra shell between his fingers for a fast follow-up shot.

with an average weight of 12 pounds, although some specimens—most notably those with thick, special order barrels—tipped the scales at 25 pounds or more. The rifle's jam-resistant action was proven and strong; in fact, many lock parts were carryovers from the percussion guns, which had already established their reputation in combat.

Not only was the 1874 accurate and rug-ged, it was easy to maintain. With a single, removable steel pin, the entire breechblock and hinged lever could be dropped out of the frame for cleaning. The machine-rifled barrels of the new 1874 had a 1:20 twist, with shallow lands and grooves. Barrel lengths ran from 21½ inches to 36 inches and could be had in round, octagon, or half-round/half-octagon configura-tions. The earliest guns featured a distinctive

A Sharps 1874 Sporting Rifle, shown with an original paper-patched .45-70 cartridge.

The original breech stamping on an 1874 Sporting Rifle.

"Hartford collar," a milled ring around the base of the barrel where it joined the receiver. When the company moved to Bridgeport, in 1876, this decorative feature was dropped. In April of that same year, the rifle's nickname, "Old Reliable," began being stamped on the barrels.

Stocks were plain, oil-finished American black walnut, although fancier wood could be ordered. The earliest 1874 models featured pewter-tipped Hartford forearms. After 1877, this attractive feature was replaced with a schnabel tip, although both the earlier Hartford collar and pewter fore-end could be special ordered for an extra charge. Receivers were case hardened, with all other metal parts being blued. Single and double-set triggers were offered, and the variety of front, rear, tang, and telescopic sights was enough to satisfy the demands of the most discriminating customers.

Indeed, the numerous models of the 1874 Sharps were as varied as the shooters who ordered them. Cataloged versions included Sporting Rifles, Lightweight Sporting Rifles, Creedmore and Schuetzen target rifles, Business Rifles, a full-stocked Military Rifle, a bare bones Hunter's Rifle, and a saddle carbine, among others. Of course, a plethora of options, including straight or pistol grip stocks,

Vernier tang sights are a popular feature on Sharps rifles, whether replicas or originals.

Below: This early Shiloh Sharps is stamped with the original Farmington, New York, address that is sought after by some collectors.

runners" carried one or more Sharps rifles, firing volley after volley at the big, shaggy beasts, at ranges that often exceeded 400 yards, and switching guns when the barrels became too hot to handle. Another notable long-range event occurred in 1874, during the Battle of Adobe Walls, when a young hunter named Billy Dixon borrowed a "Big .50" Sharps from none other than Bat Masterson and toppled a Kiowa chief at what was later confirmed to be 1,538 yards (⅞-mile).

In spite of these and other success stories, economic woes continued to plague the Sharps Rifle Company. With the unexpected cancellation of a large British order, the firm was finally forced to close its doors; the last gun was shipped in 1881. Although it was an internationally renowned rifle whose inventor never got rich, the 1874 Sharps had amassed enough glory in seven years to create a legacy that continues today.

Originals are the centerpiece of many a collection. Fortunately, there are now excellent replicas made by Italian firms such as Pedersoli and Chiappa. In addition, firms such as C. Sharps Arms and Shiloh Sharps, both located in Big Timber, Montana, are emulating the original Sharps Rifle Company by handcrafting 100-percent custom-built rifles for the discriminating sportsman. I own more than one of these heavy hitters, and, with them, have taken everything from a Rowland Ward recordbook impala in Africa, to a 2,000-pound bull bison on the plains on Montana. No wonder this nineteenth century single-shot is on my bucket list.

special barrel lengths and weights, and engraving could be special ordered—and often were. In short, the 1874 Sharps was a very labor intensive, custom-made rifle, facets that were reflected in the price. While Winchester's breechloading repeaters were selling for as little as $10, a basic single-shot Sharps was priced at $33. Nonetheless, with specialized cartridges like the .40-90, .44-77 bottleneck, .45-100, and .50-100, the 1874 Sharps soon became *the* big-game rifle among savvy frontiersmen and serious hunters.

The Sharps proved itself on target ranges as well. During one memorable 1,000-yard match, in 1877 at Creedmoor, Americans firing long-range Sharps rifles soundly defeated a British team. But it was in the hands of buffalo hunters that the 1874 Sharps lived up to its "Old Reliable" reputation. Most of these "buffalo

WINCHESTER
MODEL 21

After a long quest by the author, this Model 21 is finally back in the field. The hand-checkered buttstock is protected by a Galco recoil pad, which also adds a half-inch to the length of pull.

I suspect I'm not the only one who does this, but sometimes I lie awake at night thinking about certain guns that I simply must have, no matter how costly or rare they may be. As a matter of fact, that's how this book got started. As an example, for decades I felt this way about the Winchester Model 21, technically and aesthetically the finest shotgun ever created by American craftsmen and perfected by American ingenuity. Produced by Winchester Repeating Arms Company from 1930 until 1988 (after 1981, it was under the auspices of U.S. Repeating Arms Company), this side-by-side boxlock was the ultimate smoothbore for serious upland and waterfowl hunters, as well as for highly competitive trap and skeet shooters.

It took seven years of development by T.C. Johnson, Winchester's chief designer, and further refinement by Edwin Pugsley, their factory manager who would go on to become its vice president, but the company had created a masterpiece. Interestingly, it was the first double-barreled shotgun Winchester ever produced, as all of its previous side-by-sides had been imported.

The Winchester 21 owed its fame to a number of manufacturing techniques and design features that had never before been incorporated in a side-by-side shotgun. For one, the action broke open at an unusually shallow angle, to reduce ejecting and reloading time. Moreover, the Model 21 ignored traditional shotgun

Hacker proudly poses with his Model 21, after taking these Nebraska pheasants.

manufacturing techniques by foregoing the standard practice of brazing the twin barrels together, a process that often weakened the steel. Instead, the right and left tubes were each forged with an integral chopper lump lug, which, in turn, was cut with a dovetail that locked into the corresponding dovetail of the matching barrel and then soldered. Winchester referred to this as its "interlocking grip." Because of the incredible strength of these dovetailed barrels, the Model 21 didn't require a rib extension. To give additional strength to this already muscular design, the receiver and barrels were forged of Winchester's proprietary chrome molybdenum "Proof Steel," which was developed especially for the Model 21, but, because of its unprecedented durability, ended

up being used for other Winchester firearms, as well.

The entire shotgun was so well machined and the parts matched to such close tolerances that it could easily withstand over 2,000 high-velocity "proof loads," a feat that, in an actual field test, completely decimated the actions of other top-grade American shotguns, including the sidelock L.C. Smith and the venerable Parker boxlock. Only the Model 21 emerged unscathed from this grueling trial, a fact that was subsequently touted in ads featuring the surviving rock-solid Model 21 resting atop a stack of spent proof load casings, dramatic testimony to the gun's mechanical superiority.

Of course, all these innovations came with a high price tag. Making its ill-timed appear-

The Model 21's inertia-driven single selective trigger prevents doubling and enables the shooter to choose either right or left barrel by pushing the button to the right or left. Originally developed by Louis Stiennon, one of Winchester's research and development men, it has never been improved upon.

Because of the incredible strength of the "interlocking grip" dovetailed barrels, the Model 21 does not require a rib extension.

ance on the eve of The Great Depression, the Model 21 was an extremely expensive shotgun to produce and sell. In fact, if not for John Olin, whose Western Cartridge Company purchased Winchester Repeating Arms in 1931, the Model 21 would have been discontinued because of its unprofitability, its unsurpassed excellence as a sporting arm notwithstanding. But Olin was an avid wingshooter who knew a good thing when he saw it, and he devoted the rest of his life not only to keeping the Model

21 in the line, but improving and upgrading it. Under his direction, the original double triggers were replaced with a sturdy single trigger that featured a push-button barrel selector, a faultless inertia-driven design that was regulated to the trigger pull (thus making "doubling" impossible), and which was the brainchild of Louis Stiennon, one of Winchester's research and development men. That innovation has since been copied by numerous other companies.

The author's Skeet Model 21, with 26-inch barrels and ventilated rib, was shipped from the factory on December 12, 1946.

In addition, the Model 21's splinter fore-end was reshaped into a more hand-filling beavertail, first offered as an option in 1934, but becoming standard by 1941. Whether it was the plain Field Grade, the specialized Trap, Tournament, Skeet, or Duck (Magnum) models or, in later years, the more elaborately engraved and artistically checkered Custom Built, Deluxe, and Custom Deluxe grades and the stratospherically priced Pigeon Grade and Grand American showpieces, the Winchester 21 had evolved into the epitome of a classic, side-by-side American shotgun. And, in the true spirit of American equality, no matter what its grade or price tag, internally every Model 21 exhibited the same superb degree of mechanical perfection and workmanship. When that boxlock action softly snapped shut, it locked up tighter than the hatch on a Bradley Fighting Vehicle.

Even back in my early pre-gun writing days, I sensed this shotgun was unique. My hunting buddies often spoke of it in hushed tones, as if it were something sacred. In gun stores, there were nodding heads and murmurs of reverence among customers of the fabled Winchester 21. Clearly, I wasn't the only one to come under this double gun's spell, and, as I learned more of the Model 21's attributes, it only increased my desire to own one.

My acquisition of this shotgun was perpetually thwarted by its high price tag, always just out of reach of my meager budget. By the 1980s, when my income had finally risen to a point where I thought I could afford a Model 21, I was shocked to discover that the cost of a new plain Field Grade had also risen. It was now over $5,000, and an engraved Custom Grade would break the bank (my bank, for sure), at more than $11,000. Once the gun was discontinued, prices on the higher grades and rarer 20- and 28-gauges and the scarce .410-bore rose even more. Besides, with only an estimated 32,500 guns having been made, there just weren't that many Winchester Model 21s around; they never wore out, and shooters who owned them obviously were in no hurry to get rid of them.

Occasionally, I would find a used Model 21, but they invariably featured options that priced them well out of any negotiating range. At one point, I lucked into a Field Grade 12-gauge in the used gun racks of a favorite sporting goods store. Even though the gun had been reblued and featured a non-factory Simmons ventilated rib, the price was $4,500 (the Model 21 is one of the few collectibles in which wear and refinishing don't seem to affect value as dramatically as they do with other guns). *A bit steep*, I thought, as I left the shop and drove home. Then something snapped: What was I *thinking*? Here was my dream gun, the first one I had seen for sale in years. *Go back and buy it, you idiot!* The next day, I returned to the shop, armed with a bevy of credit cards. As I entered, an empty spot in the gun rack confirmed my fears. During my brief absence, the gun had been sold! As my long-suffering wife can attest, that was a sad day at Hacker House.

Undaunted, I continued my search. At one point, I discovered that my friend, the late cowboy movie star Roy Rogers, had an exquisite two-gun set of Grand Americans, each with a separate set of barrels.

"Would you like to see them?" Roy asked one afternoon, as I was telling him about my quest for a Model 21. I began mumbling incoherently and salivating, which Roy took to mean "Yes." Years ago, he had visited the Winchester factory to be measured for the stocks and to select engraving patterns for these fabulous guns. After all, no matter what its grade, the Model 21 was always a hand-built firearm, and Winchester offered any option the customer wanted and could afford. Each of Roy's Grand Americans sported finely figured, *fleur de lis*-carved, black walnut stocks and was fully engraved with gold inlays of Roy, Trigger, his dog Bullet, and other western and hunting motifs. Roy was an excellent shotgunner and occasionally competed with these showpieces. I, of course, would have been settled for a plain 12-gauge Field Grade, should I ever again stumble onto one that was affordable.

A few years later, at the Wally Beinfeld International Sporting Arms Show held each year in Las Vegas, I thought that day had finally arrived. It's worth the price of admission just to see some of the world's finest rifles and shotguns

on display and for sale. And it was here that I discovered the Mecca of Winchester Model 21s—every grade, gauge, and barrel length, with price tags to match. Entranced, I was able to cover only half the show and decided to return the next day to continue my quest. On the way back to my hotel, I shared a cab with a fellow who seemed remarkably happy.

"Get anything good at the show?" I asked, curious as to the cause of his beaming countenance.

"You bet!" he enthused. "I just bought the shotgun of my dreams."

"What was it?" I had a bad feeling about this.

"A Model 21!"

I was immediately filled with a mixture of admiration and blatant envy. "What did you have to give for it?" I dreaded asking, but I had to.

Wide-eyed, he turned to me and said, "Only $2,500. Can you believe it?"

Don't get me wrong; I was happy this guy had struck the mother lode. But I couldn't help thinking that, if I'd walked the show a little bit longer or a little bit faster, that gun could have been *mine*! Needless to say, there were no other $2,500 Model 21s at the International Sporting Arms Show the next day. Or the next year.

Then, once again fate dealt me a hand that made me believe ownership of a Winchester 21 might become a possibility. At the annual Shooting Hunting Outdoor Trade (SHOT) Show, a trade event for firearms dealers and manufacturers, I met Anthony Galazan, owner of Connecticut Shotgun Manufacturing Company. Tony had purchased all the remaining inventory of Model 21 parts and machinery when USRC ceased manufacturing the shotgun. CSMS is now the official factory repair center for Winchester 21s and has resurrected the production of custom Model 21s but, of course, without the Winchester logo. Naturally,

I told Tony of my eternally frustrating pursuit of this fabled and elusive shotgun.

"Come on down and visit my factory," Tony offered. "I've got the largest selection of Model 21s anywhere."

Indeed he had, for Tony has been buying up all the Model 21s he can find (contributing, I might add, to their scarcity on the open market). As it just so happened, a few months later I was in Connecticut on a business trip. I extended my stay an extra day to visit the Galazan operation. Tony's factory is a beehive of activity, with craftsmen busily hand-building Model 21s just, I imagined, as they must have done at the Winchester plant many years ago. Bluing, engraving, hand fitting of parts—it was like stepping into a time warp. But the best part was the showroom, a wood paneled shrine of shotguns that lined the walls—Parkers, Remingtons, L.C. Smiths, indeed, double guns of all vintages and descriptions. And there, taking up one whole wall, was a case full of Winchester 21s, some all original, others reconditioned by CSMC to "factory mint."

"Why don't you look around and see if there's something you like," Tony offered.

Left alone in the room, I began to hyperventilate as I picked up and examined virtually every Winchester 21 in the place. By this time I knew what I wanted: a single trigger, pistol-grip gun with open chokes for upland wingshooting (no way was I going to take a shotgun like the Model 21 into a wet, muddy duck blind). After a couple hours, I had selected three Model 21s that fit me and my criteria. I laid each of them on a table and called for Tony to come in, all set to do some hard and fast wheeling and dealing for one of them. This was as close as I had ever gotten and I was fully prepared to max out my credit cards and end my quest that very day. But, after hearing me out and glancing at the three shotguns on the table, Tony said, "Listen, you've waited so long for a Model 21, why don't you let me build a gun for you? That way you'll have exactly what you want—chokes, beads, everything. It will be made to measure and I'll even put some fancy wood on it."

By golly, he was right—why shouldn't I have the ultimate custom-made shotgun? Okay, so I wouldn't leave Connecticut with my goals finally attained, but I would, eventually, get a Model 21, even though it wouldn't have the Winchester name stamped on the barrels. So I agreed. We never discussed price, but CSMC Model 21s are not cheap. However, I rationalized the decision by thinking this would probably be the only shotgun I would ever need. And so I got professionally measured for the stock: length of pull, cast on, cast off, drop at heel, grip at comb, all the same criteria Winchester called for on its original Model 21 order forms. If I was going to plunge into debt, I was going to do it in style.

I sent my measurements to Tony, along with my choice of chokes, WS-1 and WS-2, Winchester's well-researched Skeet combination known for its superb close-range patterning. And then I waited. And waited. Bird season came and went. Twice. At the next SHOT Show, I caught up with Tony. To his credit, he was trying to save me money by looking for an original Model 21 receiver, which evidently was harder to find than original guns. Of course, he was also busy filling orders for his A.H. Fox doubles, as well as his Galazan Over & Under and Round Body Sidelock, both of which feature no visible screws or pins. Another year passed, and this time I saw Tony at the Las Vegas show. He had Model 21s on his table, but he had convinced me: after so many years, I wasn't going to settle for anything that wasn't exactly to my specifications. Again I was advised that the wait would be worth it. I had to admit, CSMC's Model 21s looked every bit as good as the original Winchesters. The problem was, I began to fear that if I ever I got the gun, I would be too old to shoot it.

Then, one day, as I was perusing Cabela's latest catalog, I noticed a blurb on the order form for the Cabela's Gun Library. I must have glanced over this innocuous announcement numerous times, always thinking it was a listing for gun books. This time I read it. "We Buy Guns, Antique and Modern," it said. Of course, it was just like wine libraries. Older, high-end collectibles. I immediately got on the phone to Cabela's flagship store in Sidney, Nebraska. With trepidation, I asked if they had any Model 21s in stock. The Gun Library manager pulled up his computer listings for all seven Cabela's stores. They had 16 of them! But, by now, my lengthy search had made me even more specific about the gun I wanted.

"Listen," I said, "it's got to be a 12-gauge, with a pistol grip, and have 26-inch barrels with a ventilated rib, and choked WS-1 and WS-2. And another thing; it's got to have above average wood."

A moment passed while the manager searched through the 16 guns on his computer screen. "Well, look at this!" he exclaimed. "Our Michigan store has a Model 21 in 12-gauge with a pistol grip, factory vent rib, 26-inch barrels choked Skeet 1 and Skeet 2 … and its got the prettiest wood you ever saw!"

I had him e-mail me a jpeg image of the gun, which I used as a screensaver for weeks afterwards. Cabela's Gun Library manager was more than accommodating. Learning I had a December deer hunt scheduled in Nebraska, he offered to have the gun shipped from their Michigan store to Sydney. They would hold it for me so that I could see it firsthand after my hunt. Was that service or what?

From Cabela's, I obtained the Model 21's serial number and contacted the Buffalo Bill Historical Center, where, for a fee, they can supply information from Winchester factory records. It turned out that this particular Skeet model was shipped on December 12, 1946. Unfortunately, it was not only used but abused, for it was returned to Winchester on February 28, 1979, for a complete overhaul, which included rebuilding the receiver, rebluing the barrels, and refinishing the wood. Then it went off to a new owner, who took much better care of it, until he finally sold it to Cabela's. In short, to use the Gun Library manager's words, it was "as close to a factory new Winchester 21 as you're likely to get." In addition to this research, I paid a modest fee to verify the approximate value by contacting the Preferred Customer Service division of Steve Fjestad's *Blue Book Publications*. After all, in spite of Cabela's extremely competitive prices, this was still going to be a major purchase for me. *The Blue Book* report was money well spent for the peace of mind it brought.

Cabela's store in Sidney is huge, but, after my hunt, I rushed past the racks of outdoor gear, stuffed wildlife dioramas, and Christmas decorations and headed straight for the Gun Library, a separate area from the regular sporting guns department. Inside the gun-filled room, the manager and his assistant were waiting with the Model 21. I took it from them like a long lost friend and threw it up to my shoulder. As expected, the factory's standard 14-inch length of pull was a little short for me, but, when they slipped on a leather Galco recoil pad (which also protected the hand-checkered butt), the fit was perfect.

"Maybe you'd like to take it out and shoot some pheasants," the manager joked. Plenty of time for that, I thought, as we wrote up the sales receipt and arranged for an FFL delivery. Later on, I called Tony and changed my order. I now wanted one of his new Model 21 Over & Unders, which he had just started building at a very competitive introductory price. It would be a perfect companion double. But for now, almost 70 years since it was originally shipped from the New Haven factory, my quest for a Winchester Model 21 was over.

GRIFFIN & HOWE

The author's 1930s-era Griffin & Howe is as much at home in the field as it is in a display case.

Around the turn of the last century, American sportsmen were transitioning from blackpowder to smokeless and from single-shots and lever guns to bolt-actions. World War I accelerated the crank-handled rifle's appeal, and, by the early 1920s, a plethora of surplus 1903 Springfields and 1898 Mausers made the field ripe for numerous custom gunsmiths like Sedgley, Newton, and Wundhammer to set up shop and sporterize these well-made and relatively inexpensive military rifles.

One of the 1903 Springfield's staunchest admirers was a young New York cabinetmaker and gun hobbyist named Seymour R. Griffin. Back in 1910, Griffin had read the just-published *African Game Trails* by popular ex-president Theodore Roosevelt, a recounting of his recent African safari. Roosevelt wrote glowingly about the 1903 Springfield rifle he and his son Kermit used on the Dark Continent. Griffin immediately purchased one of these rifles and, being a skilled woodworker, he used a premium grade of Circassian walnut to carve an exquisite new stock for his be-

loved Springfield. But it was a short-lived love affair, because a friend saw Griffin's handiwork and offered him a price for the rifle that the cabinetmaker couldn't turn down.

Griffin promptly purchased another Springfield, made another finely carved stock for it, and was subsequently offered another sum of money for it. Soon, Seymour Griffin was augmenting his cabinetmaking income by creating stylish Springfield sporters for a small but affluent coterie of serious shooters. His well-finished guns were especially noted for their finely crafted inletting and featured schnabel

The author used his vintage Griffin & Howe .30-06 to drop this trophy Rambouillet-Navajo ram.

fore-ends and Griffin's trademark: a sharply sloped cutaway in the stock by the bolt.

Eventually, Griffin's stock-making skills came to the attention of Major Townsend Whelen, who happened to be one of the most influential early post-war gun writers. Whelen's nationally published articles praised Griffin's skills and brought him to the attention of even more shooters. But Whelen was also the commanding officer at Frankford Arsenal and director of research and development at Springfield Armory. It was there, in 1921, that he encountered another talented individual, a gunmaker from Pennsylvania named James Virgil Howe, whose specialty was metalworking. At the time, Howe headed up the Armory's Small Arms Experimental Department. Whelen conceived of forming a gunmaking company that would combine the complementary talents of Seymour Griffin and James Howe. Both men agreed and, on June 1, 1923, the firm of Griffin & Howe opened its doors at 234 East 39th Street, in New York City, with Whelen serving as advisor. This new-found entity was short-lived, however, because, in September of that year, Howe quit the company that bore his name and went to work for a competitor, the Hoffman Arms Company of Cleveland, Ohio.

"He only stayed long enough to get his name on the door," noted Paul E. Chapman, Griffin & Howe's current Vice President, Director of Gunsmithing.

Undaunted, Seymour Griffin maintained the Griffin & Howe name and assembled a small but talented group of American and European gunmakers and engravers. Together, they firmly established Griffin & Howe's reputation for building some of the world's finest custom bolt-action sporting rifles. Superbly grained walnut stocks, fine line checkering, folding leaf express sights, intricate engraving, and inlaid gold, silver, and platinum motifs and coats of arms were the norm.

Most rifles were built on plentiful Mauser and 1903 actions, the latter of which were better finished than the 1903A3 Springfield actions. Super-accurate barrels were usually obtained from the equally famous Niedner Rifle Corporation. More than 14 different chamberings were regularly produced (though customers could have any caliber they desired), including propriety cartridges such as the .350 G&H Magnum (a necked-down .375 H&H) and Col. Whelen's .400 Whelen and the .35 Whelen, which was originally developed by Howe while at the Springfield Armory and which is still being commercially loaded today.

For a while, the firm even had its own brand of ammunition.

Griffin & Howe also developed a detachable scope side mount, which the company patented in 1927, and again, with improvements, in 1931. By simply flipping up a lever, the scope could be lifted off the rifle for transportation or open sight use. By repositioning the scope and rotating the levers down, the scope would be locked in place, with no loss of zero. This scope mount was also adapted by Griffin & Howe for M1 sniper rifles during World War II, and is still in the company's line today.

For all its gunmaking skills and reputation, it is estimated that Griffin & Howe produced less than 2,000 rifles between 1923 and the outbreak of World War II, which effectively put its gun making on hold. The Great Depression hit G&H especially hard, as its rifles were scarcely for the shooter on a budget. Thus, Seymour Griffin must have given a sigh of relief when he was approached in 1930, by James S. Cobb, president of the well-known sporting goods outfitter Abercrombie & Fitch, with an offer to assimilate G&H into the more secure A&F stronghold.

When Abercrombie & Fitch liquidated in 1976, an entrepreneur named Bill Ward purchased Griffin & Howe and continued its

The factory has no records of many original owners, leaving Hacker to wonder who "CSC" was on his G&H .30-06 and exactly when he ordered this rifle.

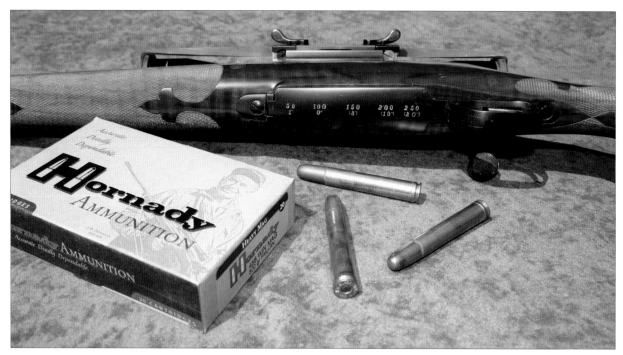

Hacker is still waiting to take this Griffin & Howe Model 70 to Africa or Alaska. Note the custom trajectory readings the company engraved on the floor plate at the request of the original owner.

One of the earliest known rifles made by Seymour Griffin, featuring his now-classic, sharply sloped cutaway in the stock by the bolt.

tradition of building rifles for sportsmen who demanded the best. When Ward over-expanded in 1986, the firm was acquired by businessman and sportsman Joe Prather and another investor. Prather served as president until he retired and became Chairman Emeritus. He was succeeded in March 2007 by Guy A. Bignell, who had been associated with the company since 1993 and is now the fifth president in Griffin & Howe's history.

All Griffin & Howe rifles are extremely collectable and have maintained their values. Griffin & Howe often renumbered its early rifles, exchanging the original Springfield and Mauser serial numbers for its own. The rifles were artistically engraved "Griffin & Howe, Inc. New York" on the barrel, along with the gun's G&H serial number. Yet I have G&H barrel-engraved rifle #110, which was purportedly made sometime during the late 1920s with the serial number stamped on the receiver and hidden by the bolt. There is also a number "9" engraved under the barrel, hidden by the stock. Most G&H rifles have meticulously engraved checkering on the bolt and an engraved blued steel pistol grip cap.

The serial numbers of many of these early guns, including those purchased by luminaries such as Ernest Hemingway, Clark Gable, and Bill Ruger, can be confusing at times, but as a point of reference, G&H No. 1001 starts in 1930 with the takeover by Abercrombie & Fitch. In 1942, just prior to our entering WWII, the ledgers show serial No. 1708. The year 1963 ends with serial No. 2504. Another G&H rifle in my collection is a Rock Island Arsenal Model 1903 rifle, caliber .30-06, serial No. 51111, which Bignell, Chapman, and Prather believe dates prior to 1923 and represents "… one of the earliest known examples to have been sporterized by Seymour Griffin, as it exhibits many of Mr. Griffin's craftsmanship trademarks." These features set the tone for the Griffin & Howe rifles that were subsequently made by that firm.

Griffin & Howe is still very much in business, headquartered in a 100-year-old building in Bernardsville, New Jersey. Its lodge-like showroom is lined with game heads and stocked with the finest new and used sporting rifles and shotguns. Another room stocks shooting accessories, clothes, and books. In back, the gun repair department does everything from stock bending, metal refinishing, and engraving to hand crafting complete rifles, just as they did more than 80 years ago, although due to the high costs of labor and material, less than four guns a year are now produced. In addition, they have a gun store in Greenwich, Connecticut, and a shooting school in Andover, New Jersey.

Today, there are once again many custom firearms craftsmen throughout the country. But Griffin & Howe is the sole survivor of America's Golden Age of early twentieth century rifle makers. The company's quality has never waived. It still produces truly magnificent rifles, albeit at truly magnificent prices. Even so, a few years ago I managed to plunge myself into debt and acquired a Griffin & Howe Winchester Model 70 in .458 Winchester Magnum that had originally been custom-made for a prominent member of an old firearms-related family. Although my intention was to take it to Africa, I have yet to put a round through that big bruiser. However, I still occasionally hunt with my G&H rifle No. 110 in caliber .30-06, which, to me, is akin to driving a Bentley to the grocery store. It's a lot of over-qualified luxury for the job, and for that reason, these guns are on my bucket list.

SMITH & WESSON
MODEL 29

The Model 29 with an 8⅜-inch barrel is the ideal gun for knockdown targets and hunting. The rosewood grips are from Eagle Grips.

There are only a few firearms whose legendary status is derived from the fact they can be defined by a single cartridge. One such gun is the Smith & Wesson Model 29, which was never chambered for anything other than the .44 Magnum.

The saga of the S&W Model 29 began in the early twentieth century, with a coterie of big-bore pistolero handloaders, hunters, and lawmen whose combined efforts gave us the .357 Smith & Wesson Magnum in 1935. But that wasn't enough for those who favored pushing bigger bullets at higher velocities. Forming an

Hacker's 1957-era Model 29, with aftermarket ivory scrimshaw grips, was originally shipped to a gun writer in New York for testing. The Dirty Harry shoulder holster was made by The Original Dirty Harry Shoulder Holster Company of Wild Guns Leather.

Using this Galco DAO holster, the author hunted with this reissue S&W Classic Model 29 in Arizona, where he harvested a javelina of undisclosed proportions with a single shot.

Although chambered for .44 Magnum, the Model 29 digests .44 Specials with equal aplomb.

unofficial group known as "The .44 Associates," they focused on stoking up the .44 S&W Special, to see if they could take it to a world of ballistics where no cartridge had gone before.

Chief among these proponents was a pistol-packing Idaho rancher named Elmer Keith, whose experimentations and gun magazine writings describing his handloading and hunting exploits put him front and center in the post-war development of what would become the .44 Magnum. The .44 Special had been developed in 1907 as a longer-cased, smokeless powder version of the .44 Russian. Smith & Wesson had created the .44 Special as an inau-

gural chambering for its New Century revolver, also called the First Model Hand Ejector of 1908, an ultra-sturdy double-action more popularly known as the Triple Lock (described in detail elsewhere in this book).

Due to the fact that the smokeless powder loading of the .44 Special was more accurate when kept at the blackpowder velocities approaching that of the older .44 Russian, this newer cartridge was not factory loaded to its maximum potential. Thus, with extra room in the case for more powder, it was the perfect candidate for Keith's ".44 Special Magnum" cartridge, as he wanted to call it. His ongoing

This Model 29 from the 1970s has all the bells and whistles: 6½-inch barrel, nickel plating, recessed cylinder, pinned barrel, and original case and accessories—and it has never been fired!

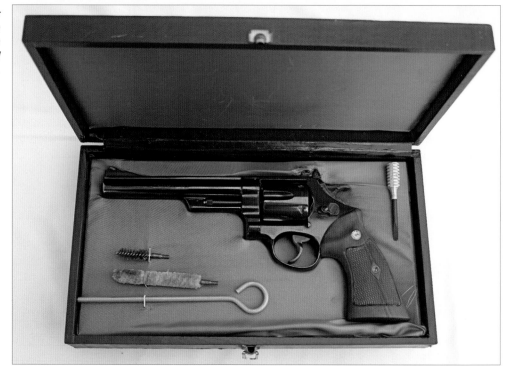

A first year production Model 29, with original case and accessories.

experimentations succeeded in blowing up a few cylinders, but at last he had a cartridge with which he was satisfied. He convinced Remington Arms Company to produce it, but first the case had to be lengthened a tenth of an inch more than the .44 Special to prevent shooters from duplicating Keith's cylinder-splitting exploits, much the same as the .357 Magnum case had to be made longer than the .38 Special, upon which that round was based. The result was the .44 Remington Magnum, which held a semi-jacketed 240-grain bullet that thundered out of the barrel at 1,400 fps and struck with more than 750 ft-lbs of energy at 50 yards—almost double that of the .357 Magnum, which up until then, was the most powerful commercially available handgun cartridge. Now that title was about to be transferred to the new .44 Magnum.

As for a handgun, Smith & Wesson had just the revolver, the Triple Lock, which had gone through Second and Third Model pre-war variations and now existed as the Hand Ejector Fourth Model, or 1950 Target (later known as the Model 24). But first some beefing up had to be done to ready this six-shot wheelgun for the muscular .44 Magnum. A longer cylinder closed the gap between it and a thicker barrel, both of which bumped the weight of the gun to 48 ounces, which helped tame the excessive recoil. In addition, the cylinder featured recessed chambers which enclosed the cartridge heads.

The first gun, one of five sequentially numbered prototypes built in Smith & Wesson's Experimental Department on what would eventually become the company's N-frame, was serial No. S121835, with the "S" prefix denoting a hammer-block safety. On December 15, 1955 the first actual production gun, serial No. S130927 was completed. On December 29 the second gun, S130806, was presented to R.H. Coleman of Remington Arms Company, and on January 19, 1956, the revolver was officially announced to the public. It was simply called "the .44 Magnum," and the price was $140.

The .44 Magnum was fitted with Goncala Alves target grips and offered in blued or nickel finishes, both with case hardened hammer and trigger. The revolver came with adjustable sights and a four or 6½-inch barrel. The gun was housed in a black, wooden, satin-lined case embossed with ".44 Magnum" and the S&W logo on the lid. Included were a screwdriver and a cleaning rod with wire brush and cotton swab attachments. Of the next five models produced, all in January 1956, S130942

was shipped to Julian Hatcher, Technical Editor of the *American Rifleman*, and on January 27, No. S147220 went to Elmer Keith. Other notable gun writers of the day also received 6½-inch barreled versions.

Hatcher's review broke in the March 1956 issue of the *American Rifleman* and other articles appeared soon after. Needless to say, the .44 Magnum was an immediate success, especially among hunters (no doubt enamored with Keith's exploits of having dropped a deer at 600 yards with his .44 Magnum) and a few law enforcement personnel who liked the cartridge's potential to effectively crack an au-

The author considers the Model 29 the only handgun a hunter needs.

Smith & Wesson has reissued the Model 29 in both a four-inch barrel (shown) and the original 6½-inch length.

The author's factory laser-engraved four-inch Model 29, which was produced only in 2012. The custom leather rig was made by Galco Gunleather, of Phoenix, Arizona.

tomobile's engine block. Others soon realized .44 Specials (which could also be chambered in the 44 Magnum) made this hefty handgun much more comfortable to shoot over the long term, adding flexibility to the guns popularity.

In 1957, reflecting a change in designation throughout the Smith & Wesson line, the .44 Magnum became the Model 29, starting with serial No. S179000. An 8⅜-inch barrel was added in 1958, and the black wooden case was changed to mahogany in 1960. The Gun Control Act of 1968 changed the "S" serial number designation to an N-frame prefix, beginning with N1 and ending in 1983 with N96000. After that, a new serial number series featured three letters followed by four numbers. In 1979 the 6½-inch barrel was shortened to six inches to standardize production with other guns, and in 1981, the counterbored cylinder chambers and pinned barrel were eliminated as being unnecessary. Later, the pivoting, hammer-mounted firing pin was changed to a frame-mounted design.

Over the years, the Model 29 underwent many variations, including Model 629 stainless steel versions, silhouette guns, and limited edition Performance Center specials, all of which proved popular. But nothing compared with the unprecedented publicity the Model 29 received in 1971, with the movie *Dirty Harry*, in which Clint Eastwood uttered these now-immortal words: "This is a .44 Magnum, the most powerful handgun in the world, and it can blow your head clean off." Sales soared and for a while Model 29s were selling for three times their suggested retail price—if one could be found for sale, that is.

The Model 29 was discontinued in 1999, but has been brought back recently as a limited edition Classic in four and 6½-inch barrels. In my collection, I own Serial No. S171XXX, which, in 1957, was shipped to a gun writer in New York, who, unfortunately, marked his test guns with a six-dot punch pattern. When I acquired it, the gun had been fired so extensively with full-house loads that I had to screw the barrel back a full turn to close the cylinder gap. This early gun still has the pre 29-1 right-hand thread on the ejector rod, so it backs out and jams after a few cylinderfuls of .44 Mags. But, as the second gun writer to own this Model 29, I feel I'm continuing a legacy started by the late Elmer Keith, Skeeter Skelton, and other members of the .44 Associates, all of whom felt that when it comes to handguns, bigger is better.

COLT NEW SERVICE

You've got to admire a beefy, no-nonsense handgun, and this revolver, which is almost too big for my medium-sized hands, has got an "I gotta have one" countenance about it. Looking at its classic, husky profile, it is hard to believe the Colt New Service was introduced in 1897. Yet, with its smooth and reliable action, it remained in the line until 1943 and, in fact, helped inspire the Colt Python many years later. Indeed, the Colt New Service had a long and colorful career and was a favored sidearm of the Royal Canadian Mounted Police (which ordered more than 3,000 of the guns between 1904 and 1942), numerous municipal police departments, and Colt's exhibition shooter John Henry FitzGerald, who carried two cutaway New Service "Fitz Specials" in special leather-lined trouser holsters. Not surprisingly, the New Service, as it name implies, also owes its existence, in part, to the armed forces, as it helped us win two World Wars in the guise of the Model 1917. But more about that later.

By the turn of the last century, Colt's double-actions had finally found acceptance by the military in the New Model Army and Navy revolvers of 1892 through 1903. But those mechanisms were complex and fragile, which caused springs to break and actions to get out of time. Nevertheless, the New Model Army and Navy Model had been adopted by the Army, which soon learned that the gun's .38 Long Colt chambering proved to be less of a man-stopper than the gun and cartridge it had replaced, the Single Action Army chambered in .45 Colt.

As a stopgap, the Army refurbished and reissued surplus single-actions, but it was clear the double-action was a superior choice for battle. Riding to the rescue was the New Service, the largest "self cocker" Colt's had ever produced. Fully loaded, it tipped the scales at a hefty three pounds. With a revamped and strengthened lockwork that would become the basis for the liquid-smooth Colt Python action many years later, this hefty sixgun proved an immediate success, especially in its larger

chamberings.

Initial calibers included the "holy trinity"—.38-40, .44-40, and .45 Colt—but also encompassed the .44 Russian, .450 Eley, .455 Eley (which the Mounties adopted), and the .476. Three standard barrel lengths were offered, 4½, 5½, and 7½ inches. A milled topstrap served as the rear sight, while the front sight was a "shark's fin" blade with a scalloped rear edge to reduce glare. Although a few guns were nickeled, the majority were finished in a luxurious polished blue, with case hardened hammer, trigger, and ejector rod tip. A lanyard ring on the butt added to the authoritarian bearing of the New Service.

In 1909, the U.S. Army selected the 5½-inch barreled New Service chambered in .45 Colt as its official sidearm. That same year the lockwork was improved with a Positive Lock, which prevented the gun from firing unless the trigger was pulled completely to the rear. Triggers for the Army guns were blued instead of case hardened, and hammers were fire blued with polished sides. Rather than the checkered rubber grips found on civilian guns, military versions featured smooth walnut;"U.S. Army Model 1909" was stamped on the butt. There was also a Navy variation, along with a Marine Corps version that featured a slightly rounded butt configuration and hand-checkered walnut grips. In all other respects, including hand fitting and finishing, these military arms were standard New Service revolvers exhibiting the highest level of workmanship.

The Army's pre-WWI adoption of the New Service as its official sidearm is not often recounted, perhaps because that association lasted only for two years, as the revolver was soon replaced by the Government Model 1911. Still, the military enlistment of the New Service was actually just beginning. On April 2, 1917, the United States entered World War I. With a shortage of Government 1911s, both Smith & Wesson and Colt's were contracted to supply large-framed revolvers chambered for the .45 ACP cartridge. For Smith & Wesson, it was its Second Model Hand Ejector, while the New Service was the obvious choice from

Colt. Regardless of manufacture, both guns would be officially designated as the Model 1917. Thus, the Colt New Service, which had briefly been the Model 1909, now became the Model 1917, a title it would hold for 26 years, eventually creating an entirely new category for collectors.

Unlike the luxurious blued finish of the Model 1909, the Model 1917 did away with external polishing, resorting to a brushed blue or matte finish. Also, the 5½-inch barrel was given a graceful taper and the cylinder was shortened for the squatter .45 ACP round. To accommodate this rimless cartridge, Smith & Wesson and Springfield Armory had developed a three-round half-moon clip that could be engaged by the extractor. Thus, two clips were required to load six cartridges. According to Bob Murphy in his book *Colt New Service Revolvers*, the earliest 1917s had bored-through cylinders that mandated the use of clips, but machining changes eventually enabled .45 ACP rounds to be loaded and fired without a clip, although spent cases had to be

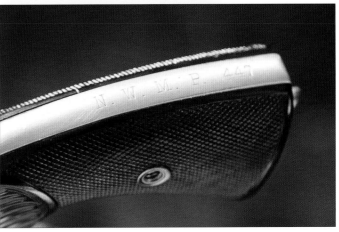

individually punched out.

Instead of being stamped with the viewed and proofed "VP" of civilian guns, Model 1917 revolvers were marked with the initials of the inspectors, GHS for Col. Gilbert H. Stewart, or JMG for Lt. Col. J.M. Gilbert. Later, the inspectors' initials were replaced by a stamped eagle's head over a one- or two-digit number. The bottom of the barrel was stamped "United States Property" and the butt was marked, "U.S. Army Model 1917," followed by the Army service number, which had nothing to do with the revolver's serial number.

World War I ended on November 11, 1918, and the last Model 1917 was shipped on February 19, 1919. In all, 151,700 guns were produced. Of these, 96,530 were returned to government warehouses. In addition, leftover parts were eventually assembled for the civilian market. In fact, during the 1920s and '30s the NRA offered surplus M1917s to members for $15 each. Other M1917s were issued to agencies such as the Border Patrol and the U.S. Post Office.

Although the Model 1917 had been retired from active duty, it was mustered back into service with the bombing of Pearl Harbor and America's entry into World War II. Both Colt and Springfield Armory were charged with the task of overhauling these WWI veterans and getting them back into action. One of the easiest ways of spotting such guns is by their Parkerized WWII finish.

Most of these reconditioned Colt 1917s were issued stateside, or to the Military Police, which explains why many examples found today are in comparatively well-maintained condition. However, as Bruce Canfield notes in his excellent book *U.S. Infantry Weapons of World War II* (Andrew Mowbray Publishers; www.manatarmsbooks.com), Colt Model 1917 revolvers were also deployed overseas during WWII, primarily for use by Signal Corps and crew served weapons personnel, as well as by headquarters staff. One such gun was issued to a young officer in France, Captain Harry S. Truman, who went on to become President of the United States and, it is rumored, kept his Model 1917 after his tour of duty ended.

Even though by then it was out of production, post-war movie-goers got to see the New Service in the hands of the bandidos in *The Treasure of Sierra Madre* (1946), used by Steve Kanaly in *The Wind and the Lion* (1975), and brandished by Jack Nicholson as Jack Napier/The Joker in the original *Batman* (1989).

Although World War II effectively halted the manufacture of the Colt New Service, in both its civilian garb and military guise as the Model 1917, it has served our country and its citizens far longer than anyone had ever envisioned.

MAUSER **K98**

I've got to admit, I have mixed emotions when it comes to writing about—let alone shooting—the Mauser K98, or the Karabiner 98 Kurtz, as it was officially known, though sometimes abbreviated as K98k. On one hand, the K98 reflects what I consider to be the height of Peter Paul Mauser's gunmaking genius, with the muscular claw design of its controlled-feed bolt, three-position wing safety, and oval bolt slots that dispelled gases away from the shooter's face.

On the other hand, this was the same rifle that had its 8mm muzzle prominently pointed at American troops for almost 50 years, beginning with the Spanish American War and lasting through World Wars I and II. Moreover, during World War II, for security reasons, Mauser K98 actions were manufactured in different arsenals in various parts of Germany, but the final guns were assembled by prisoners in concentration camps—those prisoners who were skilled as wood carvers and metalworkers were sometimes spared a death sentence so they could work on assembling the Mausers—under the ruthless gaze of the Gestapo, who were constantly on the lookout for sabotage. Somewhat ironically, because of the Gestapo's scrutiny, these concentration camp rifles are some of the best-built weapons of World War II, with many exhibiting double inspection stamps. As a re-

Hacker found ejection to be swift, although not as smooth as the Springfield 1903A3.

sult, they are quite collectable today.

The story of the K98 actually had its beginnings in 1860, when two firearms designers from Oberndorf am Neckar, Germany, Peter Paul Mauser and his older brother Wilhelm, produced their first bolt-action rifle. A single-shot weapon, it incorporated a bolt that cocked upon opening and a wing-type safety, features that would end up, albeit in much more refined versions, on the K98 three decades later.

For their new rifle, Paul Mauser designed a rimmed 11.15x60Rmm cartridge that fired a 386-grain paper-patched bullet at 1,423 fps. It was the first of a number of military cartridges he would create. Also known as the 11mm Mauser, it ended up becoming extremely popular among European and East African hunters. Because of its effectiveness, the rifle for which it was chambered—the Mauser M71—was adopted by the German army and renamed *Infanterie-Gewehr 71*; military versions were stamped "I.G.Mod.71."

Not being content with the M71 as a single-shot, an Austrian army officer and gun designer named Alfred Ritter von Kropatschek created, in 1884, an eight-round tubular magazine, similar to that found on the Winchester 1873, for the Gewehr 71, thus turning it into Germa-

ny's first repeating rifle. It was subsequently renamed the *Gewehr 71/84*, or Model 71/84, and remained Germany's official rifle until the acceptance of the *Gewehr 88*, or *Reichsgeweh*, which was created by the German (Infantry) Rifle Commission at Spandau Arsenal, not the Mauser brothers. Having not participated in its development, the Mauser factory decided to abstain from its manufacture.

Nonetheless, the Model 1888 Commission Rifle, as it is also known, was the first to fire a smokeless powder round, the 7.92x57mm IS (*Infanterie Spitzer*), which utilized a spitzer bullet. Loaded with a slightly heftier powder charge, this cartridge would become the 8mm Mauser, chambering in the K98 and, consequently, becoming Germany's official cartridge throughout two world wars. In yet another bit of irony, it was a cartridge that Mauser didn't invent. It was the popularity of the K98 that tagged the cartridge with the Mauser name.

For whatever reason, the Spanish Mauser 93 used against our troops during the Spanish American War was chambered for the less powerful 7x57mm Mauser. However, this rifle utilized a staggered five-round internal magazine that was loaded via a stripper clip inserted into the breech end of the receiver.

Some of the many accessories that were issued with the K98 included triple ammo pouches, a cleaning rope with weight, oil can, sling, and stripper clips.

This rifle's serial number and a double "SS" stamping on the barrel indicate that this K98 most likely underwent two inspections, one before and one after test firing.

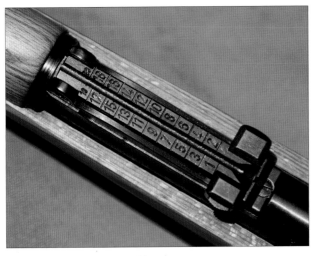

The rear sight is graduated in meters.

This same system would be incorporated in the K98.

Although Wilhelm passed away in 1888, Paul Mauser continued to produce an almost bewildering procession of new models for a number of armies around the world, including the Model 1894 for Brazil and Sweden, the M1895 adopted by Mexico, Chile, Uruguay, and China, and the M1896 which, by virtue of its use by Sweden, resulted in the development of a stronger "Swedish Steel," which was used in the manufacture of all subsequent Mauser rifles, including the *Gewehr 98*, the Mauser *Standardmodell* and the *Karabiner 98b*.

All of this culminated, in 1935, with the K98, or *Karabiner 98 Kurtz*, which translates into "Carbine 98 Short." Weighing 8½ pounds and chambered for the 8x57mm IS cartridge, the K98 sported a sharply angled bolt handle for greater leverage, a smooth, solid action, and a unique three-position safety. When the thick steel tab located near the end of the bolt was turned down all the way to the right, the bolt is "frozen" and cannot be manipulated. Turning the tab straight up frees the bolt so that it can be worked to eject cartridges from the magazine, but the trigger remains locked. Interestingly, this position also blocks the shooter's view of the rear sight, another bit of confirmation that the rifle cannot be fired. Finally, with the tab rotated all the way to the left, the bolt can be opened (thereby cocking the firing pin), the trigger is operational, and the gun

Loading is by five-round stripper clip. Note the stripper clip loading guide cast into the receiver.

can be fired. As a visual reminder that the gun is cocked, the rearward portion of the bolt protrudes out from the bolt body.

For all its sophistication, the sights of the K98 are rather crude, even though they are optimistically calibrated out to 2,000 meters. Still, the rifle is accurate enough to hit a man-sized target at 500 yards, although from my experience, three- to four-inch groups at 100 yards is the norm with military ammunition. It should be noted that the military two-stage 8½-pound trigger pull doesn't aid accuracy.

The visual appearance of the stock is not helped by the fact that it is made of laminated plywood, obviously done for both economic and ease of maintenance reasons. But it pales by comparison to the walnut used on our own World War II 1903A3 and Garand rifles. (In an interesting turn of events, while the K98 was being developed, America was fine-tuning the Model 1903A3, which employed a modified Mauser action, for use against the Germans.)

There can be no denying that the K98 was a well-respected rifle mechanically. At the end of World War II, with Germany's surrender, the last of the K98 Mausers were made in 1945 under French supervision, then the tooling was destroyed. After the Armistice, a great number of surplus K98 Mausers were shipped to the United States, where, like their counterpart, the Springfield 1903A3, their actions became the basis for superb sporters by such post-war gun makers as Griffin & Howe and Frank Pachmayr.

Today the K98 Mauser, though not exceedingly expensive, has become collectable, especially with Nazi stampings such as the Third Reich's *Totenkopf* skull-and-crossbones "Death's Head," or post-war "RC (Russian-captured) markings. The rifles also are still coveted for their actions for competition and hunting—noble pastimes for a rifle that once challenged our freedom.

WINCHESTER
MODEL 70

If ever there was the epitome of a classic bolt-action sporting rifle, it has to be the Winchester Model 70, an innovative firearm that emerged just as American hunters were starting to embrace the new-fangled crank actions for big-game hunting.

Ever at the forefront, Winchester had already captured much of this audience with its Model 54, its first big-bore bolt-action since the introduction of its .45-70 Hotchkiss Model of 1883. The Model 54 had been introduced in 1925, officially ushering in a new era and by an industry leader previously best known for its lever guns. Initially chambered for the popular Government .30-06 and .270 (a cartridge that had been created especially for the Model 54), Winchester's new bolt-action enjoyed a fair modicum of success, although it was hampered by a rather sluggish trigger pull and a bolt design that wasn't always conducive for use with a scope (although, to be fair, scope-mounted sporting rifles were still in their infancy during this period). Nonetheless, competition was catching up and shooting styles were changing; more scopes were being seen afield and newer cartridges were emerging.

Winchester answered this challenge by discontinuing the Model 54, in 1936, and introducing the Model 70 in January 1937. The Model 70 designation was part of a new numbering system, in which Winchester was revamping its older models or introducing newer ones. For example, the Model 69 was a new .22 bolt-action repeater that had been introduced in 1935, while the Model 71, brought out the same year as the Model 70, was an updated version of the Model 1886 lever-action. Thus, the newer models were not named after the years of their introduction (such as the older Models 1873 and 1892).

Rather than being thought of as an "improved Model 54," the Model 70 was a new bolt-action altogether (although it had its roots in the Mauser 98 design), and was more the result of the Winchester R&D boys having the conversation of, "What are the shortcomings of the Model 54 that we can overcome to make a better rifle?" The result was what the late, highly opinionated but extremely knowledgeable gun writer Jack O'Connor rightfully dubbed, "the rifleman's rifle."

For starters, the Model 70 featured a new stock design more attuned to the twentieth century shooter. It was graceful, sturdy, well balanced, and featured a better angle with which to absorb the increased recoil of the newer cartridges. Mechanically, the Model 70 set the stage for scores of bolt-actions since. The safety has now become a classic—a three-position horizontal lever that, in addition to "On" and "Off," enables the shooter to lock the firing pin while working the bolt, so that cartridges could be quickly and safely ejected. Moreover, the bolt and safety lever were designed so they would not interfere with a mounted scope.

Like the Model 54, the magazine held five cartridges, but the floor-

This is Winchester's current top-of-the-line Super Grade Model 70, featuring fancy grade checkered walnut stock, decorative steel crossbolt for added strength, and pre-'64 style controlled round feeding system. (Photo courtesy Winchester Repeating Arms)

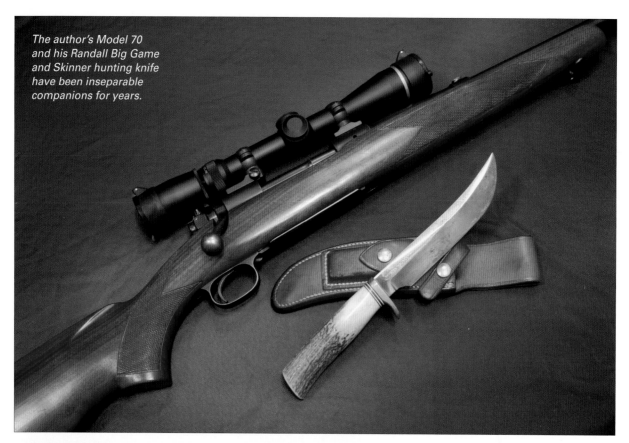

The author's Model 70 and his Randall Big Game and Skinner hunting knife have been inseparable companions for years.

The Model 70's hinged floorplate was an improvement over the fixed floorplate of the previous Model 54.

plate was hinged for ultra-fast unloading without having to cycle the bolt. What became known as the Winchester Speed Lock permitted faster cycling and, combined with a redesigned bolt stop, the Model 70's new controlled round feeding ensured reliability, a big selling point for hunters in pursuit of dangerous game. In fact, the action of the Model 70 was so smooth and strong, ballistics laboratories for velocity and pressure testing of experimental cartridges often used it. Everything about the new bolt-action, in the words of the late Harold F. Williamson, in his classic book, *Winchester—The Gun That Won The West*,

had been "calculated to make the Model 70 the best bolt-action on the market."

Initially, a Standard Grade and a Super Grade rifle were offered, with the Super Grade boasting fancier wood, a cheekpiece, black fore-end tip, and hand checkering. Both had 24-inch barrels, although there were variations. Initially, customers could pick from seven calibers: .22 Hornet, .250-3000 Savage, .257 Roberts, .270 Winchester, 7mm Mauser, .300 Savage, .220 Swift, and, of course, the classic .30-06. Later that year, the .300 and .375 Holland & Holland Magnums joined the lineup. Indeed, highlighting the Model 70's versatility, no less than 23 different calibers were eventually offered, ranging from .22-250 to the .458 Winchester Magnum. There were also National Match, Target, and Bull Gun target models, along with a 20-inch barreled "carbine" and a full-stocked Mannlicher. Numerous other variations were subsequently offered, including the Featherweight, African, Varmint, Westerner, and Alaskan, to name a few. Even with a halt in production from 1942 to 1947 caused by WWII, by 1960 more than a half-million Model 70s had been made.

Among the many celebrated owners of the Winchester Model 70 were General Curtis LeMay and Hollywood actor William Holden,

The author outfitted his vintage 1948 Model 70—originally purchased by the father of a high school friend—with a Leopold Vari-X scope.

The three-position safety of the Model 70 has become legendary.

who took his .458 Magnum to Africa. In addition, a number of Model 70s were called into service as sniper rifles by the United States Marine Corps, during the 1950s and in Vietnam.

Then, in 1964, the Model 70 (beginning with serial #700,000), along with every other gun in the Winchester catalog, fell victim to an ill-advised cost-cutting rampage that has forever given the rifle two identities: post-'64 and pre-'64 models, with pre-'64 versions commanding the most attention among today's collectors and shooters. Changes to the post-'64 Model 70 included pressed checkering, doing away with the much-heralded "controlled round feeding," and a stamped rather than forged trigger guard, among other less than desirable aspects. By 1991, the company, under the then-auspices of U.S. Repeating Arms Corporation (which served as Winchester's licensed manufacturer from 1976 to 2006), had returned to making rifles with pre-'64 quality, although they still lacked the cachet of pre-'64 Model 70s among collectors. By 2006 the Model 70 legacy among shooters kept on with the introduction of stainless steel Camo models chambered in WSSM calibers, a synthetically stocked Shadow Elite, and checkered classic walnut Super Grade, Safari Express, and Sporter III models.

But then a hiccup occurred in Winchester's history. The New Haven plant, where the gun had always been made, was closing. Ironically, this announcement came exactly 70 years after the date of the Model 70's introduction. Thankfully, and although the prices of currently made guns took a brief but dramatic swing upwards, the disruption was short-lived, as Browning soon assumed the Winchester banner. Today, the Model 70 is once again being produced in the U.S. by FN Herstal in Columbia, South Carolina, thus ensuring hunters will still be able to go afield with a gun that set the standard for the bolt-action rifle in America.

My Model 70 is a pre-'64 Standard Grade rifle that was made in 1948. I bought it from one of my old high school buddies whose father was the original owner, and who had the gun drilled and tapped (they didn't come that way back then) and outfitted it with a Redfield Widefield scope notable for having an ocular lens shaped like a TV screen. My friend's father had taken the rifle on many a successful elk, deer, and moose hunt. At one point, the sling swivel came loose and the rifle took a summersault backwards off his shoulder. As a result, it lost its front sight and sight hood. For some reason, I can't seem to find a proper front sight and hood to replace them, although I have purchased a number of them and now have the largest collection of Model 70 front sights and hoods on my block. Nevertheless, the rifle still retains most of its original blued finish, which is somewhat amazing, considering all the hunts it has been on between my friend's father and myself. The stock, which plainly shows the brunt of its hunting battle scars, had an aftermarket recoil pad on it, so I have since purchased an original 1948-era Model 70 stock with an original steel buttplate which upgraded the gun dramatically, although I still swap it out with the original stock for hunting. I also replaced the Redfield scope years ago with a Leupold Vari-X III, which has superior optics compared to the older glass. As a result, I'm continuing to keep the hunting tradition alive for this classic Winchester bolt-action.

COLT SINGLE ACTION ARMY

The Single Action Army is the quintessential "cowboy gun," and has been seen in practically every western ever filmed. The top gun is stamped "S" over its serial number, to denote ownership by Stembridge Studios, which supplied many such sixguns for the "B" westerns of the 1930s and '40s. The bottom gun is a current third generation SAA in nickel finish—still a favorite with producers of westerns, although today you are more likely to see Italian replicas being used due to their lower costs. The classic "B" western buscadero rig, such as worn by many silver screen stars, has been authentically replicated by Jim Lockwood of Legends in Leather (www. legendsinleather.com).

Without a doubt, the Colt Single Action Army—or the "Colt New Model Army Metallic Cartridge Revolving Pistol," as the SAA was initially called, or Model P, as it was originally designated by the factory—has become one of the most recognized, collectable and, dare I say, legendary firearms in the world. Perhaps the greatest testimony to its immortality is the fact that, although its design has been copied by numerous manufacturers in America and abroad, this venerable sixgun is still being manufactured in the USA by the same company that introduced it more than 140 years ago.

A classic Single Action Army, with blue and case hardened finish, 4¾-inch barrel, and aftermarket, one-piece steer horn grips.

The three standard barrel lengths of the Single Action Army are (top to bottom): 7½, 5½, and 4¾ inches.

The years after the Civil War ended saw Colt's emerge as the acknowledged revolver manufacturer in America, with two clear winners under its belt, the 1860 Army and the 1851 Navy. But times were changing, and the self-contained metallic cartridge loomed on the horizon, thus dooming the opened-topped revolver design. Cartridge conversions were only a temporary fix. A new sidearm was needed, one adapted to the Army's dictum for a .45-caliber bore diameter.

Interestingly, the Single Action Army was originally developed as a .44-caliber handgun, as the Army's official sidearm at the time was the .44-caliber Colt 1860 cap-and-ball. Plus the Ordnance Department had already given a cursory nod, though without officially adopting it, to the Smith & Wesson No. 3 First Model (also known as the American), which was chambered in .44 S&W Russian. Thus, Colt factory superintendent William Mason assumed the government preferred the .44 designation. But

The three-inch barreled Sheriff's Model (top) and four-inch Storekeeper (bottom) are still made occasionally by the factory as limited editions. Both are prized by collectors and shooters alike, even though they don't have ejector rods underneath their barrels and, thus, require special frames. Note the "smokeless" frame on top and the "blackpowder" frame on the bottom.

The author regularly packs a Single Action Army when hunting, hiking, or camping, for informal plinking or an impromptu opportunity to bag something for the pot. It's also a good deterrent for predators.

Two third generation SAAs (top) in nickel finish and (bottom) blued and case hardened. Both are classic representatives of the Old West and are still rugged and reliable handguns today.

adopting the philosophy that bigger is better, at the last minute the Army decided that what it really wanted was a .45-caliber sidearm. It turned out to be a fortuitous move for the Single Action Army, as the .45 Colt cartridge provided the perfect combination of balance and firepower, a fact that became immediately apparent and appreciated by cavalry troopers during the Indian Wars. Its only drawback was that cartridges had to be loaded and ejected one at a time, an operation that required two hands—a difficult feat at best while astride a galloping horse.

Nevertheless, in the autumn of 1872, after beating out six other revolver manufacturers, including Smith & Wesson, Merwin & Hulbert, and Remington, the U.S. Ordnance Department selected the Colt Single Action Army as the government's official sidearm, with an initial order for 8,000 guns. This number would eventually climb to 39,063 Single Action Armies ordered by the government by 1892, when the SAA was replaced with the 1892 Colt Army and Navy Model double-action .38.

Even then, the SAA remained a far superior weapon, even though it had to be manually cocked for each shot.

Thanks to the inventive adaptations of Colt's engineer Charles B. Richards and factory superintendent William Mason, the SAA was a culmination of the many Colts that had come before it. The topstrap was adapted from Colt's 1855 Sidehammer. The plow handled backstrap and trigger guard came from the 1851 Navy, which had, in turn, lent it to the 1871 Open Top. Likewise, the initial 7½-inch barrel length also came from the Navy. But the internal cocking mechanism had its origins with the 1848 Walker. Of course, increased advances in metallurgy enabled the Single Action Army to weigh in at a respectable 2½ pounds, substantially less than the massive, large-caliber, 4½-pound Dragoon horse pistols of a few decades earlier. In fact, the SAA is one of the best-balanced handguns ever produced, a fact not lost on the trick shooters of early Wild West shows and, later, the silver screen. And not only was it reliable and rugged, if need be,

This is one of the author's original SAAs, a second generation gun that was purchased new and outfitted later with tea-stained stag horn grips.

The Single Action Army was the official sidearm of the United States Army, from 1873 until 1892. It is shown here in the 5½-inch barreled Artillery Model (top) and the original 7½-inch Cavalry Model, (bottom), although these are collector's terms; the guns weren't called that by the factory.

it could be fired with half its parts broken or missing.

Another thing the Single Action Army had going for it was its perfect pairing with its propriety cartridge, the .45 Colt. Packed with 40 grains of blackpowder (the same charge previously used in the mighty Colt Dragoon), and pushing a 255-grain bullet out the muzzle at 810 fps, this was a formidable round, especially when one considers that the 1860 Army (of which many were still in use) only fired a 28-grain charge of powder behind a 133-grain round ball. Need-

less to say, the Single Action Army proved to be a much more potent man-stopper.

Like many other military guns, the SAA was immediately embraced by the civilian population as well. In fact, one major firearms distributor, B. Kittredge & Company, of Cincinnati, dubbed the new sixgun "The Peacemaker," borrowing a nickname that had been attributed to Samuel Colt many years earlier. Throughout its existence, the SAA garnered other sobriquets, too, including Thumbuster, Hogleg (referring to the 7½-inch barreled version), and my favorite, Judge Colt and His Jury of Six (although this sixshooter was in reality a five-shooter; with its fixed firing pin, the hammer was always kept resting on an empty chamber, lest the gun be accidently discharged should it be dropped).

The initial finish was blue, with a handsome bone charcoal case hardened frame and hammer. Grips were one-piece walnut, then later offered in black checkered gutta-percha. Owing to its civilian popularity, a nickel finish was soon brought out. In 1875, a 5½-inch barrel was introduced, which collectors have since dubbed the "Artillery Model." During the Philippine Insurrection, a number of retired 7½-inch barreled "Cavalry Models" were cut down to 5½-inch barrels and re-issued to troops who discovered that the .45-caliber single action was far more effective in dealing with adrenalin-pumped Moro warriors than the standard issue double-action Colt New Army & Navy. A 4¾-inch barrel, called the "Civilian Model" by collectors, came out in 1879.

Colt's offered non-standard barrel lengths, charging a dollar an inch for anything over the "Cavalry" length. Single Action Armies with factory barrels as long as 18 inches and as short as two inches, although rare, are known to exist. Many stretch-barreled SAAs were fitted with long-range sights and often came with detachable shoulder stocks. Barrel lengths less than 4¾ inches did not have ejector rods, and the most notable variations of these are (using collector's terms, as the factory never referred to the guns as such) four-inch Storekeepers and three-inch Sheriff's Models. But, as noted Colt collector and author, the late James Serven, once wrote in his classic book, *Colt Firearms*, "I doubt that any self respecting sheriff would arm himself with a Single Action Army Colt with a 3" barrel."

In 1878, Colt's secured its place in the annals of frontier Americana by chambering its Single Action Army for the .44-40, which was achieving an immortality of its own in Winchester's 1873 rifle and carbine. Thus, for the first time since the .44 rimfire was chambered for both the Henry Rifle and the 1871 Open Top, a frontiersman could carry the same box of cartridges for rifle and pistol—and the centerfire .44-40 could be reloaded. This chambering became so popular that .44-40 Colt single-actions were designated as the Frontier Six Shooter, a moniker that was etched, and later roll-stamped on their barrels.

Next in line for single-action chamberings were the .38-40 and .32-20, and Winchester acknowledged the single-action's reputation by following suit with identical chamberings for its lever-actions. These three calibers, along with the .45 Colt (which was so popular the gun was often called a "Colt .45" no matter what bullet it fired), comprised the most popular SAA calibers. I have since dubbed them "The Holy Trinity." However, due to the adaptability of its design, the Peacemaker was eventually chambered for no less than 41 different cartridges, ranging from .22 rimfire to the massive .476 Eley.

Around 1892 the method for retaining the cylinder base pin was changed from a frame-mounted screw to a spring-loaded pushpin. Many have erroneously assumed that this marked the switch from blackpowder, but it wasn't until 1900, starting with serial No. 192,000, that the factory warranted its single-actions for smokeless powder. In addition to 976 flat-top target models, from 1894 until 1915, 44,350 Bisley target versions were produced. The SAA also proved a ready canvas for the engraver's artistry. Approximately 3,500 factory engraved pre-war guns were produced and have become highly valuable collector's items. But its antiquated design, the Great Depression, and World War II all combined to halt production of the SAA in 1941, with 357,859 guns having been manufactured.

In 1947, Colt's Manufacturing Company announced in *The American Rifleman* that it would not be resuming production of its famed Single Action Army. But the popularity of TV westerns and the resultant sport of fast draw resulted in the old Thumbuster being resurrected in 1955, in what collectors now call "second generation Colts." With a brief hiatus in 1975 to update machinery (to produce what has become known as "third generation guns"), the Peacemaker remains in production to this day.

Like many baby boomers, my fascination with the Colt single-action began at an early age, while watching it perform multi-shot miracles (far exceeding its six-shot cylinder capacity) on the silver screen and, later, television in the hands of cowboy heroes such as Hopalong Cassidy, Gene Autry, and Roy Rogers. Later on, I would salivate over the sixgun on back-to-back TV westerns such as *Gunsmoke, Have Gun-Will Travel*, and *26 Men*.

I remember my first SAA, a pre-war .45 with a 4¾-inch barrel and stag grips and an Arvo Ojala holster that I bought from a down-and-out acquaintance for $65. I have since acquired numerous other Single Action Armies since then, because, like good days in the saddle, you can never have too many of them.

The only irony is that Sam Colt never lived to see the most famous gun his company had ever produced. He died on January 10, 1862, 11 years before the Single Action Army was born.

RUGER SINGLE SIX

For shooters, the word nostalgia means any gun that reminds them of their youth. For me and others of the baby boomer generation, that definition certainly qualifies for the Ruger Single Six. This trend-setting .22 rimfire revolver made its appearance in 1953, and the timing could not have been better. It was on the eve of the golden age of television Westerns. Gunsmoke had not yet made its appearance, but the earliest cowboy heroes—Hopalong Cassidy, Gene Autry, The Lone Ranger, and the Cisco Kid—were already rounding up posses of youthful fans as they galloped across the new-fangled television screens that were becoming as commonplace as toasters in practically every home in America.

The three-screw Super Single Six, shown here with a 6½-inch barrel, was introduced in 1964, and featured a ramp front sight and an adjustable rear sight that was integral with the frame. Chambered in .22 Long Rifle, this model also came with a matching 22 Magnum cylinder. The Super Single Six was discontinued in 1972 to make way for the New Model transfer bar series, which is still in the line.

What's more, six years earlier, Colt's had voluntarily dropped the reins on its 76-year hold of the penultimate "cowboy gun," the Single Action Army. In 1947, the company announced, in the *American Rifleman*, that it would not be resuming production of the Model P after its wartime interruption. That left the single-action field wide open for a couple of young gunmakers named William Batterman Ruger and Alexander Sturm, whose fledging Sturm, Ruger & Company was flush with the success of their first product, the .22 semi-automatic Mark 1 Standard Pistol. But the pair needed a follow-up act, and for Bill Ruger, there was

no doubt as to what that would be. A youthful fan of "B" Western movies, he and his partner would build their own version of the classic cowboy six-shooter.

Unfortunately, Alexander Sturm died suddenly in 1951, leaving Bill Ruger to continue with his dream. Already having achieved success with a .22 rimfire, Ruger decided to stick with what he knew. Still, he realized that a single-action based on the full-sized SAA frame but chambered for the diminutive .22 would be excessively heavy and prohibitively costly, given the technology of the time. The obvious solution was to scale down the gun, yet still keep the basic profile of the time-honored

Peacemaker. An inveterate antique automobile aficionado, Bill Ruger christened his new revolver the Single Six, after the 1920 Packard Single Six Model 116 sedan. It was a fitting play on words, as his new revolver would be a six-shot single-action.

Manufacturing problems kept the little gun from being completed as soon as Ruger would have liked, but given the pending Western craze about to sweep America, the delay proved fortuitous. Ruger quickly realized that milling the gun out of a solid block of steel, as Colt's had done and as Ruger tried with the first few prototypes, would make his single-action too expensive. As a result, Sturm, Ruger

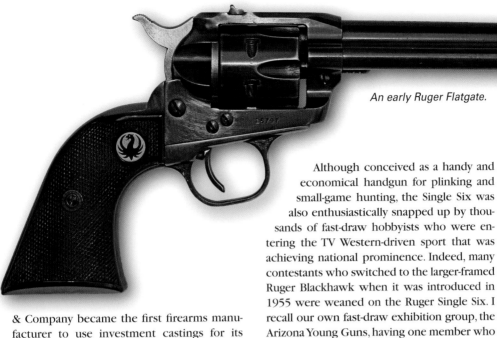

An early Ruger Flatgate.

& Company became the first firearms manufacturer to use investment castings for its major components, including the chrome-molybdenum steel frame. As a result, the Ruger Single Six debuted in June 1953 with a very affordable price tag of $57.50, making it an immediate "must have" for anyone who had longed for, but couldn't afford, a Colt Single Action Army.

Indeed, the Single Six clearly took its inspiration from the SAA. Yet in spite of its traditional upswept knurled hammer, angled ejector rod housing, and plow handle grips, there were some improvements that separated the Single Six from its predecessor. The black anodized one-piece cast Alcoa aluminum backstrap and trigger guard and an unbreakable coil mainspring were two notable features. The gun also sported a fixed notch rear sight. However, the most apparent change was the unique flat loading gate, which Ruger had devised as yet another way to reduce manufacturing costs. Collectors have since dubbed this early Single Six the Ruger Flatgate, which has assumed a collectable's status all its own. The Flatgate era lasted only until 1957, when consumer demand resulted in the adoption of a more traditional rounded loading gate, which was incorporated around serial No. 70,000.

Another improvement occurred, in 1955, when Ruger added Nylok screws to keep the gun from "shooting loose," a common malady with the old Peacemaker. In that same year, the company brought out an aluminum-framed version of the Flatgate, the Lightweight Single Six. In 1964 the Super Single Six was introduced, featuring adjustable sights and an interchangeable cylinder for .22 Magnum rimfire.

Although conceived as a handy and economical handgun for plinking and small-game hunting, the Single Six was also enthusiastically snapped up by thousands of fast-draw hobbyists who were entering the TV Western-driven sport that was achieving national prominence. Indeed, many contestants who switched to the larger-framed Ruger Blackhawk when it was introduced in 1955 were weaned on the Ruger Single Six. I recall our own fast-draw exhibition group, the Arizona Young Guns, having one member who dressed in black and sported a Ruger Single Six. Chuck was fast, even though .22 rimfire blanks were harder to come by than the centerfire blackpowder blanks the rest of us used.

Initially the Single Six was offered only with a 5½-inch barrel, but throughout its lifetime 4⅝-, 6½-, 7½-, and 9½-inch tubes have been added. Although a few experimental Flatgates had case hardened receivers, this was quickly abandoned for a more practical all-blued finish. Interestingly, some of the very earliest cast frames ended up with a purplish hue, and this forms the basis for another sub-category of Single Six collecting today.

In 1973, the Ruger Single Six went through a dramatic but necessary metamorphosis, when a transfer bar safety system was incorporated, thus permitting it (and other Ruger single actions), to be safely carried with six rounds instead of five. This variation has subsequently been dubbed the New Model Single Six, and pre-transfer bar guns are now know as the Old Model Single Six. Although free conversion kits are still offered by the company, many collectors prefer to keep their early guns original, even though it means carrying the Old Model Single Six with the hammer resting over an empty chamber. Subsequent New Model Single Sixes have been offered in stainless steel and in additional chamberings for .17 Mach 2 and .17 HMR, and the gun remains as coveted today as when it was first introduced more than 60 years ago. Indeed, while the 1921 Packard Single Six was not very popular in its day, the namesake Ruger Single Six has more than made up for it.

WINCHESTER
MODEL 94

This hand-colored photo, taken in the early 1900s, shows a transplanted Pennsylvanian who ventured to the Pacific Northwest and became an adept hunter and guide. He is shown proudly carrying his Model 94 carbine and meat for the table.

I have a special affinity for this classic deer gun, because it was the first big-bore rifle I bought. However, I initially viewed it not as wood and steel, but as a black-and-white line drawing in one of the chapters of the late Harold F. Williamson book Winchester— The Gun That Won The West.

I remember, as a kid, pouring over that book—which I still own and is now torn and tattered—and studying every line of that illustration of the Winchester Model 1894 carbine: its square-shouldered receiver, the noticeably large trigger guard (especially when compared with those of the earlier Winchester saddle carbines), and the graceful, complementary taper of the barrel, magazine tube, and walnut forearm.

Of course, back then, I was too young to purchase, let alone afford, a Model 94 carbine. But one day that moment came. I remember it distinctly. It was at the old Pinney & Robinson's Sporting Goods store in the Park Central Shopping Center in Phoenix, Arizona. I had walked in to browse the gun racks, as I often did, and there it was, a slightly used, flat-band Model 94 carbine in the coveted .30-30 caliber, which everyone knew was *the* deer cartridge. If you want to go after black bear, the old-timers told you, you bought a 94 in .32 Winchester Special, but, if it was venison you wanted for the table, then only a .30-30 would do.

Of course, the reality is that both cartridges are practically identical, ballistically speaking, and the only reason the .32 Special was developed in 1895—the same year the .30-30 was introduced as America's first smokeless powder round—was that unlike the faster 1:12 rifling of the .30 WCF, the slower 1:16 twist of the .32 Special was more suited to stabilizing the bullet when reloading that cartridge with blackpowder, obviously to appeal to those hunters back then who didn't trust a cartridge whose smoke they couldn't see.

Needless to say, I was mesmerized by that 94 flat band (a unique post-war feature of Model 94 carbines produced from April 1946 through December 1948) in Pinney & Robinson's used gun rack. To make it even more

tantalizing, the carbine came with a saddle scabbard stamped "Marfa, Texas." The rancher who had previously owned that Model 94 had brought it in to Pinney & Robinson's to trade for a "modern" bolt-action rifle. I was glad he had, and often thought it would have been interesting to meet him after the fact.

As I recall, the asking price for gun and leather was $50, and I ended up trading a .22 Springfield Model 87A semi-automatic rifle and $30 cash for the 94 and scabbard; although I have acquired numerous Winchester 94s since, I still have that scabbard. Later that year after acquiring that first rifle, I took my first mulie with it, thus perpetuating the Model 94s reputation of having taken more deer than any other rifle in America. To be sure, the Model 94 and the .30-30 cartridge were so indelibly intertwined that the gun was often simply referred to as a "thuty-thuty," no matter what its caliber when I was growing up in Arizona. In fact, for a long time I was under the

The author, with a wild boar taken by him with a single shot from a Model 94 carbine made in the early 1940s.

impression that all pickup trucks came with a rifle rack and a .30-caliber Model 94 carbine in the cab's rear window.

Like many other great guns of the late nineteenth and early twentieth century, the Model 1894 came from the fertile mind of inventor John Moses Browning. It was the culmination of all the tubular magazine lever-actions that had come before it—including the Browning-designed Winchester Models 1892 and 1886. Moreover, the Model 94 was the first repeating rifle to be adapted to smokeless powder cartridges, specifically the .25-35 and the .30 WCF, which, of course, came to be known as the .30-30. Winchester Repeating Firearms paid Browning $15,000—the same amount he had previously received for his Model 1886 and 1892 patents—for rights to manufacture the Model 94.

The new gun quickly earned a reputation as a hard-hitting, close-range hunting rifle. These attributes were primarily due to its smokeless powder chamberings and an action that, while not quite as smooth as in the Models 1873 and 1892 (both of which were still in the line at the time), was one that was noticeably stronger. A single, solid steel rod slid up and locked behind the closed bolt, thus providing greater safety to the shooter, a solid selling point in those transition years between blackpowder and smokeless. Also unique to the Model 94 was its hinged floor plate that pivoted down when the action was opened. Of course, the rifle's nickel steel barrel was a big feature, even though initial metallurgy problems kept the two new smokeless powder chamberings from appearing until 1895. Thus, ironically, the first smokeless powder repeater was initially available only for two older blackpowder rounds, the .32-40 and the .38-55. It wasn't until a year later that the Model 94 came out in the much-touted .25-35 and .30 WCF chamberings.

Rifles with 26-inch round or octagon barrels were standard, as was a 20-inch barreled saddle ring carbine, which proved to be extremely popular, especially in its .30-30 chambering, as the same sight picture could be used out to 125 yards and still result in a lethal hit on deer-sized targets. Small wonder the Model 94 quickly became a favored firearm not only for hunters, but also as a working tool on ranches and farms. And, because the large trigger guard could readily accommodate gloved hands, it was the rifle and carbine of choice during the 1897 Alaskan Gold Rush, resulting in the Winchester 94 being christened "The Klondike Model" during its earliest years.

Gold seekers and cowboys weren't the only fans. Law enforcement agencies, including the Los Angeles and Glendale California Police Departments, various railroad police, and such diverse organizations as the Texas Rangers and New York State Troopers added the Winchester 94 to their gun racks. During World Wars I and II, approximately 1,800 special ordnance-marked Model 94 carbines were issued to U.S. troops stationed along the Mexican and Canadian borders, as well as to Home Guard

units and members of the Army Signal Corps, which, according to noted author Bruce N. Canfield in his book *U.S. Infantry Weapons of The First World War* (Andrew Mowbray Publishing), used them to guard our spruce forests from enemy saboteurs, as, in those days, Sitka spruce was one of the primary materials used for airplane construction.

Besides rifles and carbines, special order Model 94s were produced up through the first half of the twentieth century. Options included half-round/half-octagon barrels, takedown versions, special engraving and checkering patterns, and a variety of barrel lengths, including rare Baby Carbines (since dubbed "Trappers" by collectors) that sported 14-, 15-, and 16-inch barrels.

Over the years, a number of changes have taken place with the Model 94. In 1924, the rifle was discontinued and in 1951 the longer wood of the carbine's forearm was shortened. In 1964, in what is now recognized as an ill-advised move, manufacturing procedures were modified to reduce costs. Thankfully, by 1967 the company realized it had done something terribly wrong and steps were gradually taken

Although this High Grade Oliver F. Winchester Limited Edition, the first "new" Model 94 to be produced by Miruko of Japan in 2010, was intended to be a collectable, the author could not resist the temptation to see how it shot. It is shown with the cartridge that helped make the Model 94 famous, the .30-30.

The author, in his teenage years in Arizona, proudly poses with his first Winchester 94 carbine, a flat band .30-30.

to restore the Model 94 to its former glory. Nevertheless, that chapter in the Model 94s history has provided collectors with the designations of "pre-'64" and "post-'64" Winchesters, with pre-'64 guns commanding more money on the collectors' market.

In 1981 "Side Eject" was added, so that for the first time, it became easier to mount a scope on the Model 94, for those who favor such things on an otherwise handsome carbine. In the 1990s the traditional half-cock was removed and replaced by a trigger-block safety and a trigger return spring, along with an ugly dished-out push-button safety that, thankfully, was removed, in 2003 and replaced by a tang-mounted safety. However, those traditionalists among us still prefer the older half-cock, which of course is only available on older guns.

The closing of Winchester's historic Hartford, Connecticut factory in 2006 was a momentous event that caused a buying frenzy for Model 94s—especially pre-'64 versions—that is still having residual effects today. After a brief hiatus, the guns are now being expertly made by Miruko in Japan, still with rebounding hammers and tang safeties, but nonetheless with a quality of workmanship that rivals the guns of yesteryear. Thus, while the Winchester '73 may have been "the gun that won the West," the Model 94 was the gun that galloped past the closing days of the frontier and maintained Winchester's lever-action lead throughout the twentieth century and, now, well into the twenty-first. In fact, even today, I can't pass up a pre-'64 Model 94 carbine without asking the price and if it is affordable, I'll relive those early years in Pinney & Robinson's and buy it.

BROWNING
SUPERPOSED

You would think a company that had made a fortune from the numerous single-shot, lever-action, and smoothbore inventions of just one man over the years would have been an eager and anticipatory purchaser for any firearms design that particular individual brought to them. But such wasn't the case in 1903, when firearms genius John Moses Browning presented his concept for a semi-automatic shotgun to Winchester president T.G. Bennett. Bennett turned down the gun, infuriating Browning and consequently ending his 19-year association with the company. Browning eventually found an eager audience for his shotgun with Fabrique Nationale of Liège, Belgium, and the gun that Winchester didn't want went on to become the famous Browning Auto-5.

Twenty years later, Browning had another idea for a unique shotgun that would become just as legendary. Because the top barrel was affixed to the bottom tube, rather than alongside it, as was common with double guns at the time, Browning called his new smoothbore the Superposed. In 1923 he was granted the first of two patents for what would become the world's first commercially made over/under shotgun. It has been reported that this stacked barrel concept was actually suggested to Browning by his friend Gus L. Becker, an Olympic trap shooter and skilled upland hunter. Whether or not this is true, it is known that once the gun got into production, the very first Superposed was shipped to Becker.

In reality, the concept of a stacked-barrel scattergun wasn't new. It existed as early as the eighteenth century with swivel-breeched muzzleloaders. But

Browning's design would become a benchmark for what remains one of the most popular shotgun designs today.

Of course, like most things Browning invented, the concept was a little ahead of its time, and companies were hesitant to take a chance on his stacked barrel smoothbore. Undaunted, Browning once again turned his gaze overseas, to Fabrique Nationale. As FN produced other successful Browning designs after the Auto-5, Browning felt the skills of its European workers would do justice to the complexities of his new shotgun. Although it was mass produced, the Superposed would require a lot of hand fitting, not just of the frames to the barrels, but for the precise meshing of internal parts as well. As the Superposed progressed, the artistry of FNs engravers and woodcarvers would also come into play.

Unfortunately, what many feel was John Browning's most sophisticated firearms design was also his last. On November 26, 1926—the day after Thanksgiving—John Browning suffered a heart attack and died in his son Val's office in the Fabrique Nationale factory in Belgium, while working on the Superposed. The responsibility and, consequently, the credit for finally getting the gun into production fell to the capable hands of his son. Indeed, it is Val

Browning whom author Ned Schwing credits for the success of the Superposed in his now out-of-print (and highly collectable) book, Browning Superposed: John M. Browning's Last Legacy (Krause Books).

Initially, doubling was a problem with the innovative smoothbore, even though the very first guns, which were produced in 1926, had double triggers. To correct this situation, in 1933 the innocuously named Superposed Twin Single Trigger was patented by Val Browning, who had proven to be a brilliant firearms inventor in his own right. The Superposed Twin Single Trigger was unique in that pulling the front trigger fired the bottom barrel first, and then, with a second pull of the same trigger, the top barrel was fired. Or the shooter could pull the rear trigger and fire the top barrel first, then fire the bottom barrel with a second pull of that same trigger. Of course, any shotgunner used to a traditional double trigger and automatically shifting his finger from the front trigger to the rear for a fast second shot would find that particular barrel had already been fired. To alleviate this problem, a non-doubling single trigger was developed.

The Superposed was officially launched in 1928, with a price tag of $107.50. First brought out in 12-gauge, a 20-gauge was eventually add-

ed and finally, 28-gauge and .410-bore models. (A 16-gauge version was never made.) Immediately it broke new trails that would, subsequently, be well traveled by other over/under shotguns that followed it. In 1931, the Superposed won eight state championships, as well as the World Live Bird Championship in Monte Carlo. The cover of Browning's 1935 catalog shows no other than Gus Becker, proudly posing with a Browning Superposed with which he broke 401 consecutive clay targets with-

out a single miss. Inexplicably, the shotgun is called a Browning Overunder in the catalog.

Over the years, the Superposed has been produced in escalating and constantly changing levels of excellence, including Grades I through VI and going on from there. S.P. Fjestad's *Blue Book of Gun Values* lists more than 50 variations. The different grades primarily reflect external engraving and precious metal embellishments, with many of the engravers signing their work. Indeed, a great number of

Superposed shotguns were museum masterpieces as much as they were well-built shotguns.

One Superposed variation slightly less desirable than the rest is the so-called "salt wood" guns. During the 1960s and '70s, many Superposeds suffered from a malady that resulted in almost instant rust in the wood-to-metal areas. This was caused by a salt curing process Browning used at the time in order to dry their wood without kilns. Unfortunately, not all the salt was leeched out of the wood before it was fashioned into stocks. Once this problem came to Browning's attention, the company offered to replace the stocks and repair the damage on Superposeds sent in by the original purchasers.

Grade I, Diana, and Midas Superposed shotguns were discontinued in 1977, but the Presentation grade was introduced that same year. A Superposed rifle/shotgun combo was brought out in 1978 in celebration of Browning's centennial. As evidence of the Superposed continued favor as a hunting arm, a Waterfowl Superposed was debuted in 1980, and then a Black Duck Waterfowl version in 1983. The Midas, Pigeon, and Pointer were reintroduced in 1985. By then, prices had escalated to encompass the $3,700 to $8,600 ranges. In an effort to keep costs down, a greatly modified version, the Citori—made in Japan by Miroku—was introduced, in 1973, and is now one of the flagships in the Browning line.

Today, the FN Browning Custom Shop in Liège, Belgium is once again offering the Superposed, specifically the B-125 and B-25, both highly personalized guns that range from single, tasteful engraving to highly stylized chiseled relief metal sculpting. Made up of more than 70 individual parts and requiring 155 different assembly steps, the Superposed remains an extremely labor intensive and, consequently, a very expensive gun to make. None are cataloged in the U.S., although they may be special ordered from a Browning authorized dealer. To that end, and thankfully, the Browning Superposed is still being hand built in Belgium to discerning customer's specifications. Each gun is individually crafted and remains an example of what many consider to be the finest over/under shotgun ever devised.

The first time I saw a Superposed I was a newlywed, many decades ago, having recently moved to Southern California from Arizona, and it didn't take me long to discover Kerr's Sport Shop on Wilshire Boulevard in Beverly Hills. Championship shotgunner Alex Kerr was the owner, and it was a monthly ritual for me to stop into the shop, where I once just missed seeing Elvis Presley buy a gun for a complete stranger (gee, if I had only entered the store a few minutes sooner, that guy could have been me!), and listened to Robert Blake doing his Baretta routine for the clerk and customers. The gun racks were always full of some of the highest-grade rifles and shotguns to be found, and it was there that I saw my first Superposed, although in my ignorance at the time, I called it a Super*im*posed.

Sadly, Kerr's is long gone now, but in compiling my bucket list for this book, and after adding the Browning Superposed as one of the guns I absolutely had to have, I stumbled upon a Browning Lightning model with a Broadway rib (so named because of its wide sighting plane running the length of the barrel), that was made in 1965—about the same time I first stepped into Alex Kerr's shop. Best of all, the barrel was factory stamped "Kerr's." It is not too farfetched to surmise that this may have been one of the very guns I had drooled over decades ago.

Whoever originally bought it from Kerr's shot it, but shot it well, and the over/under now had a luxurious patina—kind of like myself, I like to think. Yes, I bought it, thus completing that portion of my ever-expanding bucket list.

WINCHESTER
MODEL 1873

Although many firearms have claimed the title, the original sobriquet of "The Gun That Won The West" must go to the Winchester Model 1873. It was the pivotal firearm of America's quest for manifest destiny and played a major role in the opening and settling of the frontier.

The famous Winchester '73 (top) set the stage for the next two Winchester lever-actions that came after it, the 1876 (center) and the 1886 (bottom), which did away with the toggle-link system altogether.

Prior to the Model 1873's appearance, Oliver Winchester had already made a mark upon the shooting world with his Henry Repeating Rifle and the subsequent "Improved Henry," or the Model 1866, as it came to be known. But both of these guns had a failing with their .44-caliber Henry Flat rimfire cartridges, which held a weak, 13-grain (later bumped to 28-grain) powder charge. Anything more powerful and the soft copper casings—necessary for detonation of the rimfire primer—would split. So, with the perfection of the .44-40 centerfire cartridge, a new rifle was born.

True to its nomenclature, the .44-40 held 40 grains of blackpowder, which pushed a 200-grain bullet—basically the same slug used in the .44 rimfire—out the barrel at 1,310

Evidence of the replica 1873's prominence in Cowboy Action Shooting, one of Uberti's newest offerings is its Competition Rifle, featuring a short-stroke action and non-slip rubber butt pad, two things the originals never had.

With its 16-inch barrel, the Uberti Trapper '73 Carbine makes a handy brush gun.

fps, a substantial improvement over the older .44 Henry Flat. Moreover, owing to its stronger brass case and separate primer, the .44-40 could be reloaded. The Winchester New Model of 1873, as it was initially called, came out concurrently with the .44-40 and, like the trapdoor Springfield and the .45-70 of that same year, was one of the historically great gun and cartridge teamings.

With the Army's adoption of the 1873 Springfield, Oliver Winchester had to give up his dream of landing a military contract with his new lever gun and cartridge combo. But he soon discovered he had tapped into the much more influential and lucrative civilian market with his Winchester 73 and its sole .44-40 chambering. Here at last was the world's first reliable centerfire cartridge, paired up with a newer, stronger repeating rifle using an internal mechanism that had already proven itself in the Civil War and countless Indian skirmishes. Indeed, the Model 1873 utilized the same toggle-link action as the Model 66 and the Henry rifle before it. The difference with the Model 73 was that, instead of the softer, bronze-brass alloy receiver used by its predecessors, the Winchester 73 receiver was made of more durable iron. This not only made the gun stronger and lighter, but less expensive to produce. In addition, a sliding dust cover was added to protect the otherwise exposed bolt and inner workings, a source of complaints with the Henry and Model 66. The Winchester 73 was further improved in 1884, when the

iron forgings were changed to steel. Other minor mechanical improvements were made through the years, and it's small wonder the Model 73 accounted for the majority of Winchester's total sales for the first 16 years of its manufacture, even outselling the bigger-bored Models 1876 and 1886 that came after it. In all, 720,610 Model 1873s were made before the gun was discontinued in 1921. Inventories continued to be sold up until 1924.

The Winchester 1873 was produced in rifle, carbine, sporting rifle, and musket configurations, most of which came with a three-piece cleaning rod stored in the buttstock. The musket was supplied with a bayonet and was the least attractive, in my opinion, of all the models. In fact, I can remember back in the late 1950s or early '60s, of seeing a barrel full—literally—of Winchester '73 muskets that had come out of Mexico and were for sale at the old Jewel Box Pawn Shop in Phoenix, Arizona for the then-hefty price of $90 each. In our youthful wisdom, some of my other gun buddies and I toyed with the idea of buying one of these guns, sawing off the barrel to even it up with the magazine tube, and removing enough forearm wood to make the musket more closely resemble a '73 rifle. Such was our shrewdness in those early years. Fortunately, for today's collectors, none of us had enough money to even buy a box of .44-40 shells, let alone an entire rifle. Today, of course, unaltered Model '73 muskets are extremely desirable among collectors.

My teenage gun-redesigning aspirations aside, the Winchester 73 was notable for the number of factory options that could be ordered. Everything from engraved and plated versions, extra-long and ultra-short barrels having round, octagon, and half-round/half-octagon configurations, deluxe wood, and special sights could be had. Many of the shorter barreled "Trapper" models (initially called "Baby Carbines") went to South America for use on rubber plantations, but the majority of the carbines and rifles were used by lawmen, outlaws, hunters and trappers in this country. In fact, during the latter part of the nineteenth century, the .44-40 was the most ubiquitous cartridge to be found in general stores and supply posts throughout America.

After the Battle of the Little Big Horn, on June 26, 1876, the army was under pressure to re-think their single shot Springfield strategy, and retested the Winchester 73. However, the .44-40 cartridge was found to be woefully underpowered when compared to the .45-70. Indeed, Major Ned Roberts, a highly respected muzzleloading devotee and author in the early twentieth century, once wrote of being on an

eastern black bear hunt and emptying the entire 15-round contents of his Winchester 73 rifle into a bruin before it finally expired (no doubt weighing it down with lead, more than anything else). On his next hunt, Major Roberts abandoned the lever-action for a front-loading double rifle, which was far superior in killing power.

Many years earlier, Col. William F. "Buffalo Bill" Cody had a similar, yet different story to tell, one praising the new repeater. In 1875 he wrote the following letter to Winchester:

I have been using and have thoroughly tested your latest improved rifle. Allow me to say that I have tried and used nearly every kind of a gun made in the United States and for general hunting, or Indian fighting, I pronounced your improved Winchester the boss.

An Indian will give more for one of your guns than any other gun he can get.

While in the Black Hills last summer I crippled a bear, and Mr. Bear made for me, and I am certain that had I not been armed with one of your repeating rifles I would now be in the happy hunting grounds. The bear was

Although he still shoots his original Winchester '73, the author was duly impressed with the swift, smooth action and the accuracy of the new Miroku-made Winchester Short Rifle.

not thirty feet from me when he charged, but before he could reach me I had eleven bullets in him, which was a little more lead than he could comfortably digest.

"Believe me, that you have the most complete rifle now made."

Needless to say, Cody's letter was reprinted in Winchester's 1875 catalog. If this hadn't been praise enough, the trim, lightweight rifle received another popularity boost in 1878, when Colt's decided to chamber its equally famous Single Action Army for Winchester's .44-40. This sixgun even had its own designation—Frontier Six-Shooter—etched (later stamped) on the left side of the barrel. Now for the first time a frontiersman could carry the same box of cartridges for both rifle and pistol.

Returning the favor, Winchester introduced a .38-40 chambering for its '73 in 1880, and a .32-20 in 1882, thus making three Model 73/Colt SAA combinations possible. In 1885 a .22 Short/.22 Long chambering was added to the Model 73 line, but this never proved as popular as its bigger-bored brethren, and only 19,552 of the rimfires were made before that chambering was discontinued in 1904.

From a collector's standpoint, the *ne plus ultra* of Winchester 73s are the One of One Thousand and One of One Hundred rifles, guns that possessed barrels of extraordinary marksmanship ability. Those shooting the best targets during factory proofing were designated One of One Thousand and sold for $100 each. Rifles shooting the second best targets were engraved One of One Hundred and priced at $20 over the regular $27 cost of a standard gun. Both versions were outfitted with set triggers, special engraving, and other embellishments. Only 133 One of One Thousand and eight One of One Hundred Model 73s were ever produced.

One of the best tributes to the Winchester 73 was the 1950 Universal picture named after the gun. The movie *Winchester 73* starred Jimmy Stewart and featured a studio-doctored One of One Thousand. As part of the movie's publicity, a nationwide search was conducted for owners of real One of One Thousand Winchester 73 rifles. Twenty-four such guns were discovered. Today, of course, an original Winchester One of One Thousand can easily command a figure well into the five-digit range. Cimarron Fire Arms makes a substantially less expensive handsome replica of a One of One Thousand, and countless replica rifles, carbines, and sporting rifles are offered by firms such as Navy Arms, Cimarron, and Benelli/Uberti. Even Winchester has gotten back into the act by reintroducing its Model 1873 Short Rifle, although the version produced today is made by Miroku in Japan. A blued version was introduced in 2013, and (in my opinion) a much more attractive case hardened edition came out in 2014. Although Cowboy Action shooters have been responsible for many of the replica '73s also being chambered in .45 Colt and .357 Magnum, calibers that never existed in the prototypes, for my personal bucket list there is nothing like having a shootable Model 1873 in the time-honored .44-40 caliber, thus keeping the tradition of "The Gun that Won the West" alive.

BERETTA 92FS/ M9

The only real drawback to the M9 is the fact that its 9mm ammunition, as issued to our troops, is not the most effective battle round. Far better self-defense ammo is available to civilians.

Beretta is not only one of the most recognized and respected firearms manufacturers in the world, it is also the oldest, having started in Brescia, Italy in 1526. But Beretta has another claim to fame, having created one of today's most popular yet disputatious pistols, the M-9, the U.S. military version of the civilian Beretta 92FS.

The M-9 first emerged in 1975 as the Beretta 92, the result of a five-year collaboration between Beretta designers Carlo Beretta, Giuseppe Mazzetti, and Vittorio Valle. Through a long and complex lineage, the 92 had its roots in the Model 1915, Beretta's first semi-automatic handgun, and the vastly improved Beretta Model of 1951 (more popularly known as the M951), which, in one variation, was capable of both full and semi-automatic firepower.

Although the Model 92 was semi-automatic only, it was unique. For one thing, it sported an aircraft-spec aluminum alloy frame, a high-capacity staggered 15-round magazine, a loaded chamber indicator, a decocking lever, and an ambidextrous safety. It could also be fired both single- and double-action. In addition, the press-turn disassembly latch made takedown simple.

Chambered for the 9mm Parabellum (9x19mm) NATO round, the gun was immediately adopted by the Brazilian armed forces, with other military and police organizations quickly following suit. In 1976, the Italian police requested a hammer drop safety, and the 92S was the result. The 92G came about when the Gendarmerie Nationale French military wanted a decocking lever, but one without a manual safety. In 1980, with the Joint Service Small Arms Program (JSSAP) already exploring a new U.S. service pistol chambered for the 9mm NATO round, the 92SB was developed,

The author found that the Beretta 92FS/M9 was accurate enough for close range self-defense, which is what this pistol was designed for.

reversible magazine release for right- and left-handed shooters, quickly aligned three-dot sights, and weighing a scant 35 ounces, it seemed as if the Beretta 92SB-F, as it was now called, had evolved into the ideal combat handgun. At least the United States Army certainly thought so, because on January 14, 1985, it announced that this version of the Model 92 (which the Army renamed the M-9), had successfully beaten out seven other candidates (including Smith & Wesson, SIG Sauer, and Heckler & Koch), to become the new, official U.S. military sidearm, replacing the venerable Colt Government Model 1911A1.

And that's when the M-9's troubles began. There was an immediate uproar over the loss of the slab-sided warhorse that had defended our shores in two World Wars, Korea, Vietnam, and countless other conflicts. Moreover, insult was added by the fact that the new service pistol was made by an Italian firm. It was nothing short of degrading to have to exchange the .45 ACP for the 9mm NATO round, just so our troops could be "logistically compatible" with our allies' ammunition. There was also the stigma of the aluminum frame, in spite of the fact that, during one test, the M-9 fired 17,500 rounds—far in excess of the U.S. government's mandate that it withstand 5,000 rounds—without a single malfunction. To overcome the "Italian situation," it was agreed the guns would be manufactured in the new Beretta

which featured an automatic block that prevented the firing pin from being released until the trigger was in its most rearward position. In 1983, further JSSAP tests resulted in the 92F, which sported the now familiar curved combat trigger guard. This gun was also given a non-glare black matte Bruniton finish.

With its checkered front- and backstraps,

The author found the Beretta M9 to be fast firing and reliable under simulated combat conditions.

The Beretta M9 replaced the Model 1911 in 1985. In its civilian guise, it is known as the 92FS—basically the same gun.

This Beretta 92FS has been enhanced with the addition of Crimson Trace laser grips.

USA factory in Accokeek, Maryland.

Philosophical prejudices aside, there were some very real problems with the initial M-9s. Due to a rush to get the pistols into production, some of the very first slides were not made in the U.S. Soon, tales of cracked slides and frames were being reported. The barrel mounting block, which absorbs most of the energy during recoil, was the culprit. In actuality, only four such incidences were confirmed, three of which were traced to Navy S.E.A.L.S., who were putting 3,00 to 5,000 rounds a week through their M-9s in extensive testing. The fourth failure was from a similar situation in the Army.

Although four frame-slide failures are miniscule when taking into account the original order for 321,260 M-9s, a design change was immediately made and all production was quickly moved to Beretta USA, where the guns have been made since 1988. There have been no reports of cracked frames or slides since then.

Far more realistic complaints against the M-9 concern its over-penetration and lack of stopping power, but this is obviously the fault of the M882 NATO cartridge, a 124-grain full metal jacket 9mm round our troops are required to use. Obviously, civilians have far more effective alternatives, such as Hornady's 115-grain Critical Defense FTX (Flex Tip Extreme) loading. Likewise, failure-to-feed complaints can be traced back to inferior aftermarket magazines rather than the original factory mags. On a personal note, I have fired hundreds of rounds of factory ammunition, both full metal jacket and hollowpoint, through an M-9 with nary a malfunction.

There are also reoccurring tales of the M-9 not being a "tack-driver." One must take into consideration that its official designation is a "close personal defense weapon," for supplemental use with the M4 rifle and for members of crew served weapons. In that light, firing military ammunition at close combat distances, I can easily keep a five-shot string within 1¾ inches. And using highly tuned M-9s, the U.S. Army's Marksmanship Unit at Ft. Benning, Georgia, regularly shoot 10-shot groups under 1½ inches at 50 yards.

So far, there have been 50 variations of the Beretta 92, with the current 92FS being the exact civilian counterpart of the M-9, the only differences being slide stampings and serial numbering. In addition, the M9A1 is one of the latest military variants, featuring a U.S. Marine-mandated Picatinny rail. On January 29, 2009, the U.S. Army ordered an additional 450,000 M-9s from Beretta, the largest firearms contract since World War II.

As much as I admire the 1911A1, I think the Beretta 92FS belongs on my bucket list not only as a representative of our official military sidearm, but one that even with its controversy is a versatile although gun that, like the company that makes it, is nonetheless going to be around for a long time.

RUGER NO. 1

I have always had a penchant for single-shot rifles, especially when going after big and dangerous game. It's not that I have a death wish. Far from it. It's just that, for me, the single-shot hunting rifle magnifies everything we as shooters hold sacrosanct: sight picture, breath control, trigger pull, and making that first shot count—because one shot is all you're going to get. Moreover, single-shot rifles are comfortable to carry and quick to shoulder, because they generally are better balanced (with their shorter actions) than repeaters. Too, by the very nature of their more simplistic internal mechanisms

The author's Ruger Tropical No. 1 rifle in .405 Winchester, before its gold engraving, but he has already embellished it with a Galco Braided Cobra Sling.

For all these reasons, I have spent a lifetime hunting with single-shots—both originals and replicas of the trapdoor Springfield, Winchester High-Wall, and 1874 Sharps—taking game in Africa and North America. However, there was one single-shot rifle I had never taken afield: the Ruger No. 1.

Introduced in September 1966, the No. 1 is an updated version of the Scottish Farquharson falling block hammerless design of 1872, and reflected the late Bill Ruger's admiration for this gun, which he collected extensively. The No. 1 also reflected Ruger's penchant for another Scottish gunmaker, Alexander Henry, well known for his highly accurate muzzle-loading rifles of the 1860s. These rifles were often characterized by their unique wood or grooved ebony fore-ends. This "Alexander Henry fore-end," which serves no purpose other than being decorative, was adapted as a design feature on the Ruger No. 1, adding to its already handsome countenance. In fact, in his book *Ruger & His Guns*, (wilsonbooks.com) author and firearms historian R.L. Wilson rightfully calls the No. 1, "The ultimate evolution of the single-shot rifle."

Why didn't I have one? It wasn't that I didn't share Bill Ruger's enthusiasm for the gun. But even with an original price tag of $280, my chance of acquiring this new gun at the time of its introduction was as distant as the moon. Besides, the No. 1 was initially chambered for relatively "modern" cartridges, and I was wedded to things like the .44-40, and the .45-70, stretching only as far forward into the nineteenth century as the .30-30. I must admit that

in 1978 I took a serious look at acquiring a No. 1, when a limited number of Lyman Centennial models were produced in .45-70. However, I never quite got my wallet opened.

My priorities were refocused, however, when Ruger brought out its No 1-H Tropical, a thick barreled, muscular big-game rifle chambered in .375 H&H, .458 Winchester Magnum, and .416 Rigby—all potent, close-range bone crushers, and each with an historic African heritage. With its 24-inch barrel and weighing in at nine pounds (almost two pounds heavier than the standard sporter), here was a rifle that seemed to be just straining at the leash to pursue dangerous game. But though I considered the No. 1 Tropical the most enticing gun and chamberings in Ruger's single-shot lineup, increased demands of writing and travel diverted my attention.

All that changed in 2004, when Ruger announced the Tropical No. 1 was coming out in .405 Winchester. I could no longer ignore this rifle. After all, this was Teddy's cartridge! Originally developed, in 1904, for the Winchester Model 95, the potent round went on to prove itself on Roosevelt's safari and well beyond. Although the Winchester 95 was cataloged until 1934, the .405 cartridge continued to be factory loaded until 1955, when, with a lack of rifles being made for it, the .405 was eventually discontinued. But the power of its 300-grain semi-jacketed round nose bullet, with a muzzle velocity of 2,200 fps and a muzzle energy of 3,325 ft-lbs, had become legendary.

I owned an original deluxe Winchester Model 95 in this caliber, and, as some of my

magazine readers may recall, used a Browning Model 95 in .405 Winchester to drop a bison with a single shot a few years ago. Although not a tack-driver, the .405 Winchester, which is currently loaded by Hornady, is more than capable of taking any critter on the planet if the shot is placed right, and can definitely make one-shot kills on anything that roams the North American continent. Both my original and replica Model 95s produce 3½-inch groups with open sights at 100 yards. I could only speculate what Ruger's No. 1 Tropical would do. There was but one way to find out. And though, over the years, the Tropical's price tag had risen to $966, my newly increased credit card limit made acquisition of this rifle possible.

Physically, the rifle was not disappointing. In fact, it inspired me to start thinking about certain metallic embellishments to go along with its finely grained, black walnut stock. But first to the range to see how the gun performed. Using Ruger's folding leaf notched rear sight and gold bead ramped front post, I was able to punch out 3½-inch groups – same as my

Model 95 lever-actions. Of course, the inclusion of a pair of Ruger scope rings with the No. 1 and the integral scope mounts milled into the rear sight base told me no one was expected to shoot this rifle with open sights. That, of course, is a common mistake made by many of the best firearms manufacturers and, in my opinion, doesn't do justice to the quality of the guns they produce. But no, the No. 1 deserved something better. Like express sights, in keeping with its "tropical" motif. And a more visible front sight. Plus, there was something else, something a little more, shall we say, cosmetic? Quite frankly, the No. 1 practically demanded to be engraved. Some of the photos in Wilson's book and a brochure from the recently established Ruger Studio Of Art And Decoration bore this out. But, first, we had to get the mechanics in order.

Aside from Marble Arms, I know of only one other U.S. firm that makes quality, accurate, and affordable express sights, and that was New England Custom Gun, Ltd. "Classic" one, two, and three-leaf models are offered. I, of course, wanted the three-leaf model, which

The Ruger No. 1 is an updated version of the Scottish Farquharson falling block hammerless design of 1872.

A standard blued Ruger No. 1 Tropical rifle (bottom) compared with the author's Baron-etched and gold-plated rifle (top).

also features a fixed 50-yard "V" for snap shots at charging game. Given the relatively close-range trajectory of the .405 and the type of hunting I would be doing with it, I anticipated the three flip-up leafs would be filed in a deep "U" for more precise aiming, and would be graduated to 50, 100, and 200 yards. A visit to NECG's website also fulfilled my front sight wishes: NECG offers a number of front sight replacements for the No. 1, including four white beads of varying dimensions, a red fiber optic bead, and a retro-looking brass "sour-dough" Patridge blade.

I immediately discarded the fiber optic front sight possibility. Practical as it may be, it wasn't in keeping with the spirit of the gun. On the other hand, while the sourdough blade looked old-timey, it didn't provide the visibility I wanted. I opted for a 3/16-inch white bead (smaller dimensions are available for those with better eyes), set upon an NECG Masterpiece banded ramp and topped with NECG's steel "window hood," which provides natural illumination through the sides and locks onto the ramp via a hood lock button.

A call to NECG's Mark Cromwell put my plan to create the "ultimate No. 1 single-shot" into action. I sent the gun off to Mark, along with two boxes of Hornady .405 ammo for regulating the sights. I had Mark shape the express sight base to mirror the scalloped lines of the Ruger base, because I liked the way it looked; the front sight base was scalloped to match. While I was at it, I had him adjust the trigger pull to three pounds and slightly re-

shape the tang safety in an attempt to prevent .405 cases from hanging up on it during ejection, a rather disconcerting characteristic I had encountered at the range. I also asked Mark if there was anything he could do to muffle the rather audible "click" of the safety.

"As for the safety," he e-mailed back, "No. 1s are known for that 'clank,' as you throw the safety off. We have not worked on the safety other then to modify the lead end to not stop the ejected cases as it did before. I tried easing the safety off, as you might in a hunting situation, and by pushing down on the tail end of the safety and just behind the raised button you can ease it off without too much noise. (I say this and laugh, as what sounds quiet in a shop with phones, lights and machines making noise and what it may sound like in the middle of nowhere may be different)."

While NECG was putting the finishing touches on my No. 1, I contacted David Baron of Baron Technology, Inc., the firm that has gained international fame for lavishing gold and silver embellishments upon thousands of commemorative firearms, including Colts, Winchesters, and Rugers. As it happened, David was working with the Ruger Studio of Art and Decoration on a number of custom guns, some of which were No. 1s. He sent me a selection of receiver patterns, many of which were created by Paul Lantuch, Master Artist and former Chief Engraver for Ruger. Paul has a 30-year history of artistic gun embellishment and had engraved many guns for Bill Ruger's collection. There could be no better tribute to my "ultimate No. 1" than to have it reflect Paul's talent. However, because of budget considerations, I decided to have Baron Technology etch the receiver, rather than have Paul hand-engrave it.

I ended up selecting two classic rococo patterns that, although they looked like they dated from the late nineteenth and early twentieth centuries, were actually created by Paul, in 1981. On the left side of the receiver would be, appropriately enough, Diana, Roman goddess of the hunt, holding her bow and hunting horn, a dog at her side in pursuit of a stag racing through vineyards. On the right side was another scene from the legend, depicting a pair of nymphs, a highly stylized, devilish-looking buffalo skull, and two hunting dogs, which symbolize fidelity. "These are very limited patterns," Paul said of my choices. "They are not often seen."

When my No. 1 was completed by NECG but not yet blued, I sent it to Baron Technology for the etching. I gave Dave a budget, stating that I wanted some gold on the gun to accent the etchings. What I finally got back exceeded my expectations and reaffirmed why Baron is the leader in their field. The receiver and even the lever had been etched and then plated in 24-carat gold. Moreover, the breechblock and lever release were polished and jeweled. "It's just something I think is needed on all presentation grade No. 1s," David said matter-of-factly.

Needless to say, my "ultimate No. 1" was the focal point at Angeles Shooting Range in Los Angeles, when I took it out to see how it shot. The deeply cut U-notch express sights and reduced trigger pull produced 1½-inch groups at 100 yards. Both Hornady spire point and round-nose bullets printed the same. But the real test came a month later on a wild boar hunt in Paso Robles.

The gently rolling, oak studded hills and valleys of central California's Camp Five is a virtual Mecca for wild boar, as well as deer, turkey, and upland birds. Camp Five's accommodations range from a "Primitive Vista" cabin with indoor plumbing but no electricity, to an "Upper Lodge," a 2,400-square-foot, three-bedroom ranch house with sweeping vistas, TV, Jacuzzi tub, and outdoor barbeque. Naturally, this is where I stayed.

I was met by head honcho Doug Roth, accompanied by his trusty "pig dog," Moose, a diminutive Jack Russell terrier who enjoyed local celebrity status due to his ability to track down and hold the biggest of boars—well, once they were shot.

"Ah, the man with the Golden Gun," Doug exclaimed as he eyed my Ruger. Moose just circled around and stared.

Before going afield, I made a quick stop at Camp Five's shooting range to reaffirm the Ruger's sights. At 100 yards, I printed 2½ to 3-inch groups, wider than I had gotten from a benchrest at Angeles Shooting Range. I can only attribute this phenomenon to "shooter malfunction." Still, it was more than adequate for pigs.

The next two days were spent traversing the rugged countryside looking for descendants of porkers the Spaniards had brought to California more than 500 years ago. We saw plenty of pigs, but they were all in the 50 to 70-pound class, way too small to even consider taking with the .405. After all, I did want to have some meat left to take home.

It was in the long, golden glow of late afternoon of the second day that Moose and I both spotted a huge grayish mass partially hidden by tall grass. Earlier, I had missed an opportunity at a rust-colored boar, because I was carrying the No. 1 with the action open and empty. This time I was carrying the No. 1 fully charged, muzzle up, safety on, finger off the trigger, and two additional round-nosed .405s between my first and third fingers. Without notice, a 200-pound boar burst through a grove of oaks. I snapped the rifle to my shoulder, the 50-yard express sight instantly finding its mark on an angling shot as the boar crashed into the brush. The bullet hit from the rear and punched through his entire body, rolling him down a steep hill. He was lost in the brush, but Moose the Wonder Dog was hot on his trail. We soon heard barking, telling us where he was.

"I hope that boar's dead," I said, as Doug and I raced downhill towards the commotion.

"Don't worry," said Doug. "If he's not, he's gonna have 18 pounds of whup-ass on him!"

We spotted the boar 30 yards away, just in his final death throes, with Moose bobbing and weaving around it like a miniature prizefighter. I couldn't get a clear finishing shot for fear of hitting the dog. At our approach, Moose broke off his "attack," giving me an opening. I fired into the shoulder of the pig. The impact of the bullet tumbled the huge boar all the way down the steep hill, the massive body coming to rest in a cloud of dust on the dirt road below.

The Ruger had proven itself, and it has gone on to inspire others. One well-respected gun writer friend of mine, on seeing my .405, ordered a similar engraved No. 1. I'm sure there will be others. But it won't be as easy to get the caliber you want as it once was, because now Ruger is making only one caliber a year for the No. 1. As for my No. 1, it is now ready for bigger things. I'm thinking of elk this fall, and perhaps Africa next year. The No. 1 is certainly capable of all this and more. Although there may be fancier guns, as far as I'm concerned, mine is the "Ultimate Single Shot."

WINCHESTER
MODEL 1886
& MODEL 71

The Winchester Model 71 was a modern replacement for the Model 86.

The Winchester Model 1886 Extra Light Weight came out in 1896, and was available in .45-70 and .33 Winchester (shown).

You may be wondering why I have grouped these two Winchesters as one. The reason is that the Winchester Model 1886 ended up proving so popular over the years that by 1935, it was in need of an update to make it more compatible with twentieth century hunters. Here's the complete story.

The Model 71 was only chambered in one caliber, the .348 Winchester.

Although Winchester had found a modicum of success in creating a big-game lever-action by beefing up its Model 1873 and transforming it into a much heftier Model 1876, the big gun was still hampered by the older toggle link mechanism, thus making its action too short to handle one of the most popular hunting rounds of the late nineteenth century, the .45-70 Government cartridge. It fell upon Browning firearms designing acumen to come up with a complete departure from the older Winchester lever-action design, replacing it with one that was more than capable of digesting .45-70 rounds, among others.

The Model 1886 rifle was unlike the toggle-link Winchesters of 1873 and 1876. For one, it had a stronger, beefier action, one that was eventually offered in 10 calibers ranging from .33 Winchester to .50-110. This, then, turned out to be an ultimate medium-range hunting rifle that could pretty much take care of anything that walked or crawled on this side of the hemisphere.

The product of brothers Matthew and Jonathan Browning, the Model '86 owed its popularity to an action as smooth as warm butter yet strong as a tank, thanks to twin vertical locking bars that slid up through the receiver. When the Browning brothers showed their Model 1886 prototype to an executive at one of the country's leading firearms dealers, Schoverling, Daly & Gales, in New York, they were told their rifle held the key to Winchester's future. Indeed, it put Winchesters in the hands of serious big-game hunters, not the least of which was Theodore Roosevelt. In fact, it was TR who indirectly focused on one of the rifle's faults: it was heavy. Roosevelt responded by ordering an '86 with a half magazine to reduce the nine-pound weight of the 26-inch octagon barreled rifle.

Winchester also took note of its popular lever-action's heft and introduced the 1886 Extra Light Weight in 1896. Chambered in .45-70 and offered with a 22-inch round tapered barrel, half magazine, hard rubber shotgun buttplate, and straight grip stock, this was also Winchester's way of eliminating many special order options (though an optional takedown version was available). In 1902 the Extra Light Weight was also chambered for the .33 Winchester, albeit with a 24-inch barrel.

By that time all four lever-action rifles designed by Browning for Winchester had proven their versatility, easily vaulting the turn-of-the-century fence and landing well into the first part of the twentieth century. But one of those rifles was to be given a new identity, enabling it to remain in production well into the post-war years. That gun was the Model 71, a revitalized persona of the Winchester 1886, the first lever-action Browning had created for Winchester. The famous twin locking bolts, soon to be replicated in the smaller Winchester 92, were encased in the aforementioned fortress-like receiver and a smooth-as-melted-ice-cream action, which made the Model 86 a favorite with hunters, especially in chamberings such as .50-110 Express, .38-56 WCF, and, of course, .45-70.

But by the early 1930s, Winchester realized it had better do something if it was to maintain the company's lever-action legacy among outdoorsmen. Bolt-actions were all the rage by then, and Winchester's Models 1892 and 1894 were deer rifles at best, certainly not intended for larger game such as moose and brown bear. With the Model 1895 discontinued in 1931, Winchester was left with only one big-game lever-action, the 1886, which by that time was offered in just two calibers, .33 Winchester and .45-70. Moreover, the Winchester '86 had become expensive to produce. While still popular, the old gun had to be reinvented

for a new generation of hunters.

Winchester began thinking about modernizing the 1886 as soon as it discontinued the Model 95. Although 45 years old at the time, the Model 86 was still mechanically one of the strongest lever-actions ever built. It just needed some tweaking, a process that encompassed the next four years. What finally emerged, on November 2, 1935, was a gun that, with its pistol grip, checkered stock, and three-quarters magazine tube, looked every bit like a Model 86 with factory options, but it was now known as the Winchester 71. The year the 71 appeared, the 1886 was discontinued, thus ushering in the era of a lever-action that would become legendary in hunting camps for the next 23 years.

Although there was no mistaking its 1886 roots, the Model 71 was truly a redesigned gun. At the forefront, the metallurgy had been updated with forgings of Winchester's chrome mo-

Browning's design for the Model 1886 featured two locking bolts, making for an extremely sturdy action. Shown are the Model 86 (top) and Model 71) (bottom).

The Lyman No. 56 peep sight fitted to the receiver was one of three options on the Model 71.

The author has hunted with this Model 71 all over the West.

71, which also incorporated a gracefully contoured lever for rapid repeat shots. A choice of a semi-buckhorn Lyman 22K open rear sight or a bolt-mounted peep was offered. Later post-war 71s did away with the sometimes disconcerting bolt-mounted peep and, instead, had a Lyman No. 56 peep sight fitted to their receivers. Underneath a 24-inch barrel was a three-quarters tubular magazine that held four cartridges. A hooded ramp front sight with steel post and bead was standard.

This initial version is referred to as the "Deluxe Model" by collectors. From January 6, 1936, until 1947, a lower priced, non-checkered variant without a pistol grip cap and sporting a 20-inch barrel was offered, which collectors now call the "Model 71 Carbine." Up to approximately serial number 15,000, the Model 71 tang measured 3⅞ inches in length; these early rifles are now labeled "Long Tang" models. Later guns, until the end of production, had tangs measuring 2⅞ inches and are called "Short Tangs," but no such designations were ever used by Winchester for this one-inch difference.

Just as impressive as the new Model 71 was the cartridge created for it, the .348 Winchester. With the exception of a very few special order early-production Model 71s in .45-70, it was the only cartridge for which the gun would be chambered—nor was the .348 Winchester ever factory chambered in any other rifle.

Initially in developing the Model 71, Winchester realized it already had an action of unprecedented strength, so it turned the company's attention to developing a suitably strong cartridge. Rather than choose the .45-70, which was considered adequate but obso-

lybdenum "Proof Steel," originally developed for John Olin's no-cost-is-too-great Model 21 shotgun. Internally, the action had been simplified and strengthened, while still retaining its coveted butter-smooth operation. In addition, the flat springs of the 1886 were replaced by sturdier coil springs. Later versions perfected the action further, by incorporating a split trigger safety catch that prevented the hammer from being tripped until the lever was completely closed and locked. And before that could happen, the bolt had to be fully seated into the breech, making the 71 not only one of the strongest, but also one of the safest rifles of its day.

Externally, the crescent buttplate of the 86 had been changed to flat, checkered steel. A factory rubber recoil pad was an extra-cost option. The wood was now beefier, featuring a checkered varnished pistol grip and a beavertail forearm, and the eight-pound rifle came equipped with quick-detachable swivels and a leather sling. A pistol grip cap, an extra option on the 1886, was now standard on the Model

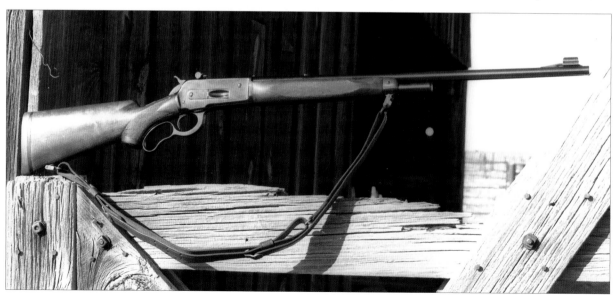

lete, they focused on the popular (at the time) .33 Winchester, which had been introduced, in 1902, specifically for the Model 1886. With a muzzle velocity of 2,220 fps, the .33 WCF had already proven its elk-busting capabilities. It also had a better trajectory than the rainbow-arching .45-70. Any new cartridge would have to be noticeably more powerful.

The .348 Winchester sported a necked-down case based upon the old .50-110 black-powder cartridge originally developed for the Model 86 in 1899. Just as the Model 71 was, in reality, an improved 86, the .348 was basically an improved .33 Winchester. The factory loaded cartridge was initially offered by Winchester and Remington in 150-, 200-, and 250-grain bullets, although the 150-grain loading proved to be ballistically inferior. Consequently, it was the 200- and 250-grain slugs that found favor with big-game hunters. The 250-grain bullet was preferred for its greater knockdown power, but with a muzzle velocity of 2,320 fps, it also produced noticeably more recoil. Thus, most hunters compromised by opting for the 200-grain bullet. In 1962, the 150 and 250 loadings were discontinued, but a 200-grain Silvertip is still offered by Winchester. In addition, Buffalo Bore (www. buffalobore.com) produces a 250-grain jacketed flat-nose, which would be my choice for brown bear and similar dangerous game.

With its tubular magazine necessitating blunt-nosed bullets, the effective range of the open-sighted Model 71 was about 200 yards; suffice it to say, anything on the North American continent within that range would be meat in the pot. It is hardly surprising that the Model 71 was enthusiastically embraced by hunters, and it remains both a collectable and a working rifle today. It is particularly coveted in Alaska, where many of these guns have been converted to wildcats such as the .450 Alaskan.

Unfortunately, high manufacturing costs and changing times led to the discontinuance of the Model 71 in 1958, with 47,254 rifles produced. Yet demand for the smooth-shooting, hard-hitting lever gun resulted in Browning offering a limited run of Model 1886 rifles and carbines from 1992 to 1993, and Model 71 rifles and carbines from 1987 to 1989, all of which proves that even though the Model 71 and its predecessor, the Model 86, have been discontinued, they are far from obsolete. As both a hunting gun and a collectable that evokes thick forests, crisp autumn days, and big racks, they both belong on my bucket list.

Left: The Model 71 maintains the fast shooting characteristics of the Model 1886.

Below: The author took this magnificent six-point elk with a single shot from his Miroku-made Winchester 86 Lightweight, using a 250-grain Buffalo Bore bullet.

COLT PYTHON

This 50th Anniversary Python was engraved by Colt Master Engraver Steve Kamyk and was the last Python the factory produced.

The year 1955 was a pivotal one for pistols, for in that one 12-month period, no less than four of today's most coveted and collected revolvers were introduced: The Smith & Wesson Model 29, Ruger's .357 Blackhawk, the reintroduction of the Colt Single Action Army, and Colt's new Python. Yet only the Python, arguably the most meticulously crafted and supremely accurate of the four, is no longer produced. In fact, the Python's superb workmanship and resultant accuracy were the very factors that ultimately caused the gun's demise. The Python simply became too expensive to produce.

"A limited number of gun connoisseurs will mark 1955 as a distinguished year in handgun history, with the purchase of this Colt master-work," the Python's full-page introductory ad proclaimed. Prophetic words indeed, as just one gun was produced that year. Only 299 were made in 1956. It took extra time to make a Python, as each part was hand polished and then hand fitted, before the fully assembled gun was hand tested on the factory firing range. If one didn't perform to expectations, it was taken back to the factory, disassembled, reevaluated, reassembled, and tested again until it was perfect.

"We had to hone all the parts, including inside the sideplates," recalls Al De John, who was Colt's Service Manager when the Python was being developed and who later became Superintendent of the Colt Custom Shop, where the Python was produced during the final years of its existence. "It was the only gun we did that on. We polished everything, including inside the hammer strut. There were only two of us allowed to work on the Python, myself and Don Bedford. Usually, a Colt's worker would be able to go through four guns an hour on average, but for the Python, because of all the extra handwork involved, it averaged about three guns per hour to build and fit everything just right."

Such exacting demands for accuracy—and not just in the target-punching sense—took its toll in the cost per gun. Yet, in spite of its hefty $125 price tag (especially when compared to the $87.50 cost of that "other" new .357 Magnum, the Ruger Blackhawk), the Python quickly became Colt's champion thoroughbred. Handsome and sophisticated in design, with

a superbly rigid cylinder lockup, a slightly tapered bore that tightened groups dramatically, and a factory trigger pull of 2¾- to 3½-pounds, the Python literally shot as good as it looked.

And it did look good. The Python's highly polished exterior steel surfaces received the same glass-smooth polishing normally reserved for guns that were to be nickel-plated, even though the first Pythons were blued (bright nickel guns were introduced shortly thereafter, a natural progression, as the polishing work had already been done). Thus, the Python became the first Colt to be produced in what the company called its Royal Blue finish. In fact, and other theories to the contrary, it was because of its almost shimmering blue-black countenance that Colt's new .357 Magnum was christened the Python, a name that was given even more stature thanks to a fully shrouded ejector rod housing that was part of a thick bull barrel topped by another distinctive Python feature, a full-length ventilated rib.

"We'd get together and talk about what we wanted to do [with the design of the Python]," recalls De John. "It might have been Al Gunther [Colt's factory supervisor at the time] who first suggested we put a vent rib across the top of the barrel. It didn't do anything, but it sure looked good."

Interestingly, the Python was originally intended to be chambered in .38 Special, as a more stylized version of the Officer's Model Target Revolver, which was also built on a .41-caliber frame and which, in turn, was a target version of the Colt Official Police. Thus, for all its up-to-date refinements, the Python's basic lockwork stemmed from 1927. Then, everything changed when the decision was made to chamber this revamped revolver in .357 Magnum. It turned out to be a prudent decision, for even though that cartridge had been around since 1935, at the time of the Python's introduction it was the most popular handgun caliber in America, and Colt's newest double-action was about to bring it even greater fame. But the Python's more powerful chambering created new challenges for Colt's design team.

"That meant beefing up the cylinder and frame, including the topstrap," remembers De John. "We had a lot of problems with blowback and the firing pins. In our initial testing of the new gun, the excessive pressure from the .357 Magnum kept hammering the recoil plate, which was a separate piece set into the frame."

That recoil plate necessitated frequent replacement.

De John continued, "So the recoil plate was eliminated by putting the firing pin hole directly into the frame and beefing up the topstrap. We also beefed up the crane to make the gun even stronger."

Initially produced only with a six-inch barrel, popular demand, primarily from law enforcement personnel, resulted in a four-inch

Whether for self-defense, target shooting, or hunting, the Python excels at all three. The aftermarkets grips are from Eagle Grips.

Accuracy is one of the Python's strong points. The author prefers Pachmayr grips for lengthy range sessions.

barrel being offered. Later, a 2½-inch barrel was brought out, "…which was the shortest barrel we could make and still fit a vent on the rib," remembers De John. Over the course of its 50-year lifespan, other barrel lengths were made, including an eight-inch Python introduced in 1980, and a limited run of three-inch Pythons (beware of fakes, as many of these snubbies were altered outside the factory; real ones carry a slight premium in price).

As a supplement to its Royal Blue and nickel finishes, in 1981 Colt began offering the Python with a weather resistant plating known as Coltguard. A stainless Python was introduced in 1984, followed by a super-polished stainless version known as the Ultimate Python in 1985, which basically spelled the end of the Python's original Bright Nickel finish. When Python production moved from the main factory to the Colt Custom Shop in 1997, the gun became the Python Elite and was also available with a stainless matte finish. Of course, silver and gold plating were extra-cost options on the Python almost from inception, as was engraving.

Although pricey, the Python was a goal worth obtaining, for those who could scrape up the cash. Whether used for law enforcement, hunting, or home-defense, the Colt Python stood

out from the other revolvers around it. It also achieved repeated fame and recognition in motion pictures such as *Magnum Force* with David Soul, *McQ* with John Wayne, and Tom Hanks in *Dragnet*, just to name a few of its roles in the hands of A-List actors.

In terms of historical significance, few of the many Colt Python variations can match The Last Python, which was exhibited at the 2006 SHOT (Shooting, Hunting, Outdoor Trade) Show, in Las Vegas. Two years earlier, when I'd learned that the Python, which had "officially" been discontinued in 1999 but was still being sporadically produced but was about to be discontinued completely, I suggested to Mark Roberts, at the time Colt's Director of Sales and Marketing, that it produce a final gun to commemorate the Python's 50 years of existence. Like the original, it was finished in Royal Blue, after being skillfully embellished by Colt's in-house Master Engraver, Steve Kamyk, who also accented the gun with 24-karat gold bands and a two-dimensional 24-karat gold rampant Colt on the right side of the frame, with an engraved gold oval on the left side that read, "Python 50th Anniversary." Thus, ironically, the same number of Pythons was produced in its final year of production as in its first: just one.

RUGER BEARCAT

By the late 1950s, Sturm Ruger & Company and Colt Industries were battling it out to see who would be king of the single-action revolver market. Ruger had its popular Single Six and Blackhawk sixguns, but Colt could claim title to having the original thumbcocker, the Single Action Army. Plus, Colt's new small-framed, .22 caliber Frontier Scout, having been introduced in 1957, was cutting into sales of Ruger's Single Six.

Always ready for a challenge, Bill Ruger now surprised everyone. Instead of introducing the .44 Magnum Super Blackhawk his company was rumored to be working on, he took a giant step backwards and, in July 1958, came out with a diminutive .22 single-action that was even smaller than the Single Six. Following a tradition of naming his sixguns after famous, early twentieth century automobiles (the Single Six was named in honor of Packard's five-person touring car, and the Blackhawk took its name from the 1920s Stutz Motor Car boat-tailed roadster), car aficionado Ruger dubbed his company's newest revolver the Bearcat, after the Stutz Bearcat luxury roadster, which was originally produced from 1914 through 1917.

Like the lightweight Stutz Bearcat, which was notable in that it had no doors and only a Spartan, rounded "monocle" windscreen for the driver, the construction of the Ruger Bearcat was simplicity itself. The gun weighed a scant 17 ounces and was composed of only 26 pieces (28, if you counted the two-piece grips!), screws and springs included. Plus, it was priced at $49.50—a bargain even in those years.

In appearance, the Bearcat took its inspira-

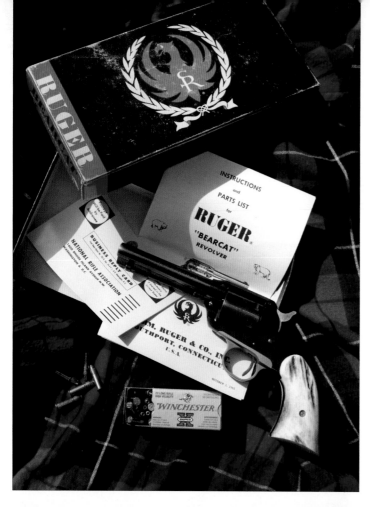

tion from the frontier-era Remington revolvers, a fact that Ruger readily admitted. The black anodized backstrap and frame were a single integral casting, while the separate trigger guard was anodized to resemble brass. Both were actually aluminum alloy, as was the cylinder. Later, trigger guards were anodized black. The 4¹/₁₆-inch barrel was blued steel, as was the ejector rod housing on the initial run of guns. Later, the housing was changed to aluminum.

The Bearcat could handle .22 Short, Long, and Long Rifle rimfire cartridges. The sights were fixed, consisting of a grooved topstrap and a thick front blade, the latter of which was serrated to prevent glare. The grips were resin-impregnated wood without the Ruger medallion. Later, around serial No. 30,000, the grips were changed to walnut with a silver-colored Ruger "rising Phoenix" logo inlay.

Like the two Ruger single-actions that had come before it, and inspired by the original Colt SAA design, the Bearcat's hammer consisted of three clicks—safety, half-cock, and full cock. The gun loaded via a gate on the right-hand side, and a spring-loaded pin on the frame released the cylinder base pin for removal of the cylinder with the gun on half-cock. Of course, like all pre-1973 Ruger single-actions, safety concerns dictated that owners carried only five rounds, with the hammer resting over the empty sixth chamber.

One of the Bearcat's most notable features, in addition to its compact size, was the fact that the cylinder was roll-engraved, much like Colt's cap-and-ball revolvers of the nineteenth century, only in this case, the design appropriately featured a fierce-looking mountain lion and a bear on opposite sides of the "Ruger Bearcat" name.

The Bearcat was "A little jewel among American handguns … It represents the 'kit gun' idea applied to a single-action," Bill Ruger gushed in a letter to his friend, gun writer Charles Askins, Jr., just prior to the Bearcat's introduction. Indeed, it did have a certain charm to it, just as the Colt 1849 pocket pistol must have had when it was first introduced. But this time there was no California gold rush, so people didn't really need a diminutive single-action—not when, for a few dollars more, they could get a slightly more hand-filling .22—the Single Six—which had a dovetailed rear sight that was adjustable for windage.

Still, the Bearcat was considered an ideal boy's gun and a revolver that women and others with small hands might enjoy, even though the Bearcat's sights were rudimentary at best.

Having one in camp certainly beat having no gun at all, and a great many of these tiny six-shooters did indeed fill Bill Ruger's "kit gun" prophesy by ending up in fishing tackle boxes or carried in coat pockets, as there were very few holsters made for this tiny revolver. No wonder the introductory ads referred to the lightweight Bearcat as "A pocket-sized single-action revolver."

In 1971, after 165,352 aluminum-framed Bearcats had been produced, the little pistol gained some heft with the introduction of the Super Bearcat, which featured a blued, investment cast, chrome-molybdenum steel frame. A total of 64,417 Super Bearcats were produced, with approximately half being shipped with anodized "brass" trigger guards and the rest having blued steel guards.

Finally, with a total run of 229,769 guns, the Bearcat was discontinued in 1973, a forced retirement mandated by Ruger's new "transfer bar" system, which did not prove readily adaptable to the Bearcat's compact lockwork. It would not be until 1993 that the New Bearcat, featuring this safety system, was finally introduced. Available in blued or stainless steel and with an extra .22 Magnum cylinder, this updated gun has an elongated frame and cylinder. It also weighs 23 ounces. Although a substantially much improved revolver, it is the beloved Old Model Bearcat that is now sought by collectors eager to complete their Ruger lineage. Even the red and black boxes bring a premium, as most were tossed out as unnecessary for what was conceived as a utilitarian sixgun.

In 2008, Ruger introduced a one-year-only 50th Anniversary Bearcat commemorative, featuring the transfer bar safety, but with a gold plated (rather than anodized) trigger guard. It was a fitting tribute to a rugged little revolver that proved, in the long run, size really doesn't matter. And that's why it belongs in our bucket. After all, it doesn't take up much room.

WALTHER
PPK AND PPK/S

Officially, this handy little slab-sided pocket pistol is known as the *Polizeipistole Kriminellmodell*, which translates into "Police Pistol Detective Model." However, it is more simply referred to as the Walther PPK, a double-action semi-automatic that first appeared on the European shooting scene in 1931, during particularly hard-pressed economic times in pre-World War II Germany.

The PPK was the product of Carl Walther GmbH, a successful and rather inventive firearms company (it also made mechanical and electric calculating machines during the 1920s), started in 1886 by Carl Wilhelm Walther, a third generation German gunmaker in the town of Zella-Mehlis. Eventually Walther brought his five sons, Fritz, Georg, Wilhelm, Erichh, and Lothar into the business. Upon the senior Walther's death, his eldest son, Fritz, took the helm and in 1908 expanded the company's products from hunting and target rifles to include semi-automatic pistols.

After a bit of a struggle in this field, the company finally achieved success in 1929 with its Model PP *Polizeipistole*, which was initially chambered only in 7.65mm caliber or, as it was more commonly referred to in America, the .32 ACP. Although considered marginally adequate for self-defense, even back then this round nonetheless achieved popularity by virtue of its light recoil, as well as for the small and compact semi-automatic pistols, such as the Colt Model 1903 Pocket Hammerless and the FN Model 1910, for which it was chambered. In addition, .380 ACP and .22 Long Rifle chamberings were soon added to the Walther PP. There were also a few models made in .25 ACP, which are quite collectable today. With its semi-arched backstrap, gently angled grip, exposed hammer, and hand-filling pointability, the Walther PP became an extremely successful double-action semi-automatic handgun, the first double-action specifically geared for military use. Small wonder it was almost immediately adopted by the German army and police.

Quickly capitalizing on this success, two years later, Walther produced a variant of the PP, the PPK, which featured a shorter 3⅓-inch barrel, compared with the almost four-inch barrel of the Walther PP. The PPK also sported a more compact grip and magazine, reducing the cartridge capacity by one round. This translated into six rounds in a PPK chambered for the .32 ACP or .380 ACP, compared to seven rounds in the PP (plus one in the chamber, of course). To augment the PPK's smaller grip, the magazine sported a finger rest on the bottom.

Both the PP and the PPK encompassed a number of innovative features, including a side-mounted combination safety and de-cocking lever, a loaded chamber indicator, and straight blowback operation with a recoil spring that slipped directly onto the barrel. There were also some drawbacks. For one thing, the 13½-pound double-action trigger pull was hardly conducive for first-shot accuracy, and even the seven-pound single-action let-off wasn't much better than the U.S. Government Model 1911. In addition, the sights were minimal, although it could be argued that this weapon was designed for self-defense, not target shooting. In that respect, flawless function was a hallmark of both the PP and PPK. Needless to say, surpassing even the PP in popularity, the PPK was enthusiastically adopted by the German police and the military, which included the Luftwaffe. Due to its more compact size, the PPK was especially coveted by Nazi officers.

After the war, the Walther factory was moved from its original location (which became East Germany under Soviet occupation, thus, few pre-war factory records exist), to the city of Ulm, in what became West Germany. Of course, in those post-war years, firearms manufacturing in Germany was prohibited, so, from 1952 until 1986 Walther licensed the manufacture of its PP and PPK models to Manufacture de Machines du Haut-Rhin (Manurhin) in France. These guns were imported into the United States by Interarms. They are easily identified, as the left side of the slide bears the "Carl Walther Waffenfabrick Ulm" stamping, while the right side is marked "Interarms, Alexandra, Virginia."

In post-war years, the PPK not only survived, but thrived as a favored carry pistol for self-defense as well as a handy kit gun, and one not much bigger than a .38 Special snubby. And that became a problem, for, with the Gun Control Act of 1968, the PPK just barely missed qualifying for importation due to its compact size.

The solution to this problem was ingenious in its simplicity. Walther simply put the shorter PPK barrel and receiver on the slightly larger PP frame. Thus, you now had a combination of both guns that got dubbed the PPK/S, which was almost as compact as the PPK but had the extra round capacity and slightly longer grip of the PP. It was the best of both worlds. In addition, a stateside manufactured PPK, which was not prohibited by 1968 laws, was built by Walther USA and also distributed by Interarms. That arrangement eventually was cancelled, and, since 2002, the PPK as well as the PPK/S in both .32 ACP and .380 ACP chamberings have been made under license by Smith & Wesson in both stainless and blued steel versions (there's a Crimson Trace variant, as well).

Weighing in at less than 23 ounces and with an overall length just under six inches, the PPK remains for many the ideal conceal carry weapon, especially in its .380 ACP chambering, as that cartridge has been improved dramatically in recent years as a self-defense round. Plus, there is very little on the gun to snag on clothing and, thus, it was a precursor of today's popular "meltdown" configuration.

For all its classic design features, the PPK is probably best known for being the personal weapon of choice by a fictional super-spy named James Bond. Indeed, although Bond originally carried a Beretta 418, he is best remembered, in both Ian Fleming's books and the subsequent films, for packing a Walther PPK. Inexplicably, he chose the .32 ACP chambering over the .380. Sean Connery kept true to Bond's PPK tradition in all except the last of his James Bond roles, and though, in 1995, Pierce Brosnan dutifully picked up a PPK in *GoldenEye*, he broke the pattern with *Tomorrow Never Dies* in 1997 when, after initially using a PPK, he switched to a Walther Model 99, a gun still retained by the current James Bond, Daniel Craig. Yet Craig is sometimes seen using a PPK with a suppressor in a 2006 poster advertising *Casino Royale*, and also at the beginning of 2008's *Quantum of Solace*, and although he loses his PPK in a plane crash, he gets another one later in the film. After all, as Agent 007 knows, the Walther PPK is too good a gun to be without.

WINCHESTER MODEL 1892 CARBINE

Friendly firearms conversation often drifts to someone eventually commenting that Winchester lever-actions were the first rapid-fire assault rifles. But that honor should really go to the forerunner of the Winchester, the 1860 Henry Rifle. After all, a period broadside for the Henry boasted it could fire "Sixty Shots Per Minute"—obviously not taking into account reloading time for the 16-shot repeater. Nonetheless, it was a formidable weapon for its time.

Teddy Roosevelt's Model 92 carbine sports a number of special order features, including John Ulrich engraving, fancy checkered walnut stocks, and nickel- and gold-plating, much of which is worn off.

That was only the beginning, for afterwards came the bronze-framed Model 1866, then the Model 1873 and its reloadable .44-40 chambering, and the '73's bulkier offshoot, the Model 1876 "Centennial" that put Winchester lever-actions in the hands of big-game hunters. Then Winchester hit an impasse, for the action of the Model '76 wasn't long enough to chamber one of the most popular cartridges of the day, the .45-70 Government. Plus, all of Winchester's lever-actions still used the basic 1860's toggle-link innards of the Henry rifle. The Winchester Repeating Arms Company needed a stronger, smoother action capable of handling some of the more powerful big-game cartridges. For the solution, Oliver Winchester's son-in-law and company president Thomas G. Bennett turned to John Browning, from whom Bennett had already

purchased the single-shot rifle that would become the Winchester 1885 High Wall. Browning responded by creating the smoothest action of any lever gun in existence at the time, the Model 1886 Winchester.

Although it was equal in scale and approximate weight to the Model '76, the Model '86 was a completely different rifle. It employed twin elongated locking lugs that slid up on either side of the bolt and anchored it shut when the lever was closed. After firing, the lever was pivoted open, which ejected the shell and dropped the twin lugs away from the bolt as it slid back in the receiver with a minimum amount of friction. The result was a lightning-fast action that was smooth as warm butter.

The Model 1886 became tremendously popular, the only drawback being its 9½-pound weight. Bennett soon realized a natural pro-

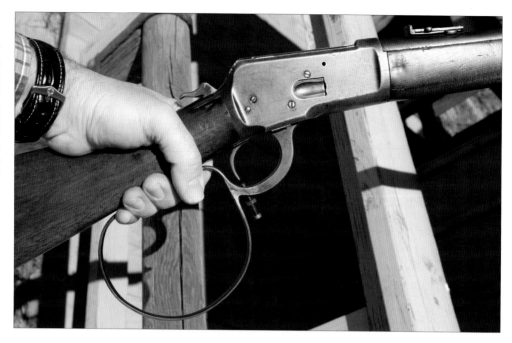

The "secret" behind Chuck Connors' rapid firing of his Model 92 carbine lies in a specially installed trigger-tripping screw, which can be backed out for conventional usage.

Two rare Winchester 92 Baby Carbines (called Trappers by today's collectors), with a 15-inch barrel (top) and a 14-inch barrel (bottom).

gression of the Model '86 would be a scaled-down version for the same three "holy trinity" of frontier rifle/revolver cartridges chambered in the 1873, the .44-40, .38-40, and .32-20. Thus emerged the Winchester Model 1892, which was eventually also chambered for .25-20 WCF and later still, the .218 Bee.

Like its big brother the Winchester 1886, the sleeker Model 1892 featured the identical slick action, just slimmed down a bit. Yet, considering the low-recoiling cartridges it was chambered for, it was still over-engineered. Nonetheless, it was less expensive to produce than the Model '73 and priced at $18, soon began outselling "The Gun that Won the West." Al-

though the '92 was introduced as both a rifle and saddle ring carbine, it was the six-pound carbine that proved more popular. Like most Winchesters, it could be ordered with any number of options, including special finishes, barrel lengths, and engraving. Interestingly, for an extra charge, the saddle ring could be eliminated. Another variation of the Model 92 isn't a Model 92 at all, but a fairly accurate copy that was made by the firm of Garate y Anitua Cia, in Eibar, Spain, during the early twentieth century and called El Tigre.

One of the most ardent users of the Model 1892 was Theodore Roosevelt, and I had the privilege of personally examining his .44-40

carbine, serial No. 53614, which is on display at the Frazier History Museum in Louisville, Kentucky (www.fraziermuseum.org). This particular carbine was shipped in 1894, after TR had left the ranching business and was living at Sagamore Hill. But he still traveled west to hunt, and it is evident this gun went with him on more than one occasion. Like many of TR's guns, this Model 92 was special ordered. It features John Ulrich engraving and checkered, fancy grade walnut stocks. In addition, the receiver, buttplate, barrel bands, and special order sling studs are gold-plated, while the rest of the gun is nickeled. But this gun's nicked stock and worn plating told me that not only did the man who would eventually become our twenty-sixth president carry his Model 92 extensively in the field, he did so in a saddle scabbard.

Rear Admiral Robert Peary took his Model 92 carbine on numerous expeditions. In a 1909 promotional pamphlet entitled "The Rifle That Helped Peary Reach The North Pole," he wrote "On my last expedition I had a Model 1892 .44 caliber Carbine and Winchester cartridges, which I carried with me right to the North Pole. After I left the ship I depended on it to bring down the fresh meat we needed … . Each of my Artic expeditions since 1891 has been fitted with these arms."

Because they were fast shooting and accurate, Model 92 carbines became indispensable tools for ranchers and cowboys throughout the West and served double duty for self-defense. They were favorites of lawmen such as the Texas Rangers, as well as those in municipal police agencies, prison guards, and even the Western Australian Police Force.

Because the Model '92 had a stronger action than the Model '73, in the early part of the twentieth century both Winchester and Remington offered a more powerful, smokeless powder, high-velocity .44-40 factory loading in addition to duplicating the original blackpowder ballistics still used today. Unfor-

The author demonstrates the rapid-firing capability of one of the 92 carbines used by Chuck Connors in **The Rifleman** television series. Notice the shells in the air and the fact that Hacker's finger never touches the trigger as the gun is fired.

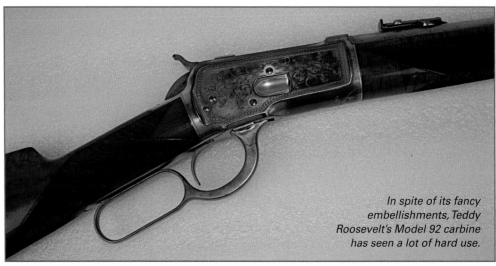

This original .44-40 Model 92 Trapper sports a rare 14-inch barrel. Note the shortened length of the forearm, one way to tell if a Trapper is original.

In spite of its fancy embellishments, Teddy Roosevelt's Model 92 carbine has seen a lot of hard use.

tunately, some folks failed to read the HV labels, and blown Model '73 bolts and mangled hands eventually caused the more potent .44-40 round to be discontinued.

One of the most collectable and romanticized variations of the Model '92 was the Trapper, or Baby Carbine, as it was officially cataloged by the factory. These special order guns were produced with 12-, 14-, 15-, 16-, and 18-inch barrels. Describing the Model 1892 Trapper in his classic book *Winchester, The Gun That Won The West*, the late Harold Williamson wrote, "One interesting use of this gun was among the trappers in the northern United States and in Canada. In running a line of traps for smaller animals these men would not infrequently catch a wolf or a bear, and a Model 92 with a fourteen-inch barrel was effective in dealing with these animals. The short-barreled 92 also proved to be popular in the jungles of Brazil for use on the rubber plantations." (It should be noted that, to be legal, any Trapper with a barrel length less than 16 inches must have an authenticating letter from the BATFE certifying it as a curio and relic. Often, this involves sending the gun to the BATFE for inspection.)

The one millionth Model 92 was presented to Secretary of War Patrick Hurley on December 13, 1932 and the carbine remained in pro-

duction until 1941, finally being unsaddled by World War II after 1,004,675 guns had been produced. But in spite of its discontinuation, the '92 carbine has always been in the spotlight—quite literally—thanks to its continued appearance in movie Westerns and on television. It has been most dramatically seen as a loop-levered Trapper spun by John Wayne in the 1939 film, *Stagecoach*, as Steve McQueen's chopped-down Mare's Leg in *Wanted Dead or Alive*, and in Chuck Connors' hands as ABC's *The Rifleman* from 1958 until 1963, where its fast-firing capability was dramatically demonstrated at the beginning of each show as Connors slammed off 10 shots in 10 seconds, thus equaling the "one shot a second" claim originally made for the Henry Rifle. This feat was accomplished by means of a trip-screw in the carbine's trigger guard that touched off the trigger each time the lever was slammed home. Today, firms such as Cimarron Fire Arms, Chiappa, and Dixie Gun Works import well-made Italian copies of the Model '92, including a loop-lever replica of the carbine carried by John Wayne in the motion picture *Rio Bravo*. Thus, aside from being smooth shooting and lightweight, the Model 92 carbine has become a part of our American western lore and as such, deserves a place on everyone's bucket list.

SMITH & WESSON
TRIPLE LOCK

Little did Horace Smith and Daniel Wesson realize in 1856 that their newly formed company would be embarking towards a classic revolver design that would transcend the centuries. Although many of the pair's large-framed single-actions, such as the American and Schofield, would become legendary, it was S&W's double-action, swing-out cylinder that came to personify the modern revolver.

The concept began in 1894, with a base pin that projected underneath the barrel. When the pin was pulled, the cylinder swung out to the left for loading. The pin was then used to "punch" out empty cases all at once, via a ratchet. Thus the term "Hand Ejector" differentiated this new design from S&Ws earlier bottom-break revolvers, which automatically ejected empties when the gun was cranked open.

The first pistol to feature this innovation was Smith & Wesson's .32-caliber Hand Ejector First Model in 1896. In 1903, the company changed the cylinder release to a more reliable latch on the left side of the frame, though the lengthened cylinder base pin remained as the ejector. These early Hand Ejectors were chambered for .22, .32, and .38 calibers, but Smith & Wesson was well aware of the potential for a larger, more powerful version of its new model. Thus, the company's Hand Ejector design culminated with what many perceive as the classic, big-bore double-action revolver, the .44 Hand Ejector Model, which was built

on what came to be known as the N-Frame.

The first version debuted in 1908, and was known as the .44 Hand Ejector First Model or, more stoically, as the Smith & Wesson .44 Military Model of 1908. It was also cataloged as the .44 New Century. However, shooters and collectors now refer to it as the Triple Lock. This was the most advanced—and, in some ways, over-engineered—handgun Smith & Wesson had ever produced. In many ways, it still is.

The Triple Lock derived its name from the fact that its cylinder locked up three different ways: with a spring-loaded catch between the end of the yoke and the tip of the extractor shroud; by a center pin indentation in the frame that secured the cylinder; and with another catch in front of the extractor. The Triple Lock was also the first Smith & Wesson to sport the now-familiar under-barrel shroud, which protected the extractor and also put more weight in front of the frame, which aided accuracy. Barrel lengths were four, five, and 6½ inches, and both fixed and adjustable target sight versions were offered. Finishes were either blued or nickeled, and standard grips were checkered walnut.

Adding to the Triple Lock's solid yet graceful heft was the fact that it was built around a new cartridge S&W specifically developed for this revolver, the .44 Smith & Wesson Special.

Although many today do not realize it, the .44 Special started out as a blackpowder cartridge and was basically a lengthened and slightly more powerful version of the old blackpowder .44 Smith & Wesson Russian. However, the .44 Special sported a slightly elongated case, thus permitting three more grains of blackpowder than the .44 Russian. But in these early transition years of blackpowder to smokeless, it was soon discovered that the .44 Special cartridge, as well as the gun for which it was designed, the Triple Lock, adapted exceedingly well to smokeless powder. Interestingly, the Triple Lock was also chambered in the less powerful .44 Russian. Later, .38-40, .44-40, .45 Colt, and .455 Webley Mark II chamberings were offered, but it was the .44 Special that garnered the spotlight. In fact, the gun is often generically referred to as the .44 New Century Hand Ejector.

The Triple Lock's high production cost of the three locking systems and the under-barrel lug hampered sales; the gun wore a price tag of $21, a sizable sum back then. In addition, with the outbreak of World War I, both the British and Canadian governments began purchasing .455 Webley-chambered Triple Locks for their troops and became concerned that the under-barrel shroud and its accompanying third locking mechanism (the most delicate feature of the gun) could collect debris and cause a malfunction. As a result, the Triple Lock was discontinued in 1915, with only 15,375 having been produced. Today, it is the most collectable of the .44 Hand Ejector series, with even a worn .44 Special in 60-percent condition bringing around $800, according to S.P. Fjestad's *Blue Book of Gun Values*. A minty version tops out over $3,000, and factory target sights bring a premium.

The .44 Hand Ejector First Model was replaced by a substantially more popular variation—you guessed it, the .44 Hand Ejector Second Model. This was essentially the same solid gun, but without the costly under-barrel lug and the locking point between the yoke and the extractor shroud. This third lock was deemed unnecessary, given the relatively underpowered loading of even the smokeless powder version of the .44 Special. With an initial price of $19, the Second Model proved to be immensely popular, especially in .44 Special. It was also offered in the same alter-

nate calibers as the original Triple Lock, but those chamberings are extremely rare. As an example, out of approximately 35,000 guns produced between 1915 and 1940 (with interruptions by World Wars I and II), only 565 were made in .44-40, while 727 were in .45 Colt.

In 1926 a crossover gun emerged, the .44 Hand Ejector Third Model, which was basically the same as the Second Model, but reintroduced the under-barrel shroud. Overwhelming demand from shooters and lawmen resulted in this new model, which remained in the line alongside the Second Model until 1940, when it replaced it completely. After World War II, the Model of 1926, as it is also known, continued in this large-frame series with the addition of a new hammer block safety. Like all the .44 Hand Ejectors, they are superb shooters, but do not have the collectability of the pre-war guns.

The .44 Hand Ejectors were favorites of lawmen like the Texas Rangers and outdoorsmen who wanted a rugged, big-bore double-action at their side. They were also chosen by hand-loading pioneers like Elmer Keith and helped set the stage for the subsequent Model 29 and its .44 Magnum cartridge. Even today, carrying a .44 Hand Ejector afield harkens back to a time when crackling campfires sent ribbons of smoke curling into a sky unmarred by jet streams overhead, and a man could arm himself with the finest double-action available, which, with all deference to the excellent Second and Third Model Hand Ejectors, was the Smith & Wesson Triple Lock.

SAVAGE 99

Most guns are reactive products of their times, fulfilling a need that exists. But the Savage 99 was ahead of the curve, in both design and calibers. Moreover, it was invented by a man as remarkable as the rifle that bore his name.

Arthur W. Savage was born in Jamaica, in 1857. The son of a British colonial official, he was schooled in England and the United States. While still in his twenties, he decided to seek adventure in Australia. He found it, for he was captured by Aborigines and held prisoner for more than a year. Finally gaining his freedom, Savage remained in Australia and created the largest cattle ranch that country had ever seen. He returned to Jamaica briefly before finally settling in Utica, New York, where he became the Superintendent of the Utica Belt Line Railroad.

Evidently he had plenty of free time on that job, because on June 8, 1887, at just 30 years of age, Savage patented a rifle based upon the Martini lever-action system. By all accounts, the gun didn't work. Undeterred, Savage kept at it, until he ended up with a rifle that featured a more conventional-looking finger-lever and a unique rotary magazine. With a group of financial backers in Utica, on April 5, 1894, the Savage Repeating Arms Company was founded. The rifle it produced was the Savage Model 1895, forerunner of the Model 99 and the world's first hammerless lever-action. Moreover, the solid brass internal magazine was revolutionary, in the most literal sense of that word. Looking somewhat like a can opener wedged in the receiver, it rotated within the

The Model 99's action is swift and smooth.

action of the gun, aligning a fresh cartridge with every crank of the lever, thus making the Savage imminently suitable to the new, ballistically superior spitzer bullets.

Mindful of its somewhat shaky financial footing, Savage subcontracted with the Marlin Firearms Company to produce tooling and manufacture the Savage Model 1895 rifles, which explains the "JM" stamp on their barrels. Although the goal of Arthur Savage was to secure a military contract with his unique rifle, the Army had already adopted the Model 1892 .30-40 Krag. So, in spite of the fact that the prototype featured a 30-inch barrel with a full-length military musket stock, Savage turned to the now-familiar half-stocked 26-inch barreled sporting rifle version (along with a much less commonly found 20-inch barreled carbine), to appeal to the civilian market. The Savage 1895 was only chambered for the .303 Savage, a round developed especially for it and ballistically equivalent to the then-new Winchester .30-30. It is obvious Savage wanted to compete with this smokeless powder cartridge on a proprietary basis.

In addition to its hammerless feature and rotating magazine, another distinguishing feature of the Model 1895 was a hole in the top of the bolt through which the firing pin could be seen. When the rifle was cocked, a stamped letter "C" was visible though the hole; when fired, the letter "F" appeared. Almost needles to say, this "safety" feature caused problems with rain and debris. Consequently, a number of improvements evolved over the next four years, culminating in the new Savage Model 1899.

The Savage 99 (as it was later called) emerged with all the attributes of a lever-action destined for the twentieth century. Small wonder it would remain in production, off and on, for the next 98 years. Its sleek, straight-gripped walnut stock, schnabel-tipped fore-end, and slim receiver combined to produce a handsome, well-balanced gun that was fast pointing and easy to carry, as its weight was centered in the receiver by virtue of the six-shot rotating magazine.

A coil mainspring provided an extremely fast lock time, and the viewing hole on the bolt was replaced by an oblong post—easy to see and feel—that popped up from the top of the bolt when the rifle was cocked. Later, around 1908, this cocking indicator was redesigned as a steel pin on the upper tang. Another notable innovation, a small oval hole on the left side of the receiver, revealed a brass cartridge counter that displayed the number of rounds left in the magazine. Fired casings were smartly ejected to the side, even though the Model 99 did not come drilled and taped for scope mounts until the 1950s. Until then, a wide variety of factory-supplied tang sights and open iron sights were the norm.

Initial chamberings were for the .303 Savage, as well as Winchester's .30-30, with scarcer variations in .25-35, .32-40, and .38-55. Some of Savage's more popular Model 99 calibers over the years included the .22 Hi-Power, brought out in 1912, and the classic .300 Savage, introduced in 1920, a round that was a stubby-necked equivalent to the .30-06 (for which the Model 99 action was too short). To me, the cartridge most representative of the Model 99 is the .250-3000 (or the Savage .250, as it is known today), which came out in 1914. Its nomenclature was derived from the fact that the original 87-grain bullet was the

first factory round to crack the 3,000 fps barrier. That feat all of itself gave the Model 99 another boost in notoriety among early twentieth century hunters. Even today, a Model 99 in .250-3000 remains a potent pairing for whitetail and antelope, although the cartridge is now offered in a heavier 100-grain bullet, which doesn't travel quite as fast. In the latter years of its life, the Savage 99 proved adaptable to numerous "modern" chamberings, including the .308 and .358 Winchester.

In 1919 a notable event occurred in the annals of Savage history—and firearms advertising. A Native American named Chief Lame Bear contacted Arthur Savage in the hope of procuring a number of the highly esteemed Model 99s for use on his reservation. Savage agreed to sell his rifles to the tribe at a discount, if he could get their endorsement. To fully grasp the significance of this transaction, one must remember that this was an era in which many could still remember the Indian

The Model 99's unique cartridge counter.

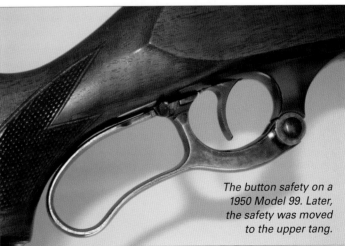

The button safety on a 1950 Model 99. Later, the safety was moved to the upper tang.

Years later, the Model 99's unique rotary magazine mechanism would inspire Bill Ruger to adapt it to his Ruger 10/22 rifle.

uprisings. The chief accepted and presented Savage with an image of his profile, which Savage promptly made part of the company logo. Thus, the rifle inventor's surname took on a new and even more romanticized imagery.

Savage went on to invent the detachable box magazine, which would appear many years later on the Savage 99C. He also became enraptured with building and racing automobiles and, in 1901, moved to California, where he established the Savage Tire Company in San Diego, and subsequently invented the radial tire. Sadly, Savage committed suicide in 1938 at the age of 81. Thankfully, his namesake rifles lived on.

Throughout its long and distinguished history, the Savage Model 99 was produced in many versions, including a takedown model introduced in 1909, and a 22-inch barreled short rifle which was made from 1899 until 1922. An octagon-barreled rifle—the 99B—was made from 1899 until 1922. There was also a Model 99 Featherweight supplied with a separate .410-bore smoothbore shotgun barrel (which had to be used as a single-shot, as the shells would not function in the rotary magazine).

In 1960, the button safety on the lever was changed to a sliding tang version, and a new 99DL incorporated a Monte Carlo stock. That same year a low-cost 99E was brought out, without the famous cartridge counter and sporting a plain, uncheckered birch stock. But the most radical departure from the famous rifle's logistics was the 99C, made in 1965 and, again in the late 1990s. This iteration featured a detachable four-shot clip, thus eschewing the famed rotary magazine. This, along with the pressed checkering (introduced in 1965), that replaced the hand-checkered workmanship of earlier years, were indications of the complexity of manufacturing the Model 99. Even an embellished Model 99CE (Centennial Edition), made to celebrate the company's hundredth anniversary, came out one year late, in 1996, thus foretelling the gun's demise.

A great gun from inception, manufacturing costs and questionable manufacturing decisions combined to close the curtain on the Savage 99 in 1997. Thus, it barely missed making the centenary mark it so richly deserved—but, at least it made our bucket list.

RUGER BLACKHAWK .357 AND .44 MAGNUM FLAT TOPS

∙∙

Back in 1955, William Batterman Ruger's fledging Sturm Ruger & Company was already batting two for two, first in 1949 with its Mark 1 Standard Pistol and then, in 1953, with the Single Six—a seven-eighths scale, vastly improved .22 version of the Colt Single Action Army. Both rimfires had hit the ball out of the park, but now the TV Western craze and fast-draw mania were starting to sweep the country. As a result, outdoorsmen, weekend plinkers, and would-be gunslingers were all clamoring for a big-bore single-action.

Ruger's New Model .44 Magnum Blackhawk.

At the time, the only options were used, first generation Peacemakers and a Great Western replica marketed by Hy Hunter of Burbank, California (although, contrary to popular belief, it wasn't made by him). Consequently, Colt's was planning to relaunch its Single Action Army, the sixgun they had declared obsolete back in 1947. But times had changed, and this was literally a whole new ball game.

For Bill Ruger, his next offering to the shooting public was obvious, especially in light of rumors that Colt's was planning to reenter the single-action arena: he would develop a full-sized single-action chambered for the powerful .357 Magnum, at the time the most popular pistol cartridge in America. Of course, Colt's had produced a scant 525 pre-war Peacemakers in .357 Magnum, but the sixgun Bill Ruger created was nothing like any single-action that had come before it.

For one thing, the frame was 4140 chrome molybdenum steel. Rather than Colt's costly case hardening, Ruger anodized the frame

black, a technique he also used on the one-piece cast aluminum trigger guard and backstrap assembly, a carryover borrowed from the Single Six. This made the gun much more economical to produce, though at the same time, Ruger incurred the extra costs of also using chrome molybdenum steel for the hammer, loading gate, trigger, and pawl, even though he admitted these parts didn't require this added strength. Still, Ruger felt it added to the gun's prestige.

Because of the .357 Magnum's higher pressures, Ruger decided to dramatically beef up the topstrap. That extra-thick bar of steel created the ideal platform to add a Micro click-

The author's finely tuned .44 Magnum Super Blackhawk, as customized by Bill Oglesby, of Oglesby & Oglesby.

adjustable rear sight, which was teamed with a Baughman-style ramp front sight having an ⅛-inch wide serrated steel blade. This was a vast improvement over the shallow topstrap groove and high front blade of the SAA, which caused the Peacemaker to shoot low. Also, Ruger opted for a spring-loaded, frame-mounted firing pin, another carryover from the Single Six. He also eschewed the flat mainspring of the SAA for a practically unbreakable coil spring. Likewise, the flat trigger bolt spring, always subject to breaking, was replaced with music wire coil springs. Finally, to solve the Model P's habit of "shooting loose," Ruger incorporated Nylok screws.

To ensure this redesigned single-action would not be misconstrued as a reworked Colt, such as those customized by pioneering firms like Christy Gun Works and King Gunsight Company, its name would have to convey the fact that it was an entirely new gun. In keeping with his passion for classic motorcars, Bill Ruger christened his new revolver the Blackhawk, after the famous Stutz roadster of the 1920s. (Three years later, Ruger would again turn to the Stutz Motor Car Company for inspiration, when he named a diminutive .22 revolver the Bearcat.)

With its black, checkered, two-piece Buta-preme grips (changed to two-piece walnut, in 1960), thick frame, and 4⅝-inch barrel, the Ruger Blackhawk was a stylish, albeit somewhat chucky-looking handgun. Although it didn't balance as well as the Single Action Army, the Blackhawk weighed the same, two pounds and six ounces, thanks to its aluminum back-strap/trigger guard assembly and ejector tube. Because of its thick, squared-off topstrap, these

early Blackhawks have since been nicknamed "Flat Tops," by collectors.

Although I was wasn't even a teenager at the time, I still remember staring in fascination at Ruger's first magazine ad announcing the new Blackhawk in the August 1955 issue of the *American Rifleman*. "The ultimate development of the single-action revolver," the copy proclaimed. This was the same year Colt's re-introduced its Peacemaker, but it was only available in .45 Colt and .38 Special. Ruger had the single-action .357 Magnum field to itself. What's more, the Blackhawk listed for $87.50, compared to $125 for the Colt SAA.

Hunters were quick to embrace the new Blackhawk, but it also found acceptance with those engaged in fast-draw, the fastest growing sport in the country. With its smooth action, the gun didn't need tuning, although snipping a coil or two off the mainspring lightened the hammer pull. Most competitors replaced the Micro rear sight with a steel blank, so they wouldn't rip off their thumbs when fast-cocking the gun. Many also removed the front sight, so it wouldn't drag on the holster when they cleared leather. (It should be noted all fast-draw contests were conducted only with blank ammunition or wax bullets—live rounds were *never* used, a common-sense safety rule that is still followed.) Like Cowboy Action Shooting today, hours of hard and fast hammer cocking put a lot of wear and tear on those Ruger Flat Tops, but the guns proved to be practically indestructible. It got to a point where Colt's finally stopped sponsoring the

Sahara Las Vegas National Fast Draw Championships, as most events were being won by Ruger Flat Tops.

In 1962, with serial No. 42,670, the era of the Flat Top came to an end, as the topstrap was recontoured that year to incorporate protective "ears" on either side of the rear sight. By that time, Ruger had retooled the original Blackhawk design, beefing it up slightly to handle the then-new .44 Magnum cartridge. However, with its standard-sized XR-3 plow-handled grips—the same size used on the .357 Magnum—the gun was almost uncontrollable

Externally, this New Model .357 Flat Top Commemorative mirrors the original 1955 version.

A rare factory engraved New Model .357 Anniversary commemorative.

with full-power factory loads, and many shooters resorted to firing .44 Specials out of it. The .44 Magnum Blackhawk morphed into the Super Blackhawk in 1959, with a 7½-inch barrel (although a few rare 6½-inch barreled guns were also produced). Even more dramatically, the Super Blackhawk featured a non-fluted cylinder, elongated walnut grips, and a Dragoon-styled square-back trigger guard.

The next significant change came about, in 1973, when Ruger revamped its entire single-action lineup to incorporate a revolutionary new transfer bar safety which, for the first time, permitted a single-action revolver to be safety carried with six rounds in the cylinder. To load these New Models, as they have subsequently been called, the loading gate was flipped open, which freed the cylinder and allowed it to rotate for loading. That eliminated the half-cock notch on the hammer, a characteristic that still trips me up after so many decades of shooting a Colt single-action. Muscle memory occasionally causes me to attempt to put a New Model Ruger SA on half-cock, which, of course, no longer exists.

The New Model Super Blackhawk gradually morphed into a sixgun sporting a more rounded trigger guard and a less elongated grip frame. However, I found myself wishing

the Super Blackhawk also sported a shorter 4⅝-inch tube, like the original Blackhawk in .357 Magnum. It would be the perfect backup gun, I theorized, for a safari to Africa. In 1985, I expressed this thought to the late Tom Ruger, who was Sturm, Ruger's Vice President of Marketing. A gun was subsequently produced for me, and the shorter barrel has now become a regular part of Ruger's lineup. In recent years, I had this gun extensively reworked and customized by Bill Oglesby of the gunsmithing firm Oglesby & Oglesby, a job that included case hardening the frame, fine-tuning the action, and outfitting it with Oglesby's patented, one-piece faux ivory Gunfighter grips.

It was the original .357 and .44 Magnum Flat Tops that established a new criteria for every big-bore single-action that came after it. Small wonder that, in 2005, in honor of the .357 Magnum Flat Top's fiftieth anniversary, and again in 2006 to acknowledge the fiftieth anniversary of their .44 Magnum Flat Top, Ruger issued limited editions (with New Model improvements) of its first bold ventures into the big-bore single-action arena. Whether original Old Models or reissued New Models, both versions have a definite place on our bucket list. Just don't try putting the New Models on half-cock.

THE HAWKEN RIFLE

Firearms development during America's western expansion has given our hobby many generic terms—"Derringer" and "six-shooter" are two that come to mind. But one that predates both of these is "Hawken." Although the name originally referred to a big-bore muzzleloading rifle specifically designed for hunting in the Far West, today it has become a label for almost any muzzleloading rifle and is often misspelled as "Hawkin" or "Hawkens," something that would have made the Hawken brothers cringe.

Jacob and Samuel Hawken were extremely skilled gunsmiths. It was Jacob who first came to St. Louis, in 1807, one year after Captains Meriwether Lewis and William Clark returned from

their exploration of the Louisiana Purchase. That expedition opened an area that had previously only been known as "The Great American Desert." This, in turn, produced a new breed of adventurers called "mountain men" who ventured into the remote wilderness—specifically "the shining mountains," as the Rockies were being called. Beaver hats had become fashionable in the eastern U.S., and there was money to be made hunting and trapping in the untamed wilderness.

It wasn't long before St. Louis became "The Gateway to the West," the last stop before leaving civilization. In the process, hunters, trappers, and adventurers were buying the best rifles they could afford in this booming city. Recognizing an opportunity when he saw one, in 1815 Jacob Hawken opened a gun shop at 214 N. Main Street, the first of a number of addresses he would occupy over the years.

At first, Jake was kept busy by the vast migration of juggernauts "Hawkenizing" their slender, small-caliber flintlocks for the unknown challenges awaiting them in the Far West. Bores were enlarged, barrels were shortened, and stocks were strengthened. Jacob dutifully stamped these reworked guns

was invented, and although the earliest rifles built by the brothers were flintlocks—using locks purchased from other purveyors—the majority of Hawken-built rifles were the more reliable and desirable caplocks.

The Hawken rifle was basically a straight-gripped halfstock, although some fullstock versions exist and a few specimens feature pistol grips. The maple stocks were carved in the Hawken shop, where the fancier curly maple was often used. Most of the furniture, including nose cap, wide crescent buttplate, trigger guard, and wedge plates were browned iron, but some guns were built with German silver or brass trim. Double set triggers were standard.

The percussion locks were Hawken-made and usually stamped "J&S Hawken" (some were occasionally left unmarked); they were often lightly engraved. Barrels were bored and rifled by the Hawken brothers themselves. Indeed, it was their deep, slow-twist rifling that made Hawken rifles so adaptable to hefty powder charges and accurate out to 150 yards or more. Calibers were rarely less than .50, with .53 being the norm, and larger bores are known to exist. Barrels were stamped "J&S Hawken," usually measured one inch across the flats, and were 30 to 38 inches in length. Consequently, the gun could handle hunting charges that ranged from 100 to 210 grains of blackpowder. Hawken rifles normally weighed between 9½ to 12 pounds, a factor that helped tame the rifle's heavy recoil. In short, the Hawken was the *ne plus ultra* of a muzzleloading big-game hunting rifle.

The Hawken had a number of distinguishing physical characteristics. Most notable were the two iron wedges set into oval iron wedge plates to anchor the heavy barrel to the stock. In addition, the trigger guard continued in a long band affixed to the underside of the stock, which helped strengthen the wrist. On the earliest rifles, this tang ended in a ring, but on later guns it finished in a graceful scrolled curve. Also helping to soften the lines of what was basically a workhorse rifle was the thick, teardrop-shaped cheekpiece on the left side of the stock. The fixed rear sight was usually a full buckhorn slanted slightly to the rear to reduce glare, while the front sight was a German silver blade. A hooked breech enabled the barrel to be lifted out of the stock (after removing the wedges and ramrod, of course) for cleaning. Occasionally, rifles were made with an iron patch box.

As fate would have it, right about the time Sam joined Jake, General William H. Ashley was organizing the Rocky Mountain Fur Compa-

"J. Hawken St. Louis," causing many a modern-day collector to assume that the Hawken shop made a wider variety of muzzleloaders than it actually did. But soon the enterprising young gunsmith found himself building a new kind of rifle for clientele that included the influential Missouri Fur Company, a gun generally referred to as a "mountain rifle" or, more specifically, a "Rocky Mountain Rifle." The caliber was bigger, the stock was thicker, and the rifle was heavier than most front-loaders of the period.

Meanwhile, Sam Hawken was busy building a lucrative gunmaking career of his own in Xenia, Ohio. When brother Jake sent word of a greater fortune that could be made by the two of them at his more strategic location in St. Louis, it didn't take much to convince Sam. In 1822 he joined his brother in St. Louis. This was right about the time the percussion cap

ny, destined to become a driving force of the mountain man era. Ashley became a fan of the rifles Sam and Jake were building and ordered a number of them for his outfitters, as well as to trade at hefty prices to trappers and hunters armed with less than adequate rifles in the Far West. Eventually Ashley ordered a massive .68-caliber Hawken with a 42-inch barrel for himself.

The Hawken brothers sold their guns for around $25, but the farther west you went, the more expensive the rifles became. In 1840 Kit Carson paid $60 in gold for a Hawken rifle and was so impressed with it, he armed his mounted riflemen with similar guns when they fought in the Mexican War. As the Hawken rifle's fame spread, so did the fame of many of its users, which included John C. Fremont, Jim Bridger, and Daniel Boone.

The Hawken was given another boost in popularity in 1849, when gold was discovered in California, bringing a new wave of adventurers into Sam and Jake's shop. But right at the height of their fame, a cholera epidemic killed Jake. A devastated Sam continued with the business until 1858, when his own health began to fail. After a brief sojourn to Denver, Sam returned to St. Louis in 1861 and sold his business to a fellow worker, William L. Watt. A young German gunsmith named John Phillip Gemmer, who had joined the shop in 1860, bought a share in the business from Watt in 1862. By 1866 Gemmer had purchased complete ownership. He continued making "S. Hawken"-stamped muzzleloading rifles, but gradually phased in his own "J.P. Gemmer, St. Louis" mark as cartridge guns became more

prevalent. One of Gemmer's more notable accomplishments was restocking Sharps rifles in the Hawken style.

Sam Hawken died on May 9, 1884, at age 92, but Gemmer kept the Hawken shop going until 1915. Interestingly, Hawken rifles continued to be used well into the cartridge era, as they were much harder hitting than most lever-actions. Gemmer died in 1919, and both he and Sam Hawken are buried at Bellefontaine Cemetery in St. Louis, thus ending the saga of America's most famous mountain rifle.

Today, although many well-made but mass produced muzzleloaders are labeled "Hawken," it's difficult to find an authentically designed Hawken rifle, unless you have one created by a custom gunmaker. For years, I have hunted with a custom Hawken that was built for me in 1976 by John Speak, a former motion picture sound engineer in Hollywood, California, and another Hawken with a 26-inch barrel (designed for use on horseback) that I ordered from the no-longer-existing Ozark Mountain Arms. Both are .54-caliber, feature the later-styled "S" curve of the elongated trigger guard, and shoot remarkably well out to 100 yards with 100 grains of 2Fg blackpowder behind a soft lead conical bullet. Recently, at the Wally Beinfeld Antique Arms Show in Las Vegas, I bumped into the fellow who had made my Ozark Mountain Hawken. He was genuinely pleased that I still hunted with it after all these years. Which got me to thinking: an authentically-styled Hawken rifle definitely belongs on our bucket list as a tribute to the mountain men who helped open the Rocky Mountain gateway to the Far West.

REMINGTON 870

One of my hunting buddies has amassed a rather impressive collection of shotguns. Securely stored in his safe are some of the finest Parkers, Brownings, and Winchesters ever seen outside a museum. He shoots them all, yet when we go upland hunting or gear up for waterfowl, there is only one of his many scatterguns he invariably selects—an old, beat-up, synthetically stocked 12-gauge Remington 870 Wingmaster. His reason? "It always works," he says.

Quoting from one of Remington's fairly recent catalogs:

The original design of the Model 870 Wingmaster is so smooth and so reliable that today—more than five decades after its introduction—it's still the standard by which all other pump-action shotguns are judged. … Its classic balance and natural pointing qualities provide the handling speed for the most evasive and challenging birds … .And because they practically never wear out, there are more Model 870s in use today than any other shotgun.

That would be well over nine million Model 870s to date, making this the most prolific and popular pump-action shotgun ever produced. But before the emergence of the Model 870, Remington had already been enjoying a fair amount of success with its five-shot Model 31, a 12-gauge pump that had been introduced in August 1931, hence the name. It had been the company's first side-ejecting repeating shotgun, but it got off to a slow start in those early years of the Great Depression. Nonetheless, 16- and 20-gauge versions were brought out in 1933. Even during a lull in production caused by World War II, a number of Model 31s were conscripted into the service to help train aerial gunners. But by 1947, with peacetime pros-

perity on the horizon and being left behind by Winchester's popular Model 12, Remington—the country's oldest arms maker—decided it was time to update its Model 31.

In January 1950, after three years of planning, the Model 870 Wingmaster made its appearance with sleek new styling, a greatly improved and strengthened action, and priced at $69.95 for the AP Standard Grade. This launched the Model 870 with a definite competitive advantage over the field grade Winchester Model 12, which was selling for $98.15 at the time. But in spite of its dramatically lower price, the Wingmaster would still end up being one of the most reliable and versatile smoothbores ever built. Its unique "twin action bars"—thin steel rails that extended into the receiver from both sides of the sliding forearm—gave the pump-action a ball bearing smoothness that resulted in quick follow-up shots on fast-moving targets. In addition, the bolt locked into a barrel extension, making for a rock-solid action.

The streamlined Model 870 featured a walnut pistol grip stock and fore-end and a swept-back trigger guard with cross-bolt safety. The smooth receiver, machined from a solid block of steel, was matted to reduce top glare. Initially chambered for 2¾-inch shells, the Wingmaster loaded from the bottom and boasted a takedown action, easily interchangeable barrels for switching to different lengths and chokes, and a tubular magazine that held five rounds; a three-shot wooden plug was standard, and 12-gauge guns came with an alternate steel "Vari-Weight" steel plug. The Deluxe versions offered a checkered pistol grip, checkered and grooved fore-end, a fully matted barrel ridge, and decorative grip cap. Internally, both guns were the same.

Remington's faith in its newest scattergun was evident by the introduction of no less than 15 different versions of the Model 870—in 12-, 20-, and 16-gauge—that very first year. Models included Special, Deluxe, and Deluxe Special Grades, in addition to a variety of trap and skeet guns, plus a 20-inch barreled riot gun. Indeed, when it came to the Model 870, there was something for everyone and it was an immediate success with hunters, competitive shooters, and law enforcement agencies, as well as the military.

The butt cap of this Wingmaster leaves no doubt as to the shotgun's intended purpose.

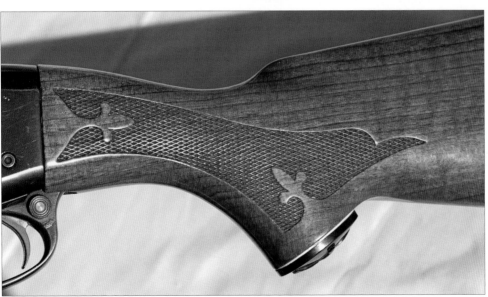

The fleur de lis checkered pattern adds a touch of elegance to the Model 870's glossy walnut stock.

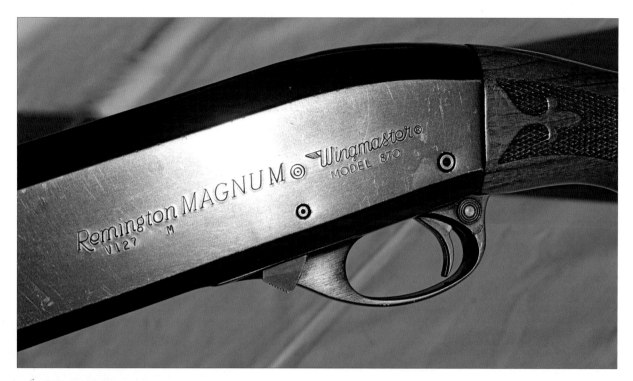

*This particular
gun was made
in 1978 and is
chambered for
12-gauge 3-inch
Magnums.*

In 1955, a magnum 12-gauge chambering for 3-inch shells was added. The versatility of the Model 870 was extended further in 1959, when the open-sighted RSS Rifled Slug Special was introduced; of course, slug barrels could also be purchased separately by those who already owned the basic 870 shotgun. A 20-gauge magnum came out in 1960, and three years later even the lowest-priced field grades were upgraded with checkering, providing ever greater value. Small wonder that by 1966, just 16 years after its introduction, more than a million Model 870s had been sold. As this also marked the one hundred-fiftieth anniversary of the Remington Arms Company, which had been started by Eliphalet Remington in 1816, that year saw the shotgun's first commemorative, the Model 870 150th Anniversary Edition,

of which 2,534 were made. Three years later, 28-gauge and .410-bore versions were brought out, featuring appropriately scaled-down receivers with lighter-weight mahogany stocks.

Over the course of its still-active lifetime, the Model 870 has existed in a mind-boggling array of variations, including the Mk-1 military model with extended seven-shot magazine, left-handed versions (which first came out in 1971), the Lightweight Deer Gun, Lightweight 20-Gauge Youth Gun, commemoratives such as the 12-gauge "100th Anniversary of Pump-Action Shotguns," and the economical 870 Express. From synthetically stocked marine models to camouflaged turkey guns to magnum duck guns to tactical models, the Remington 870 remains one of the most versatile and affordable pump-actions in the world.

FREE DOWNLOADS— NO STRINGS ATTACHED.
No, Really!

Hone your expertise on the latest concealed carry guns, AR-15 optics, ammunition options, shooting tactics and more from our collection of more than 20 topic-specific downloads at gundigest.com/free. And hey, the price is right—they're free!

GunDigest
GUIDE TO AMMUNITION
Cartridge Basics Explained

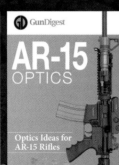

GunDigest
AR-15 OPTICS
Optics Ideas for AR-15 Rifles

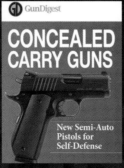

GunDigest
CONCEALED CARRY GUNS
New Semi-Auto Pistols for Self-Defense

GunDigest
ESSENTIAL GLOCK ACCESSORIES
Must-Have Glock Parts and Upgrades

GunDigest
HANDGUNS A BEGINNER'S GUIDE
Choose the Best Self-Defense Handgun

MORE DOWNLOADS BOOKMARK US! COMING SOON

Download now at
GunDigest.com

Stay on target with

GunDigest
THE MAGAZINE

DEFENSIVE SHOOTING CASE STUDIES

FEATURED: HECKLER KOCH'S P2000 SK PAGE 16

GunDigest
THE MAGAZINE
WE KNOW GUNS SO YOU KNOW GUNS
MARCH 25, 2013
VOLUME 30 · ISSUE 6

The One-of-a-Kind
BOBERG XR9-S
XR9-S

5.56 or .223?

WINCHESTER'S NEW VARMINT-X LOADS

REVIEW: FRANCHI ASPIRE

GunDigest
THE MAGAZINE
WE KNOW GUNS SO YOU KNOW GUNS
February 25, 2013
VOLUME 30 · ISSUE 4

PREDATOR-POUNDING RIFLES

▶ WEATHERBY
▶ MOSSBERG
▶ BROWNING
▶ SIG SAUER
▶ THOMPSON

THIS AR CAN HUNT!
Rock River Arms LAR-15 Hunter

SEE WHAT'S NEW FROM COLT! PAGE 7

WORLD'S FOREMOST GUN AUTHORITY FOR '70 YEARS!

GunDigest
THE MAGAZINE
WE KNOW GUNS SO YOU KNOW GUNS
January 28, 2013
VOLUME 30 · ISSUE 2

.17 WIN SUPER MAG
New Rimfire is World's Fastest!

7 New Shotguns for 2013

GLOCK vs. 1911

ARE YOU READY?
Ultimate Survival Rifles

GUN DIGEST EXCLUSIVE
FNH USA'S NEW FNX-45

⊕ **GUN REVIEWS**

⊕ **NEW PRODUCT UPDATES**

⊕ **GUNS FOR SALE**

⊕ **FIREARMS INDUSTRY NEWS**

⊕ **AUCTION AND SHOW LISTINGS**

↘ 3 EASY WAYS TO SUBSCRIBE NOW:

Order your print or digital subscription at
subscribe.gundigest.com

NOW AVAILABLE ON:

CALL **800.829.9127**

A3GNLA